*to*_____

*from*_____

Copyright © 2008 by Neilsons & D, LLC

PRIDE & HUMILITY
by Neilsons & D

Printed in the United States of America

ISBN 978-1-60477-995-0

All rights reserved solely by the author. The author guarantees all contents are original and do not infringe upon the legal rights of any other person or work. No part of this book may be reproduced in any form without the permission of the author. The views expressed in this book are not necessarily those of the publisher.

Unless otherwise indicated, Bible quotations are taken from the Holy Bible, New Living Translation. Copyright © 1996. Used by permission of Tyndale House Publishers, Inc., Wheaton, Illinois 60189. All rights reserved. As found in BIBLESOFT PC STUDY BIBLE Version 4.2B, copyright © 1998-2004. All rights reserved.

Graphic Designs by Neilsons & D.
Acrostic Poems by Neilsons & D.
Book Cover Design by Neilsons & D.

www.xulonpress.com

www.neilsonsd@yahoo.com - **for free bookmarks.**

PRIDE

&

HUMILITY

PRIDE

ITS CAUSE AND ITS EFFECT

IN PRAISE OF

HUMILITY

By Neilsons & D, LLC

DEDICATION

This book is dedicated to anyone who wants to walk in a Close Relationship with God – that they may receive His blessings and graces, leading to a true, disciplined, serious, dedicated, devotional reason and purpose for existence.

FORWARD

About the Author

It is the wish of the author to remain anonymous. The book's emphasis should be on the message and not the messenger.

I would be the first to admit that throughout my life, I have made many mistakes. Those that know me will attest to that. Only through my faith and trust in God, was I able to acquire the strength and courage that I *so* needed to put behind those situations, and to then put my focus on the reality of the true purpose of living.

Through the years of intense researching for this book, it has made me, not only more conscious of these mistakes, but more importantly, made me realize the seriousness of my journey. I have learned many things that have helped me to have a more enriched, and subsequently, more enjoyable life. I would like to share with you what I have found, to help you to become more aware of, and become more focused on, the complexity, yet simplicity, the purpose, and the important choices which then will decide our destiny. It is also my hope that you will enjoy reading the book as much as I have enjoyed bringing it to you. You may also know of someone who might want to read it to help refresh their own soul. My wish is that it will similarly help anyone to find a true and purposeful meaning in the preparation for the *good life* that is waiting to be fulfilled.

Throughout my journey, I wasn't able to accumulate many riches. I do however, want to leave this book to my family, my children, grandchildren, and whoever else can benefit from it, as an aid and reference available while going through *this* life, and getting ready for, the more important *everlasting* life.

About the Book

One of the reasons why this book was written, is because, we as a people, are living in a society that is experiencing a degrading culture, and has made morality less than secondary. God's laws are not being observed. A *worldly* attitude has become a global acceptance. Liberalism is not only allowed, but has infiltrated to a progression of decaying culture. Our Society and Culture needs to go back to the basic, fundamental, elemental, primary and foundational values of living. A focus on reapplying strong principles and integrity in our lives. This is why an intense, and intended section of this book, will be devoted to virtues. We have to reintroduce the tools and strengths that are found in these virtues – the tools to heal, reconstruct, and bring about the decency, true spirit, reason, dignity and purpose for a holier way of living.

People learn by example. If the examples are virtuous, they will learn virtue. On the other hand, if the examples are corrupt, they will experience and learn a behavior that will become detrimental to their soul and way of life.

With moral, spiritual and religious education declining more than ever – we as parents, grandparents, uncles, aunts, friends, teachers or anyone that *cares* – all of us, out of necessity, have to fill this gap. If we don't – then who will?

We have given our *time*, or we have given *things* to our children, grandchildren, or other loved ones to make their earthly life more pleasant and enjoyable. What are we doing to make their *next* life more enjoyable? The same, and even more attention, should be given to their soul, with even more emphasis because of the seriousness of the nature, and its important eternal reward – thereby helping them achieve their ultimate goal. *What a Gift!*

CONTENTS

	Page
Chapter 1 - HEAVEN.	15
What Is Heaven Like?	17
Who Is God?	23
Chapter 2 - CAUSE.	28
The Fall Of Lucifer - The Cause.	30
Satan's Course Of Action.	33
Chapter 3 - CREATION.	41
God's Plan And Purpose.	43
Creation Of The Universe.	45
Creation Of The Earth.	47
Creation Of Man.	49
The Fall Of Man.	50
The Renewal Of Man.	52
Receiving The Laws.	56
The Melange Of The Languages.	58
Chapter 4 - PRIDE.	59
Man's Sinful Nature.	62
Man Is Ego Motivated.	65
Permissiveness.	68
Doubt - Fear.	70
Disobedience.	73
Dishonesty - Deceitfulness - Hypocrisy.	74
Hate.	76
The Seven Capital Sins.	78
Pride.	78

(Contents - continued)

Avarice.	79
Envy.	81
Wrath.	82
Lust.	84
Gluttony.	86
Sloth.	88
Chapter 5 - HUMILITY.	92
In Praise Of Humility.	95
God's Humility.	101
Self-Control.	103
Discipline.	104
Love - Caring.	109
Faith - Trust - Belief.	118
Faithfulness.	126
Hope.	127
Courage.	130
Charity - Sharing.	132
Honor - Respect - Dignity.	135
Integrity.	140
Helpfulness - Kindness.	141
Goodness.	145
Consideration.	147
Cooperation - Unselfishness.	148
Friendliness.	150
Gentleness.	151
Joy.	152
Peacefulness.	154
Tolerance.	155
Responsibility.	157
Honesty.	158
Justice.	160
Purity - Prudence.	163
Decency - Modesty.	166

(Contents - continued)

Abstinence - Temperance.	169
Patience.	173
Endurance - Fortitude.	175
Suffering - Affliction.	178
Forgiveness.	183
Appreciation - Thankfulness.	186
Reciprocity.	189
Close Relationship With God.	191
God's Mercy.	198
Chapter 6 - WISDOM.	200
Who Are We?	202
What Is Wisdom?	206
Where To Find Wisdom.	210
Applying Wisdom.	213
Purpose.	219
Character.	222
Temperament.	224
Communicating With One Another.	231
Communicating With God.	238
Chapter 7 - REDEMPTION.	241
Deliverance - Salvation.	246
Acceptance.	248
Repentance.	249
Atonement.	251
Chapter 8 - CHOICE.	254
Discernment.	256

(Contents - continued)

Priority.	262
How To Find Our Faith And Destiny.	264
Obedience.	267
Perseverance - Persistency.	269
Devotion.	271
Prayer - Fasting.	273
Following Footsteps.	278
Heeding.	282

Chapter 9 - ETERNITY.   284

What Is Eternity?	287
Nearing The Final Days.	290
Getting Ready.	293
The Rapture.	296
The Tribulation.	298
The Millennium.	303
Satan's Final Defeat.	305
Judgment.	307
Enjoying The Good Life.	309

Chapter 1

HEAVEN

OMNIPOTENCE

"I am the Alpha and the Omega — the beginning and the end," says the Lord God. "I am the one who is, who always was, and is still to come, the Almighty One." (Rev 1:8)

HEAVEN

H ome, our awaiting, and final resting place;

E ager to greet us all, with such warm embrace.

A ngels with God, and all the Holy Saints abiding;

V ast, and its dwelling, sublime and enchanting.

E xpecting saved souls, in divine providence;

N urtured in bliss, endowed of omnipotence.

WHAT IS HEAVEN LIKE?

God is everywhere! However, the Kingdom, Heaven, Paradise, His Glorious Dwelling Place, the promised final resting place, in its glorious form and wonder of excellence, is not only difficult, but almost impossible to imagine, and much less possible to describe. Although much has been authored about its authentic and fundamental purpose, little has been said, written or documented about this ultimate destination's location, structure, size, beauty, or activity.

Although many of the world's greatest painters and poets have tried to depict it, and so much artwork crafted, or someone's anticipated cultural ideas of what its elegance could be – none have ever, or could ever been able to show or capture its realistic and genuine splendor in its Divine and angelic surroundings.

> "For I tell you that in heaven these angels
> are always in the presence of my heavenly Father."
> (Matt 18:11b)

For many people the thought of heaven consists of clouds, wings, halos, and harps. But this is where the imagination goes to work. Everyone picturing their own rendition. All of us trying, in some way or other, to elaborate in our own ideas what might be, in clarity, its utmost perfection. *Beauty is indeed in the mind of the beholder!* Everyone attempting, desiring, and some quite determined to fill their own personal gallery with their individual and very unique perceptions. Its actual majestic presence is therefore *beyond* our human imagination.

> "That is what the Scriptures mean when they say, 'No eye
> has seen, no ear has heard and no mind has imagined what
> God has prepared for those who love him'"
> (1Cor 2:9)

"For God has reserved a priceless inheritance for his children. It is kept in heaven for you, pure and undefiled, beyond the reach of change and decay." (1Pe 1:4)

God in His creativity and generosity, has given us so much to sustain our existence here on earth. We are living in a world of plenty – everything needed, wanted, in our reach, or attainable, to supply us with nourishment, shelter, communication, and other necessities for our well being during our short, earthly, and mortal stay.

We are able to appreciate some of God's creation now, because of our visual capacity, which only entices us to try to further understand what He has planned for those He loves, and especially for those who love Him.

There are numerous exquisitely designed gardens throughout the world, showing the beautiful flowers and plants that came from many lands. All varying in size and colors. Each one individually crafted by God for a specific appearance. Visiting a Zoo gives us such an array in diversity of creation. Some animals or birds sport stripes, others dots; males being one color, and the females of another.

As wonderful, exciting, or enjoyable that any of earthly experiences can be, nothing will ever, or could ever compare to the existence with a God in Paradise. Undoubtedly it will not only be a new, but an awesome active participation, full of unthinkable, but unlimited happiness, joy and pleasure.

We will be given *new bodies*. One would want to presume that they would be without wrinkles, deformities, disease, and that they will never show age or blemish. We will become more *ourselves*, because finally we will not be interfering with what God wants us to be. We will have become what He wanted us to be. We can now *start* to imagine that.

There will be no more worry, pain, agony, suffering, being too skinny or too fat; or having to toil at the sweat of our brow; or having to *earn a living*. Imagine, no bills to pay, no emotional problems, no more drug addictions, incest, rape or prostitution; no more insecurities or fears; no more separation from homes or loved ones; no more wars, disasters, alcoholism, divorces, or abandonments; no more hunger and starvation; no more discontent or hatred; no more tears or crying; no more racial or ethnic issues.

Finally – living in joy and peace – forever.

One of the most difficult things to understand, is that this very different environment will be enhanced by the experiencing of a new dimension of *space* and *time*. Whatever it is that God has prepared for us – it will surely be something of absolute amazement.

Let's imagine the ultimate experience!

> "This is what the LORD says: 'Heaven is my throne, and the earth is my footstool. Could you ever build me a temple as good as that? Could you build a dwelling place for me? My hands have made both heaven and earth, and they are mine. I, the LORD, have spoken!'" (Isa 66:1,2)

What could we expect to see in heaven? Here are a few things that the Bible has revealed to us.

• that heaven will be a city, equal in length, width and height, and surrounded with wall and gates:

> "The angel that talked to me held in his hand a gold measuring stick to measure the city, its gates and its wall. When he measured it, he found it was square, as wide as it was long. In fact, it was in the form of a cube, for its length, and width and height were each 1,400 miles. Then he

measured the walls and found them to be 216 feet thick (the angel used a standard human measure.)

The wall was made of jasper, and the city was pure gold, as clear as glass. The wall of the city was built in foundation stones inlaid with twelve gems: the first was jasper, the second sapphire, the third agate, the fourth emerald, the fifth onyx, the sixth carnelian, the seventh chrysolite, the eight beryl, the ninth topaz, the tenth chrysoprase, the eleventh jacinth, the twelfth amethyst.

The twelve gates were made of pearls – each gate from a single pearl! And the main street was pure gold, as clear as glass.

No temple could be seen in the city, for the Lord God Almighty and the Lamb are its temple. And the city has no need of sun or moon, for the glory of God illuminates the city, and the Lamb is its light. The nations of the earth will walk in its light, and the rulers of the world will come and bring their glory to it. Its gates never close at the end of day because there is no night. And all the nations will bring their glory and honor into the city. Nothing evil will be allowed to enter – no one who practices shameful idolatry and dishonesty – but only those whose names are written in the Lamb's Book of Life." (Rev 21:15-27)

• that there are many rooms:

"There are many rooms in my Father's home, and I am going to prepare a place for you. If this were not so I would tell you plainly. When everything is ready, I will come and get you, so that you will always be with me where I am."
(John 14:2,3)

• it is giving a direction, and a special seating arrangement:

"When the Lord Jesus had finished talking with

them, he was taken up into heaven and sat down in the place of honor at God's right hand." (Mark 16:19)

• it mentions a door, thrones, gemstones, crowns, lampstands with burning flames, and a sea of glass:

"Then as I looked, I saw a door standing open in heaven, and the same voice I had heard before spoke to me with a sound of a mighty trumpet blast. The voice said, 'Come up here, and I will show you what must happen after these things.' And instantly I was in the Spirit, and I saw a throne in heaven and someone sitting on it! The one sitting on the throne was as brilliant as gemstones – jasper and carnelian. And the glow of an emerald circled his throne like a rainbow. Twenty-four thrones surrounded him, and twenty-four elders sat on them. They were all clothed in white and had gold crowns on their heads. And from the throne came flashes of lighting and the rumble of thunder. And in front of the throne were seven lampstands with burning flames. They are the seven spirits of God. In front of the throne was a shiny sea of glass, sparkling like crystal." (Rev 4:1-6)

• about a river, a tree of life, and fruit:

"And the angel showed me a pure river with the water of life, clear as crystal, flowing from the throne of God and the Lamb, coursing down the center of the main street. On each side of the river grew a tree of life, bearing twelve crops of fruit, with a fresh crop each month..."
"No longer will anything be cursed. For the throne of God and the Lamb will be there, and his servants will worship him. And they will see his face, and his name will be written on their foreheads. And there will be no night there – no need for lamps or sun – for the Lord God will shine on them. And they will reign forever and ever." (Rev22:1,2a,b,3-6)

- heavenly meals:

    "I will not drink wine again until the day I drink it new with you in my Father's Kingdom." (Mt 26:29)

- entertained by angels, choir and signing:

    "Then I looked again, and I heard the singing of thousands of angels around the throne and the living beings, and elders. And they sang in a mighty chorus." (Rev 5:11,12)

- a heavenly city:

    "But they were looking for a better place, a heavenly homeland. That is why God is not ashamed to be called their God, for he has prepared a heavenly city for them." (Heb 11:16)

How will it be like in this heavenly city? Certainly not at all, in any way, how we've been accustomed to act or react. What about our spouses, our children, parents, friends, or even our animals? One would simply imagine that our most important, and primary focus, will be in the homage and reverence to our God.

In this awaiting divine dimension, will we, in our celestial bodies be able to become *bi* or *mutilocational*; being able to be at more than one place at the same time? What other intriguing conditions, abilities, purposes, or activities will be experienced and enjoyed?

What kind of knowledge will we possess? How will it be learned or utilized? What about our present talents and aptitudes?

We have as many probable answers, to the many possible questions, about what is to be expected in the *other* life.

WHO IS GOD?

Throughout the history of man, this question must have been asked innumerable times: "Who *is* God?" A simple answer could be:

"God Is Love."

Referring to the Bible and many other sources, we find that He has been described as being:

> **as God** – a Triune God, Abba, abounding in love and faithfulness, Almighty, Awesome, Compassionate, Divine, El-Bethel (God of Bethel), El-Elohe (God of Israel), Elohim, El-Shaddai (God All Sufficient), Eternal, Forgiving, full of unfailing love, Generous, Goodness, Gracious, Great, Inerrable, I AM, I AM THE ONE WHO ALWAYS IS, I Am who I Am, Infinite, Jealous, Jehovah, Kind, Light, Lord, God Most High, Holy, Lord your God, Merciful, our Creator, our Father, our Spiritual Father, patient, Powerful, Righteous, slow to anger, The Almighty One, the Eternal Rock, The Great I Am, The Lord your God, The Sovereign God, Yahweh.
>
> **the God of** – Abednego, Abraham, all families of Israel, all the Kingdoms of the earth, all the people of the world, Daniel, David, devouring fire, Elijah, Glory, Heaven, Hezekiah, Isaac, Israel, Jacob, Jerusalem, Justice, Love, Meshach, Nahor, Peace, the Hebrew, Gods and Lord of Lords, miracles and wonders, Shadrach, the armies of Israel, the land, the Spirit of all living things, the living, Truth, Vengeance, and your ancestors.
>
> **The Holy Spirit** – a Counselor, a giver of gifts, a Sevenfold Spirit, an advocate, like a dove, Spirit of God, one who encourages, one who inspires, the Eternal Spirit, the Father

of our Spirit, the Spirit of Truth.

As the Son – Anointed King, Avenger of God's Elect, Bread of Life, Burden Bearer, Captain of our Salvation, Chief Cornerstone, Chief Shepherd, Christ, Christ our Lord, Closest Deliverer, Dayspring and Faithful One, Eternal Sacrifice, Everlasting Love, Friend, Emmanuel, Faithful Husband, Faithful Pastor and Blessed Hope, Faithful Scribe, Faithful Witness, Firm Foundation, Friend that is closer than a Brother, Fullness of God, Gentle Shepherd, Gift of the Spirit, Glorious Promise, Glory of Israel, Glory of the Lord, God's Outpouring of the Holy Spirit, God's Mercy, Great Physician, Hidden Teacher, High Priest, Highest Authority, Interceding King, Jesus, King of Kings and Lord of Lords, King of the Jews, Kinsman Redeemer, Liberator, Light of the world, Majesty and Power, Mediator, Merciful Father, Messenger of the Gospel, Messiah, My Chosen One, My Son, Only Hope, our Brother, our Redeemer, our Salvation, our Humble Savior, Power on High, Prince of Peace, Provider and Supplier, Redeeming Prophet, Reigning King, Rebuilder, Rescuer, Restorer of God's Lost Heritage, Righteous Branch and Friend, Righteousness, Ruler of Creation, Savior and Justifier, Shepherd Song, Son of God and Wonder of Wonders, Son of Man, Sovereign King, the Bridegroom, the Heir to His Throne, the Lamb of God, the Messiah, the Morning Star, the Son of the Living God, the Son of Man, Steadfast Judge and Lawgiver, the source of David, the Spirit of Christ, the way the truth and the light, the Word, Triumphant King, Trusted Guide, Victory, Watchman and Wheel in the Sky, Weeping Prophet, Wisdom, Wise King, Wonderful, Word made flesh.

"In the beginning the Word already existed.
He was with God, and he was God." (John 1:1)

The above mentioned are but a few of the many ways that God is *understood* to be. But these are only showing some of the distinctive *abilities, qualities, features,* or *traits* of who, or how He is referred to. God has kept from us, not only His appearance, and who He actually is, but also other fascinating things about His Triune Being – His knowledge and His creativity. God is infinite and eternal in His *attributes*. He is all knowing. No one can comprehend His kind of intellect or capabilities. The Father, Son, and Holy Spirit, all three are eternally equal – being of unity of essence in the Trinity of Persons.

> "God is light and there is no darkness in him at all."
> (1 John 1:5b)

God gave us His Son, Christ, as a visible image of Himself, for the Father in His fullness took pleasure to live in Christ.

> "Since God in his wisdom saw to it that the world would never find him through human wisdom, he has used our foolish preaching to save all who believe." (1Cor 1:21)

> "Christ is the visible image of the invisible God. He existed before God made anything at all and is supreme over all creation. Christ is the one through whom God created everything in heaven and earth. He made the things we can see and the things we can't see – kings, kingdoms, rulers and authorities. Everything has been created through him and for him. He existed before everything else began, and he holds all creation together." (Col 1:15-17)

> "Oh, what a wonderful God we have! How great are his riches and wisdom and knowledge! How impossible it is for us to understand his decisions and his methods! For who can know what the Lord is thinking? Who knows enough to be his counselor? (Rom 11:33,34)

"No one can know a person's thoughts except that person's own spirit, and so no one can know God's thoughts except God's own Spirit." (1 Cor 2:11)

"The LORD, your Redeemer and Creator, says: I am the LORD, who made all things, I alone stretched out the heavens. By myself I made the earth and everything in it." (Isa 44:24)

"Where there is Love – there is God."

Whatever the purpose God had for keeping these secrets from us, it still makes it that much more desiring, in our curious nature, to take a peek at the other side. And for some same similar reason, he kept us from knowing what *our* future would hold for us.

The unknown can sometimes bring us *fear*. But our absent knowledge about God's divine existence, is like turning our *fear of the unknown*, into an *anticipation of discovery*. In the same way, our future is not revealed to us, though He knows what our fate will be. It would be very difficult to believe that anyone would *want* to know his or her fate, keeping in mind that it would be almost unbearable to live with the knowledge.

Trying to describe God, is almost like trying to describe someone that is talking to you over the phone, someone you had never met or seen before. The one, and probably only attribute known to us about God's physical being, is that we are created in His image. So, if we were made to look like God, then God must look like us.

"My Father has given me authority over everything. No one really knows the Son except the Father, and no one really knows the Father except the Son and those to whom the Son chooses to reveal him." (Mt 11:27)

"Not that anyone has ever seen the Father, only I, who was sent from God, have seen him." (Jn 6:46)

> "The Father and I are one." (John 10:30)

God is also a jealous God. Not jealous in the sense that Tommy is jealous because Suzie came home with an ice cream cone, and he didn't get one. God's jealousy takes on a different meaning.

> "You must worship no other gods, but only the LORD, for he is a God who is passionate about his relationship with you." (Gen 34:`14)

He wants us to, and we must, look at *Him* as being the Supreme One, above everyone and everything else. If we don't perceive Him in that way, then we would have chosen something, or someone else to be supreme. For the essentiality of reverence, the focus must be directed towards God, and God alone; otherwise the whole purpose of creation would be in jeopardy. But by focusing on God and His values, we are not drawn to other gods (worldly living). God is a loving and caring God. He cares what happens to us. We must also have that same love and caring for Him.

One of the reasons that talking about God to some, seems rather dull, is because they don't know enough of what they are talking about. It probably is not so much that they don't care, but most often could be, because they don't perceive, haven't learned, or understood the awesomeness of His power and His Being. It is difficult for people to talk about things they know little about.

> "No God – No Peace."   "Know God – Know Peace."

There is an important fact to know about the Holy Spirit, and Jesus explained it, by saying,

> "I assure you that any sin can be forgiven, including blasphemy, but anyone who blasphemes against the Holy Spirit will never be forgiven. It is an eternal sin."
> (Mark 3:28,29)

Chapter 2

THE CAUSE
(The Fall)

THISTLE
(A symbol for the curse of sin, especially the fall.)

"Beware of false prophets who come disguised as harmless sheep, but are really wolves that will tear you apart. You can detect them by the way they act, just as you can identify a tree by is fruit. You don't pick grapes from thorn bushes, or figs from thistles." (Matt 7:15-16)

CAUSE
(And Fall)

C ast from Heaven because of his evil ways;

A nnounced to him and his angels – numbered days.

U nwilling to abort their unwanted pride;

S ent by God to earth, a place where they would hide.

E ternity then theirs, to justly suffer;

A ngels fallen, with their prime self-adorer.

N estling about, in his devouring ambition;

D esiring to gain more souls, through temptation.

F alsely trying, to prove his power and might;

A ttempting to deceive us, away from right.

L ucifer, luring, in every way he tries,

L ooking for ways, to spread all his horrid lies.

THE FALL OF LUCIFER – THE CAUSE

At first thought, it is extremely difficult to imagine something this calamitous occurring, or would have been allowed to occur.

As with us mortal beings, when God created the angels who are eternal beings, He also gave them a free will. One of the most precious gifts that God so generously, and lovingly gave to his creation, was the ability to choose one's own destiny. But as we have found through our earthly existence, this power or discretion to choose, can be either beneficial or detrimental, glorious or fatal. The choices through free will are ultimately voluntary and not determined by external causes. Consequently some of these choices would so change and affect the course of existence for everlasting time; showing intensity to degeneration of culture, accelerating from generation to generation.

Angels are immortal, spiritual beings, attendant upon God. He created nine different orders of angels:

Seraphim – Cherubim – Thrones – Dominions or Dominians
Virtues – Powers – Principalities – Archangels – and Angels.

God gave three Angels higher authority:

Lucifer to oversee Infinity.
Gabriel to oversee Awareness.
Michael to oversee Eternity.

The higher authority that was given to them as Archangels, was because they were to manage God's administration; and He chose to give the most power to Lucifer, the light bearer, for God had been pleased by Lucifer's service.

When the Angels found out that God had a special place in the universe that would be bearing life, they all were fascinated by this find. However, Lucifer had the most fondness for it, and longed for it the most. God, realizing Lucifer's eagerness, authorized him to reside in this newly found dwelling place and ordered him to direct the course of life and bring it to its fundamental capacity for its further growth and development.

Lucifer soon realized and understood the full and profound meaning of God's plan for this newly found world, often referred to as the Jewel of God. The plan was to have Lucifer assist the new souls that God would be creating by the billions. When Lucifer realized that he would then have to compete with all of these new creatures, he thought that God had deceived him, and in his *pride* he wanted to maintain his status as the Highest of creation. In his conceit and arrogance he wanted to preserve his High Position of Honor. Not only did Lucifer detest God's plan, but he wanted to acquire God's Holy Throne.

Lucifer found angels to side with him, and they engaged in a war against Michael and the good angels; trying to conquer and establish themselves as the new rulers of the universe, and gain possession of God's Throne. God, having given the angels free will, allowed the ensuing course to take place and be carried through – but He averted Lucifer's stronghold and didn't allow him to win the war. Because of this rebellion, Lucifer was cast out of heaven, and compelled to go back to earth along with the other *fallen* angels.

"I saw Satan falling from heaven as a flash of lighting!"
(Luke 10:18)

"How you are fallen from heaven, O shining star, son of the morning! You have been thrown down to the earth, you who destroyed the nations of the world. For you said to yourself, 'I will ascend to heaven and set my throne above God's stars. I will preside on the mountain of the gods far away in the north. I will climb to the highest heavens and be like the Most High.' But instead, you will be brought down to the place of the dead, down to its lowest depths. Everyone there will stare at you and ask, 'Can this be the one who shook the earth and the kingdom of the world? Is

this the one who destroyed the world and made it into a wilderness? Is this the king who demolished the world's greatest cities and had no mercy on his prisoners?'"
(Isa 14:12-17)

"You were the perfection of wisdom and beauty. You were in Eden, the garden of God. Your clothing was adorned with every precious stone — red carnelian, chrysolite, white moonstone, beryl, onyx, jasper, sapphire, turquoise, and emerald — all beautifully crafted for you and set in the finest gold. They were given to you on the day you were created. I ordained and anointed you as the mighty angelic guardian. You had access to the holy mountain of God and walked among the stones of fire."

"You were blameless in all you did from the day you were created until the day evil was found in you. Your great wealth filled you with violence, and you sinned. So I banished you from the mountain of God. I expelled you, O mighty guardian, from your place among the stones of fire. Your heart was filled with pride because of all your beauty. You corrupted your wisdom for the sake of your splendor. So I threw you to the earth and exposed you to the curious gaze of kings. You defiled your sanctuaries with your many sins and your dishonest trade. So I brought fire from within you, and it consumed you. I let it burn you to ashes on the ground in the sight of all who were watching. All who knew you are appalled at your fate. You have come to a terrible end, and you are no more." (Eze 28:12b-19)

Lucifer, the *prince and power of the air,* then became the *leader of the evil angels* and also the *god and ruler of the Earth.* Never able to return to the Majestic Heaven. An eternal price to pay by him and his fallen angels for the folly of vanity and evil.

Some of the other names given to Satan, include:

Accuser of the Brethren, Adversary, Apollyon (Abaddon) – which means "destroyer", Beelzebub – which means "lord of the flies, Belial – which means Slanderer, Enemy, Great red dragon, Liar and Father of Lies, Lucifer, Murderer from the beginning, Prince of the devils, Prince of this world, Serpent, Spirit that works in the children of disobedience, Strong man, Tempter, Thief, whose mission is to steal, kill, and destroy, Wicked one.

Some of those in the Bible that encountered Satan:

Eve, King David, Job, Joshua, Jesus, Peter, Israelite woman, Judas Iscariot, Ananias, Hymenaeus, Alexander, Paul.

SATAN'S COURSE OF ACTION

Lucifer's path, or course of action, brought him from being one of the Highest Angels in God's command; the greatest and most *brilliant light*, the shining star, son of the morning, the one with exceptional beauty – to becoming, Satan, the Devil – a catastrophic dilemma, ending as being called the *Prince of Darkness*. Quite an opposite contrast in accomplishment and portrayal – from bright light to darkness.

His goal and ambition as the Prince of Darkness, with the help of his fallen angels, is to deceive and obtain as many souls as he can gather, by binding them, blinding them, filling them with doubt, fear and insecurities, keeping them in darkness, so they can not see the light of truth.

"Satan the god of this evil world, has blinded the minds of those who don't believe, so they are unable to see the glorious light of the Good News that is shining upon them. They don't understand the message we preach about the glory of Christ, who is the exact likeness of God." (2 Cor 4:4)

THE FIRST TEMPTING OF MORTALS

Satan having disguised himself as a serpent, was successful at his first attempt at deceiving the first mortals. God had given instructions, that any fruit could be eaten from the Garden of Eden, except the fruit from the tree of the knowledge of good and evil. But Satan in his serpent appearance, the shrewdest of all the creatures the LORD God had made, came to Eve, Adam's mate, and said,

> "'Really?' he asked the woman. 'Did God really say you must not eat any of the fruit in the garden?'" (Gen 3:1b)

The opposite of faith is doubt, and the opposite of honesty is deceit. Those are two of the primary tools the Devil uses to introduce his enticement on his victims. In his sly and cunning ways he was effective in utilizing these tools with Eve. As with Eve, once he gets our attention, he moves on to more seductive ways to implement his plan. He is very clever in his demonic trickery. So. because of Satan's action, God punished him.

> "So the LORD God said to the serpent, 'Because you have done this, you will be punished. You are singled out from all the domestic and wild animals of the whole earth to be cursed. You will grovel in the dust as long as you live, crawling along on your belly.'" (Gen 3:14)

TESTING JOB'S FAITHFULNESS

Job was a good man, and was ever so faithful to the LORD. One day, Satan the Accuser came to the LORD, and God asked him where he had come from. Satan answered that he had been roaming the earth, watching what was going on.

> "Then the LORD asked Satan, 'Have you noticed my

servant Job? He is the finest man in all the earth — a man of complete integrity. He fears God and will have nothing to do with evil.'"

"Satan replied to the LORD, 'Yes, Job fears God, but not without good reason! You have always protected him and his home and his property from harm. You have made him prosperous in everything he does. Look how rich he is! But take away everything he has, and he will surely curse you to your face!'" (Job 1:8,9)

God gave Satan permission to test Job, and to do whatever he wished with everything that Job possessed but not to harm him physically. Job endured and withstood all of the trials and afflictions brought about by Satan. But Job steadfastly kept his loyalty to the LORD. Because of Job's allegiance, God restored his fortunes, and in fact the LORD gave him twice as much as before! Job lived another 140 years after that, long enough to see four generations of his children and grandchildren.

THE TEMPTING OF JESUS

Satan took advantage of God's allowing him to transform himself into a human form. In order to show his demonic power, and to see if he could trick Jesus to succumb to him as the god of the earth – he was anxious to apply his devious tactics.

"Then Jesus was led out into the wilderness by the Holy Spirit to be tempted there by the Devil. For forty days and forty nights he ate nothing and became very hungry. Then the Devil came and said to him, 'If you are the Son of God, change these stones into loaves of bread.' 'If you are the Son of God, jump off!' 'I will give it all to you, if you will only kneel down and worship me.' 'Get out of here, Satan,' Jesus told him. 'For the Scriptures say, 'You must worship the Lord your God; serve only him.'"(Mt 4:1-3,6,9,10)

THE EVIL SPIRIT'S PERSISTENCY

The devil and his demonic crew are very determined in their evil quest. Therefore they are forever in function – never easing up. They are *always* on the prowl, working as diligently as they can, realizing that they have very little time to accomplish their evil mission. For this reason they are, in their tenaciousness, very obstinate in not wasting any of their allotted time. Their time is limited – and is running out!

> "When an evil spirit leaves a person, it goes into the desert, searching for rest. But when it finds none, it says, 'I will return to the person I came from.' So it returns and finds that its former home is all swept clean. The spirit finds seven other spirits more evil than itself, and they all enter the person and live there. And so that person is worse off than before." (Luke 11:24-26)

THE WHEAT AND THE WEEDS

The disciples wanted Jesus to explain a parable that he had just told the people. Jesus always used stories and illustrations when speaking to the crowds.

> "'All right,' he said. 'I, the Son of Man, am the farmer who plants the good seed. The field is the world, and the good seed represents the people of the Kingdom. The weeds are the people who belong to the evil one. The enemy who planted the weeds among the wheat is the Devil. The harvest is the end of the world, and harvesters are the angels.'" Mt 13:37-39)

SATAN IN DISGUISE

Satan wants to portray himself as the *good guy.* So his attractions can, and usually are, in the form of beauty, cleverness, something ultimately so desirable and alluring; anything that he can employ to attain his next victim's attention. He will usually attack with the promise of giving pleasure or reward, and he will become whatever that particular person's weakness happens to be. The disguise will be appropriately – *suit to kill!*

"Even Satan can disguise himself as an angel of light. So it is no wonder his servants can also do it pretending to be godly ministers. In the end they will get every bit of punishment their wicked deeds deserve." (2 Cor 11:14,15)

THOSE WHO OBEY SATAN

God told us that if we are not *for* Him, that we are *against* Him. So whoever we decide to accept and follow in our selection, is the one that is being obeyed. We, through our decision, remain to be our only source of choice in the matter – who we want to obey is up to *each and every one of us.*

"Once you were dead, doomed forever because of your many sins. You used to live just like the rest of the world, full of sin, obeying Satan, the mighty prince of the power of the air. He is the spirit at work in the hearts of those who refuse to obey God." (Eph 2:12)

"But when people keep on sinning, it shows they belong to the Devil, who has been sinning since the beginning."
(1 John 3:8)

ANGER – SATAN'S FOOTHOLD

Going from being upset over something, to becoming either – irate, angrily silent, mad, sore, furious, indignant, or showing hostility, invites the Devil to join in at the playground. There is nothing that he likes better, than to find himself in that kind of *stirred-up* environment.

> "Don't sin by letting anger gain control over you. Don't let the sun go down while you are still angry, for anger gives a mighty foothold to the Devil." (Eph 4:26,27)

THE ARMOR OF GOD

Trying to deal with this kind of enemy, Satan, on your own, is senseless. The Devil has been at his trade for so long, he cleverly knows what he's doing, why he's doing it, who he's going to do it to, and how he's going to do it. He knows which chains, or which strings to pull! Another advantage that he has, is that he can see us, and observe us. By watching certain incidents we can sometimes see his work in progress. But the only true armor we have against this hostile force, is turning to God to utilize His strength through faith, trust and prayer.

> "Put on all of God's armor so that you will be able to stand firm against all strategies and tricks of the Devil. For we are not fighting against people made of flesh and blood, but against the evil rulers and authorities of the unseen world, against those mighty powers of darkness who rule this world, and against wicked spirits in the heavenly realms." (Eph 6:11,12)

> So humble yourselves before God. Resist the Devil, and he will flee from you." (James 4:7)

> "In every battle you will need faith as you shield to stop the fiery arrows aimed at you by Satan. Put on salvation as your helmet, and take the sword of the Spirit, which is the word of God. Pray at all time and on every occasion in the power of the Holy Spirit." (Eph 6:16-18a)

SATAN'S COUNTERFEIT POWER – THE ANTICHRIST

Sooner than later, the identity will be revealed of the one who is going to deceive and cause great harm to the world. The proper time is approaching. Some say that it is approaching quite rapidly – for the recognition of this *counterfeit* power. Jesus cautioned us to look at the signs that would indicate his coming. The number of devastating disasters and calamities, floods, hurricanes, murders, suicides, rapes, abortions – and the fact that they are growing in numbers and in intensity. The countries at war, the hate and greed, are just some of the indications.

> "For that day will not come until there is a great rebellion against God and the man of lawlessness is revealed — the one who brings destruction. He will exalt himself and defy every god there is and tear down every object of adoration and worship. He will position himself in the temple of God, claiming that he himself is God. Don't you remember that I told you this when I was with you? And you know what is holding him back, for he can be revealed only when his time comes."

> "For this lawlessness is already at work secretly, and it will remain secret until the one who is holding it back steps out of the way. Then the man of lawlessness will be revealed, whom the Lord Jesus will consume with the breath of his mouth and destroy by the splendor of his coming. This evil man will come to do the work of Satan with counterfeit power and signs and miracles. He will use every kind of wicked deception to fool those who are on their way to destruction because they refuse to believe the truth that would save them. So God will send great deception upon them, and they will believe all these lies. Then they will be condemned for not believing the truth and for enjoying the evil they do. (2 Th 2:3b-12)

THE EFFECT

Consequently, *pride*, became the *cause* of Satan's Fall, and also the *effect*, causing the ensuring corruption of mankind through all other sins; thus spreading evil all over the world. Starting with the original sin that he brought about through Eve, his work has compounded itself into a global deterioration. Through his reign as the luring ruler of the world, he has deceived and enticed a multitudinous amount to their terrible and inescapable fate. He is working as efficiently, and as quickly as he can, knowing that his captivating time is limited. This is why we see the evidence of escalating corruption.

Some have asked the question,
"Will Satan ever repent?"
What do you think?

Satan, with his unsatiable malice, and because his pride far exceeds his power – seeks human aid. Through such help he always promises *himself* greater ease of victory, and in return deceitfully promises his aids greatness and pleasure.

Chapter 3

CREATION

SIX DAYS OF CREATION

"In the beginning God created the heavens and the earth...–...Then God looked over all He had made, and He saw that it was excellent in every way." (Gen 1:1,31)

CREATION

C lever are His ways, and always loving his purpose;

R adiantly forming, in a way so generous.

E arth then became, the chosen, intended dwelling place;

A dorned of beauty and plenty, for the human race.

T o be shared with each other, and animals brought forth;

I ngeniously carving life's structure, with so much worth.

O nly a God could evolve, these great gifts of splendor;

N ature, with its space and time, was granted by our Donor.

GOD'S PLAN AND PURPOSE

No one knows, or will ever know, God's full intentions, purpose and reason, for bringing about creation. He alone knows the entirety of the scope of His course, or about His probable instantaneous drawings, diagrams and designs of what He wanted to accomplish. He alone knew why He would create; how all of His ideas would come to fruition, or when and how they would be fulfilled. We cannot even start to imagine and much less understand the full complexity of His plan, and how it would be accomplished or realized.

> "I assure you, until heaven and earth disappear, even the smallest detail of God's law will remain until its purpose is achieved." (Matt 5:18)

One of the things that we know for certain, is that we have a loving God; and through this immense affection for us, He wanted to share that love through the many gifts He had for us.

> "The world is only peopled to people heaven."
> – St Francis de Sales –

Only through creation could God's existence be recognized, extolled, praised and honored. He is the cause of all causes, and everything that was, is, and is still to come, is, and will be the result of His intent, purpose, power and might. Only through creation could His immeasurable love be exposed and displayed in such wondrous effect.

For His glory, and to help Him fulfill His Majestic Plan, God created the Angels, who would then assist Him in different capacities. The Angels were brought forth as spiritual eternal beings. They will exist forever. They were created not only to serve God but to ultimately serve the forthcoming humanity, of which Christ would be the Head. The Angels would also eventually share Heaven with these

God-like souls who would be created as mortals.

The Angels roamed throughout the universe that God had created and they found a special place where life could and would exist. A place which was then called the Jewel. Once this Jewel, Earth, had been found, God revealed His ultimate plan for Earth to His Angels. God sent Lucifer and many Angels to Earth to help in its development of life.

God realized through his generous liberality (having given the Angels their freedom to choose), that they would not be ruled by sovereignty, but by free will and self-independence. And also that, through their own choice, the created Angels would obey or disobey; would, reverence Him because of their loyalty to Him, or would turn against Him because of their pride and self-love.

The Earth and the heavenly bodies were created for the mortal creatures. The creation of the human race, starting with one man and one woman, but through propagation would not only multiply itself, but bring forth a Redeemer. For even Redemption, God himself through Christ, was in God's plan; that we would live in Christ, and He in us. If through free will, sin could and would occur, then sin could also have been avoided. For this we shouldn't criticize or blame God.

> "Who are you but a mere human being, to criticize God? Should the thing that was created say to the one who made it, 'Why have you made me like this?'" (Rom 9:20)

In understanding and appreciating God's purpose and desire for having created us, we must react positively, willingly, unselfishly, and joyfully to the fulfillment of His plan for our existence. We mustn't disappoint Him in what He had in mind for each and every one of us as individuals; to find and fill that reason and purpose for having been created. However we shouldn't attempt to find this path on our own. The only way to achieve this is to let God bring out from each of us, what He would like us to become, according to, and utilizing the talents and gifts He has given us.

"Let go – and – let God?"

He loves us, and knows us better than we know ourselves. He also knows what is best for us, more than we could ever appreciate or perceive on our own. If we let go of our self-determination, and ask Him, it might surprise us to find out what He really has in store. It's worth talking to Him about!

"I knew you before I formed you in your mother's womb."
(Jer 1:5a)

CREATION OF THE UNIVERSE

"By faith we understand that the universe was formed at God's command, that what we now see did not come from anything that can be seen." (Heb 2:3)

Why did God create the immense universe, with its vast number of galaxies, traveling through space in perfect balance, arrangement, speed, orbit and order? Is it just to give us an exhilarating view of magnificent appearance and display when we're looking up to the sky? Is it to temp our human logic and intellect; to keep questioning in awe and amazement its meaningful, fascinating structure and purpose? Forming the uncountable stars and planets in this extremely immense creation that we call the universe, with not any two of them being exactly alike. But similarly to the creation of humans, each has a certain purpose for having been created. What was God's ultimate plan for such a gorgeous creation? Only God knows! One thing we do know for sure, is that it is completely, absolutely and interestingly beautiful. One of the most exciting and repetitive exposures that God has given us to show His continuous artistry, is in the daily and most predictable sunrise and sunset. Each one showing a new charming and mesmerizing, dramatic design from the other. There is a song with lyrics that describes a sunset:

"There are pretty colors, gathering all around;
creating such a splendor, only to be found...
...They wait now 'til tomorrow, for that time serene,
when that Special Artist, paints His majestic scene."

THINK ABOUT IT !

Now let's take some time to put our imagination through a little experiment. Let's see how we can envision this phenomenon. Take time now to clear your thought process. We will begin by concentrating on something quite marvelous and astonishing. Ready?

Let's start by imagining a *ball*. Imagine that ball being quite big. In fact the ball is so big, it measures thousands of miles in diameter. Now, imagine this huge ball being suspended in space, with nothing holding it up. Amazing isn't it! Then notice that the ball is covered with water which stays on it and surrounds it, but doesn't flow off.

Now imagine land, countries, cities, roads and buildings covering it. Imagine yourself sitting, walking, or driving your vehicle on top of it. The next time you are in your vehicle, or the next time you take a look at the horizon, try to imagine this reality. It certainly gives a very different sensation and perspective of where we are. The thought of being able to drive, if the roads would accommodate, all the way around this big ball, going completely around, and still staying on its surface. Imagine all these people and things around you, that are able to, and are supplying you with all your earthly needs.

Imagine that this ball is slightly tilted and at the same time, spinning on its axis, and that there is a smaller ball that is orbiting around it. Now the bigger ball, along with other companion balls are all orbiting around a much larger ball. One that is enormously bigger and seems to be on fire; a fire that has lasted for millions or billions of years, and is so bright that it illuminates all the other balls that are circulating it. And all of these balls are part of a vast and greater system that are filling an area that is so immense that it cannot be measured. Another amazing marvel, is that all of these balls of different sizes are all perfect spheres, not ragged or oblong like some rocks, but are astonishingly all flawlessly round.

Now imagine being able to think of, engineer, and create these models of excellence. God is indeed accurate and precise in everything He does, or create. In the placement of the Earth in our Solar System, if the Earth's location would have been a mere thousand miles further from the Sun, we couldn't stand the cold. If it had been placed a thousand miles closer to the Sun, we couldn't stand the heat.

To further appreciate the gigantic and significant fact of creation of unaccountable proportion, we can also imagine that it was probably brought about by *one spoken word.* Amazing! Awesome!

> "God promised everything to the Som as an inheritance, and through the Son he made the universe and everything in it. The Son reflects God's own glory, and everything about him represents God exactly. He sustains the universe by the mighty power of his command." (Heb 1:2b,3a)

THE CREATION OF THE EARTH

When God created the heavens, the Earth was an empty, formless mass, enveloped in darkness, and the Spirit of the Lord hovered over its surface. And the Lord made the light, and He separated it from the darkness.

> "God called the light 'day' and the darkness 'night'. Together these made up one day." (Gen 1:5)

Then God separated the waters from above and below, which then allowed the *sky, clouds,* and the *water* on the earth to appear. He also separated the water from the ground on the Earth, and the *land* and *seas* appeared. Then God said,

> "Let the land burst forth with every sort of grass and seed-bearing plant. Ant let there be trees that grow seed-bearing fruit. The seeds will then produce the kinds of plants and trees from which they came." (Gen 1:11)

God then brought forth and introduced the bright lights to the sky to separate day from night, and to become signs to the Earth to mark off the days, seasons, and years. The larger one, the *sun* would rule the day, and the smaller one, the *moon* would preside through the night. With them He also made the stars, so that together they would light the Earth. Then God said,

> "'Let the waters swarm with fish and other life. Let the skies be filled with birds of every kind.' And God said, 'Let the earth bring forth every kind of animal – livestock, small animals, and wildlife.'" (Gen 1:20,24)

So all of the Lord God's creation of the earth and man were completed from the first to the sixth day. And after each of the days of His creation, God saw that each creation was excellent in every way.

> "On the seventh day having finished his task, God rested from all his work. And God blessed the seventh day and declared it holy, because it was the day when he rested from His work of creation." (Gen 2:2,3)

The LORD God, therefore, being the *only one* who can give life, is the *only one* who can take it away.

> *Nota Bene – It is understandable that some believe that creation has been around for billions of years. The fact to*

*remember though, is that God has limitless capabilities. In these wondrous powers and abilities, it is then possible that he made it **look** like it had been around for billions of years. Not Science, but only God knows the exact and actual age of creation.*

THE CREATION OF MAN

Until God made rain fall, the plants and grain were being fed from the ground to keep them alive, because there was no one there to cultivate the soil.

> "And the LORD God formed a man's body from the dust of the ground and breathed into it the breath of life. And the man became a living person. (Gen 1:7)

The LORD planted an exceptionally lovely and bountiful garden in Eden, the earthly paradise that God had prepared for man. God brought the first man, Adam, to the garden where He had planted beautiful trees that produced delicious fruit. At the center of the garden He had placed the *tree of life* and the *tree of the knowledge of good and evil*. Adam was to care for the garden, but God gave him this warning:

> "You may freely eat any fruit in the garden except fruit from the tree of knowledge of good and evil. If you eat of its fruit, you will surely die." (Gen 2:16b,17)

God saw that His new creation, Adam, needed a more suitable companion than the animals He had given him to name, and accompany him. So the LORD put Adam into a deep sleep, and while he was asleep, God took one of his ribs and formed a woman from the rib, and brought the woman to her mate.

"'At last!' Adam exclaimed. 'She is part of my own flesh and bone! She will be called 'woman', because she was taken out of a man.'" (Gen 2:23)

"'...Let us make people in our image, to be like ourselves...' So God created people in his own image; God patterned them after himself; male and female he created them." (Gen 1:26a,27)

THE FALL OF MAN

Satan wanted to show his vengeance to the LORD because God had created the humans that would be regarded as higher than the angels. So disguising himself as a serpent, the devil didn't waste any time in his attempting to set apart, and cause division between the newly formed human race, with their creator. He utilized one of his primary approaches, by planting *doubt*, while asking Eve if God *really* said that the designated fruit should not be eaten.

She then expressed to the serpent that they may eat the fruit in the garden, except the one from the tree in the center of the garden – and if they would eat, or even touch it, that God had said that they would die. In using another of his most deceivingly effective tools, the *promising of a reward,* the serpent said,

"'You won't die!' The serpent hissed, "God knows that your eyes will be opened when you eat it. You will become just like God, knowing everything, good and evil.'"
(Gen 3:4,5)

The woman, in being tempted, and believing Satan's first lie to a mortal, became so convinced; the fruit looking so fresh and delicious, and remembering the promise of becoming so wise, ate some of the fruit. Then she gave some to her husband Adam, who was with her. At that moment, *shame* came upon them, for they suddenly realized their now apparent nakedness. So they found some fig leaves, and strung them together around their hips to cover themselves.

Their eyes now having been opened to shame, caused them to hide, because they had heard God walking in the garden. God called to Adam, and asked him where he was. Adam replied that he was hiding because he was naked. So God asked him who had told him that he was naked. Then God asked him if he had eaten the fruit from the garden, the specific fruit that He had commanded them not to eat. Adam admitted that he ate it, and that it was the woman who had brought him the fruit. The Lord then asked the woman how she could do such a thing. She replied that the serpent had tricked her, and that was why she ate it. So the LORD told the serpent that because he had done that, that in his punishment, and being singled out from all the other animals, he would be cursed to grovel in the dust, and that he would forever crawl on his belly.

> "Then he said to the woman, 'You will bear children with intense pain and suffering. And though your desire will be for your husband, he will be your master.'"
>
> "And to Adam he said,'Because you listened to your wife and ate the fruit I told you not to eat, I have placed a curse on the ground. All your life you will struggle to scratch a living from it. It will grow thorns and thistles for you, though you will eat of its grains. All your life you will sweat to produce food, until your dying day. Then you will return to the ground from which you came. For you were made from dust and to dust you will return.'" (Gen 3:16-19)

Because, through propagation she would become the mother of all the people everywhere, Adam called his wife, Eve. And for Adam and his wife, God made them clothing from animal skins so they could cover themselves. But the Lord didn't want them to stay in the garden He had prepared for them, for He didn't want them to eat from the tree of life, because if they did, they would live forever.

God then sent Adam out to cultivate the ground from which he had been made.

From this moment on, man has had to pay the debt of mortality to his Creator.

> "After banishing them from the garden, the LORD God stationed mighty angelic beings to the east of Eden. And a flaming sword flashed back and forth, guarding the way to the tree of life." (Gen 3:24)

Eve, after having slept with her husband Adam, became pregnant. When she delivered her first born, Cain, she said,

> "'With the LORD's help, I have brought forth a man!'"
> (Gen 4:1a)

Later the second son was born, and she named him Abel. When the brothers were older, Cain had become a farmer and Abel a shepherd. Because God was favoring Abel's gift offerings to Him, Cain, in jealousy and revenge, while out in a field one day, attacked and killed Abel. Thus evolved humanity's second calamity. Sin and evil would then follow in the path of humankind.

THE RENEWAL OF MAN

Cain, having been banished from his living area, as a punishment from God for slaying his brother Abel, re-established himself in the land of Nod, east of Eden.

From Adam there became a list of descendants. It wasn't unusual in those days for people to live to be hundreds of years old. One of these descendants was Lamech. Lamech brought forth a son at the age of 182, and named him Noah. Lamech said that Noah would bring relief from the distressing struggle of farming the ground that had been cursed by the LORD. The population had begun to grow rapidly on the earth, and evil was spreading just as fast. Then the LORD said,

> "'My spirit will not put up with humans for such a long time, for they are only mortal flesh. In the future they will live no more than 120 years.'" (Gen 6:3)

In those days, and for ensuing years, as the many unverified legends told about them, the sons of god got sexually active with human women, giving birth to giants that became heroes. It also broke God's heart, seeing the extent of human wickedness, and the trend and direction of man's living, going towards evil.

> "And the LORD said, 'I will completely wipe out this human race that I have created. Yes, and I will destroy all the animals and birds too. I am sorry I ever made them.'"
> (Gen 6:7)

The people at that time had corrupted and degenerated themselves through the love of lust and evil. They had lost all sense of normalcy and morality, and became utterly, and spiritually deteriorated.

Noah was a pleasure to the LORD, and the *only* and *truly* righteous man living on the earth at that time. He always tried to do everything according to God's will.

> "Now the earth had become corrupt in God's sight, and it was filled with violence." (Gen 6:11)

God, having observed the condition of man, found that the people had become vicious, depraved, corrupt and perverted. So He told Noah that He had decided to destroy all of mankind, because the earth was filled with crime and immorality. He then told Noah to build a boat, an ark, and gave him all the instructions necessary, not only including the plan and measurements, but a full and entire list of materials as well.

>"'Look! I am about to cover the earth with a flood that will destroy every living thing. Everything on earth will die! But I solemnly swear to keep you safe in the boat, with your wife and your sons and wives.'" (Gen 6:17,18)

Then the LORD told Noah that he should bring into the boat a pair of every kind of animals, a male and female, and also the same with the birds and the reptiles. He told him to bring enough food for themselves and the animals, and even had Noah bring in some extra animals designated for gift offerings. God also told him when the rain would start, and that it would rain for forty days and forty nights, and that all of the animals, birds, reptiles, and all of mankind that would be left behind would not survive, but die. Noah obeyed the LORD and accomplished everything that he had been asked to do.

>"He was 600 years old when the flood came, and he went aboard the boat to escape – he and his wife and his sons and wives. With them were all the various kinds of animals – those approved for eating and sacrifice and those that were not – along with all the birds and other small animals. They came into the boat in pairs, male and female, just as God had commanded Noah." (Gen 7:6-9)

After Noah, along with his wife, sons and sons' wives, pairs of animals, birds, and insects were all safely in the ark, the Lord shut them in.

On the seventeenth day of the second month of his age of 600, water suddenly, from underground pressure, swelled, exploded and emerged onto the ground, and the rain fell from the sky in a deluge. For forty days and forty nights the floods came continuously and forcefully covering the earth with water.

The boat floated safely on the water that had risen, as God had promised. The waters covered the highest peaks and were more than twenty two feet above the highest mountain. Everything that had remained behind perished – all of mankind, animals and birds, every breathing thing was eliminated from the face of the earth. The water covered the earth for a total of one hundred and fifty days.

The rain and the subterranean water having stopped, God then allowed the wind to blow across the waters to form a drying process, and the flood began to recede. After exactly five months from the time the flood began, the boat came to rest on the mountains of Ararat. Three months later the other mountain peaks appeared. After another 40 days, Noah, in his attempt to find dry land, sent out some doves to see if they would find any sign of life. One came back with an olive leaf in its beak, which told Noah that the water was almost gone. He later released the dove again, and this time the dove did not come back – a sign that it had found nourishment.

> "Finally, when Noah was 601 years old, ten and a half months after the flood began, Noah lifted back the cover to look. The water was drying up. Two more months went by, and at last the earth was dry! Then God said to Noah, 'Leave the boat, all of you. Release all the animals and birds so they can breed and reproduce in great numbers.'"
> (Gen 8:13-17)

In appreciation and thankfulness to the Lord for having spared him and his family from that devastation, Noah wanted to show his gratitude to God. So he built an altar to offer some of the animals that He had designated for sacrificing. The Lord was pleased with the sacrifice, and He said,

> "'I will never again curse the earth, destroying all living things, even though people's thoughts and actions are bent toward evil from childhood.'"(Gen 8:21b)

Then God put His blessing upon Noah and his sons, and told them to go and multiply, and have many children, in order to repopulate, and *renew* humankind on the earth. God wanted to assure the remaining few that were left from His creation, and for the many generations to come, that there would never again be another flood, and so He said to Noah,

> "'I am giving you a sign as evidence of my eternal covenant with you and all living creatures. I have placed my rainbow in the clouds. It is a sign of my permanent promise to you and to all the earth. When I send clouds over the earth, the rainbow will be seen in the clouds, and I will remember my covenant with you and with everything that lives. Never again will there be a flood that will destroy all life. When I see the rainbow in the clouds, I will remember the eternal covenant between God and every living creature on earth.'" (Gen 9:12-16)

Noah had three sons, Shem, Ham, and Japhet. Through Ham the Canaanites came to be. All the nations that are scattered throughout the earth, from east to west, originated from these three sons of Noah that survived the flood.

After re-establishing himself, Noah became a farmer, and watched over and cared for his vineyard. He lived for another 350 years. He died at a ripe old age of 950.

RECEIVING THE LAWS

The Ten Commandments – The Decalogue, is a compendium of the fundamental obligations, as a commitment to serve the Lord.

The Ten Commandments became the religious laws that governed the ancient Hebrews. They were also accepted by Christians as fundamental principles for their belief.

God had told Moses to call the people together so they could be instructed as to how *they* should reverence Him, and to make sure that they would teach His laws to their *children*. God had purposely given Moses instructions to have the people stay within a designated area at the bottom of Mount Sianai.

A huge cloud had come upon the mountain, along with a frightful thunder and lightning storm. There was also a long, loud blowing from a ram's horn. The people shook in fear. Mount Sinai was covered with smoke because God, Jehovah, had arrived to the mountain in an overwhelming manner, in the form of fire. The mountain shook from an earthquake. Moses went up to the mountain to meet the Lord, but He told him to go back to warn the people not to come up the mountain.

The people had seen the lightning and smoke billowing from the mountain and had heard the long, distressing trumpet sound as they were standing in the distance in fear.

"'Don't be afraid,' Moses said, 'for God has come in this way to show you his awesome power. From now on, let your fear of him keep you from sinning.'" (Ex 20:19,20)

Moses calling all the people of Israel together, told them to listen carefully to all the new regulations God had given him, and was bringing to them. He wanted them to be attentive, because he wanted to make sure that they would understand, learn and obey the laws.

Moses also wanted them to know that he was acting as an intermediary, because they didn't want to follow him to the mountain because they were afraid of the fire.

So God had spoken to Moses, and he was delivering the Lord's Communication to his people. He gave them the message that God,
Does not want us to worship any other gods except Him;
Does not want us to swear or misuse His name;
Wants us to observe and keep the day of the Sabbath Holy;
Wants us to honor our father and mother;
Doesn't want us to commit adultery;
Doesn't want us to steal;
Doesn't want us to lie about anything or anybody;
Doesn't want us to desire another mate's spouse;
Doesn't want us to desire anyone else's property.

THE MELANGE OF THE LANGUAGES – THE DISPERSION

People started to multiply in great numbers, as was instructed to Noah and his sons, by God. They wanted to form themselves into a settled society, for they had their ethnic and linguistic entity. The people had found a plain in the east. A place called Shinar. They had not only united themselves through their intelligence and knowledge, but had also united their forces. They decidedly were determined to build a city in *their* honor, to keep the people from *dispersing*, and to satisfy their vanity and self-exaltation. They would erect a tower, a monument to themselves, so that they would be remembered. The tower would be a *ziggurat*, a pyramidal structure of imposing height, built with successive stories, and having outside stairs, and a shrine at its top. They wanted to look at themselves as being God.

"Let's build a great city with a tower that reaches to the skies – a monument to our greatness! This will bring us together and keep us from scattering all over the world."
(Gen 11:4)

When God came down and saw the city that mankind was building, and seeing what they had accomplished while they had just started to develop themselves linguistically and politically, He knew what they would be capable of. The Lord, also might have wanted to slow down the process in order to give time for the prophesies to be fulfilled. So He gave them *different languages* so they wouldn't understand each other.

"In that way, the LORD scattered them all over the earth; and that ended the building of the city. That is why the city was called Babel, because it was there that the LORD confused the people by giving them many languages, thus scattering them across the earth." (Gen 11:8,9)

Chapter 4

PRIDE

FROG
(A symbol of worldly pleasure.)

"And I saw three evil spirits that looked like frogs leap from the mouth of the dragon, the beast, and the false prophet." (Rev 16:13)

PRIDE

P rince of darkness originated this sin;

R esulting in other offenses to begin.

I nterposing with his lies and his conceit;

D evouring though many, using deceit.

E veryone should banish this perversity,

   (affecting many, and their eternity.)

PRIDE

P   perversity, possessions, prince-of-darkness, profanity.

R   rage, rambunctious, rancorous, rampage, ravish, rebellion, recklessness, reclusiveness, reluctance, remiss, reproachful, repugnant, revolting, ridiculing, rile, rivaling, rude, rumoring, ruthless.

I   idleness, immorality, impatience, impiousness, impoliteness, impure, imprudent, inappreciable, indecent, infidelity, ingrate, insensitive, insincere, insulting, irreligious, irreverent.

D   damning, dastard, debasing, debauchery, deceitfulness, deception, defiling, dehumanizing, demeaning, demonic, demoralizing, depriving, deriding, desiring, devious, devoid, devouring, discordant, discourteous, discrediting, disgraceful, dishonest, disobedient, disorderly, dispassionate, disregardful, disrespectful, dissident, distorting, dissipating.

E   earthly, egotistic, evasive, envious, erotic, evil.

MAN'S SINFUL NATURE

God has implanted the knowledge of His existence in us from the very start of creation through conscious reasoning. Just looking around us, at the earth and the sky, we can see His wondrous and awesome works. He made Himself known to Adam and Eve, Moses and many others. People have always known instinctively in their hearts of God's existence, and also of His capabilities and power, but the knowledge of good and evil only came as a result of *man* testing God.

The Bible tells us that we are all infected with, and thus impure with sin; and if we were to display proudly our righteous deeds, that we would find them as filthy rags. If we were then to follow our *natural direction*, it would lead us away from God. If we want to be directed by *our sinful nature*, we then turn to the way that seems right to us, and although it *might* seem to be the proper way to go, it usually ends up towards destruction. In the same way, it might also feel right, that going to heaven should in some way depend on us, through our urging and our own efforts. We must remember that the *only* way to heaven is by grace through faith, not through *our* works.

"All of us have strayed away like sheep. We have left
God's path to follow our own. Yet the LORD laid on him
the guilt and sins of us all." (Isa 53:6)

Scripture tells us that the law of Moses could not have saved us because of our *sinful nature*. So God implemented a different plan in order that we would be saved. He sent His Son in a sinless human body, that through Christ's sacrifice, sin's control over us would be destroyed.

If we are dominated by our sinful nature we think about sinful things. If we are controlled by the Spirit of God, we think about things that please the Spirit. So if we let our sinful nature control our mind – that is death! But when we let the Spirit control our mind, we find that there is life and peace, because the sinful nature is always an enemy of God, it never did, nor will it ever, obey God's laws. If we are to please God, we therefore have to get rid of our sinful nature. But once we are in the control of the Spirit, we have the Spirit of God living in us. Like the term that is often used, we have to "Get with the Program!"

It seems to be a fact of life that even with the best of intentions in intending to do what is right, we sometimes inevitably do what is wrong. Even though in our hearts we want to obey God's laws, there is another force within us that is at war with our mind. That force could win the fight and make us a slave to it. Only through the Lord can we be freed from this sin-dominated life.

People easily replace the attention that should be given to God and the truth, and instead are drawn to whatever it is that they desire. Which many times leads them to shameful and sinful things. They choose to worship their *desires* and the *things* that God made, rather than to worship the *One* who created these things.

These desires caused women to turn with lust, indulging sexually with each other, and men doing the same with other men. Although God said that He abandoned them to their shameful desires – He said that they will endure the penalty which they justly deserve.

> "Don't you know that those who do wrong will have no share in the Kingdom of God? Don't fool yourselves. Those who indulge in sexual sin, who are idol worshipers, adulterers, male prostitutes, homosexuals, thieves, greedy people, drunkards, abusers, and swindlers – none of these will have a share in the Kingdom of God." (1 Cor 6:9,10)

Lives have become full of every imaginable, and unimaginable wickedness – morality being viciously depraved. Increasing degeneration of bad habits and activities of backstabbing, boastfulness, deception, divisions, drunkenness, eagerness for lustful pleasure, envy, fighting, gossiping, greed, hate, hostility, idolatry, impure thoughts, insolence, jealousy, malice behavior, murder, outburst of anger, participation in demonic activities, pride, quarreling, the feeling that *everyone* is wrong except those in your own particular and exclusive little group, selfish ambition, sexual immorality, wild parties, and the forever inventing of new kinds of sins that spread rampantly. Many children have become disobedient to their parents and authority, refusing to listen, understand, comply or cooperate. *They,* now have to be the ones that have to be looked up to by their parents – not the other way around. This reversal of honor and authority has caused many parents to succumb to this type of environment and behavior, and consequently have lost control of their children – and some unable to regain that control. Some children are also not only breaking their promises, but are becoming heartless and unforgiving, and will not only do these things, but will encourage others to do the same, while not even being aware of God's penalty for those actions. There are, however many other children who are very considerate, attentive, and well behaved.

Right is right! – Wrong is wrong!

There are *reasons* for doing good, – and *excuses* for doing bad.

Society had gotten so morally and sinfully bad in the ancient city of Sodom, that God wanted to destroy the whole city. Abraham pleaded with God, and asked Him, that if he could find fifty good people in Sodom, would God spare the city from destruction. When Abraham couldn't find fifty, he asked God to spare them for finding forty. Then he asked God if for thirty, then if for twenty. Finally God told Abraham that He would spare Sodom if he would find ten good men. Imagine how corrupt that city must have been, and how merciful God must have been if only ten good men were found!

"As the Scriptures say, 'No one is good – not even one.'"
(Rom 3:10)

It is understandable that God is then quite justified in showing his anger to those who push the truth away from themselves, and to those who don't take time to worship Him or even give Him thanks.

"I know I am rotten through and through so far as my old sinful nature is concerned." (Ro 7:18a)

We want *anything* and *everything* that is desirable. We want it *now*, and want it to be enjoyable, beautiful, beneficial, justifiable and appropriate, so as to either please ourselves, or our senses. Be it gluttony, the flesh, wagering, comfort, wealth, possessions, notoriety, etc. But the opposite of these, fasting, chastity, labor, deprivation, charity, self-abasement, etc., would be so much more beneficial, not only in causing us to humble ourselves, but in the molding of our soul, spirit, character and senses, and also to help and guide us towards a proper direction; focusing on a healthier and wealthier way of life – physically, morally, and spiritually; and also to achieve the cleansing and greatness that our souls should aspire to. The alternative to this way of life leads only to degeneration and the pornographication of the cultures.

MAN IS EGO MOTIVATED

Many things today are motivating the present culture, and leads society to satisfy three people – *me, myself,* and *I*.
Egotism could be defined as, the inclination to convey or to note of oneself boastfully or in excess. An inflated degree of self-importance; conceit. **E. G. O. Easing God Out!**
There is a large difference between humbly feeling good about yourself, or for having accomplished something that you have done well, or, bragging or making yourself shine through an ego trip. Some like to draw attention to themselves in any way they can. Some do it with either, or a combination of: clothes, fame, hairdos, homes, jewelry, vehicles, and many other kinds of worldly possessions, and some even attempt it and succeed by doing something that will make themselves look *bad.* Some make themselves look better on the

outside than they do on the inside. The only true way of making ourselves look good to ourselves and others, is through the good things we do.

> "It is not that we think we can do anything of lasting value by ourselves. Our only power and success come from God."
> (2 Cor 3:5)

Everybody is so busy! *So* busy! Everything is operating at such a fast pace, and for some, 24/7. Between family life, our work, our exercising in trying to keep physically fit, and our entertainment, there is so much left to do and so little time to do it in. Some people are working long hours, and some at more than one job. But the remaining available time seems to be concentrated more and more on selfish needs; people giving *themselves* everything they want, and in so doing, not finding the time, or not wanting or caring to take the time for God. Is this the way to live, to give shelf-life to God, He that has given us everything? In reality what we are saying is, "We are putting You, God, on a shelf, and You can wait until we are ready, or decide to spend some time with You. We are too busy now, because we're fulfilling all of our desires, needs and wants, and that keeps us pretty occupied. We'll get to You later!" How will we then explain this to Him?

In these days filled with rivalry of every sort, people will argue, until they are blue in face, trying to prove a point. Sometime even knowing that they might be, or are wrong – often just trying to save face. Nobody likes to lose a debate, but some will try all kinds of ways to prove themselves right, often times stretching the truth, or becoming just plain deceitful. The following is a cute little story that exemplifies that:

> There were three little kids bragging about their dads. The first little kid said, "My dad is so fast, he goes in the back of the house and shoots an arrow from his bow, and before the arrow has a chance to hit the target, he runs over there and

catches the arrow." The second little kid says, "My dad's faster than that! He goes on the firing range and fires his rifle, and before the bullet has a chance to hit the target, he runs over there and catches the bullet with his teeth." The third little kid isn't saying anything, so one of the other kids asked him, "Well, how about your dad?" So the third little kid replied, "Oh my dad's faster than that! My dad works for the State. He gets out of work at five – but he's home by three."

When we become jealous and we let our ambition fill our hearts with selfishness, then we shouldn't boast of being good, clever or wise. We would just be lying to God, to others and basically to ourselves. Jealousy is considered as a worldly evil tool and motivation used by the Devil to have his victims desire what others have, as he did with his desire for God's Power and Throne. Selfishness will bring nothing more than bad and false portrayal of oneself, as well as evil and disorder. A selfish ego just keeps us from finding good in others.

> "Don't be selfish, don't live to make a good impression on others. Be humble, thinking of others as better than yourself. Don't think only about your own affairs, but be interested in others too, and what they are doing." (Phil 2:3,4)

It seems that humility and self-abasement is becoming more and more *non-existent* in this world that is obsessed with ease, comfort, self-satisfaction, greed, power and self-gratification. Some will even make others look bad, or purposely find fault, in order to make themselves look better than they are – often brought forth by their insecurity. The media also has a stronghold in capturing and saturating the people's attention and minds. Through the media and many other facets of reaching the public, the emphasis seems to dwell on gossip and the importance of putting the *self* first.

Selfishness is another form of pride. It differs as it is a sign or symbol to give oneself the right to go before, or to be considered before something or someone. It is also the placing of one's needs, desires, or advantage above the needs or interests of others; quite similar to egotism, as it prompts one to be self-absorbed, self-seeking, or self-centered. It then makes the selfish person feel, that it is fitting and rightful to be supremely caring for oneself. Because it regards its own comfort and advantage, it does so as a *disregard* and usually at the expense, of others.

> "For jealousy and selfishness are not God's kind of wisdom. Such things are earthly, unspiritual, and demonic." (Jas 3:15)

Arrogance is yet another derivative of pride, the deadly sin. It involves showing signs of being boastful, haughty, insolent, lordly, overbearing, presumptuous, supercilious, and displaying oneself to be excessively and unpleasantly, self-important, or claiming rank, dignity or power. Arrogance is usually, dictatorially portrayed as showing one's superiority and importance, or looking down on others.

> "Stop acting as proud and haughty! Don't speak with such arrogance!" (1 Sa 2:3)

Arrogance precedes such things as perverted speech, corruption and many other evils. It is a deterrent from goodness, and keeps people from finding God. In the end, the proud and the haughty will be brought low, and the LORD alone will be exalted.

PERMISSIVENESS

Permissiveness usually comes about in different ways. It could be abrupt or gradual in occurrence. It is the allowing, tolerating or letting something happen that usually is forbidden, prohibited or not permitted. It is the granting of access, or allowing freedom or tolerance of behavior or indulgence.

Even with the promising traditions of economics, philosophy, politics, religion, science, sociology and the arts, our culture has failed to bring about a positive or normal human society – one in which we can live in peace, live freely and live happily.

By encouraging the wicked – permissiveness insults the great.

We are living in a society that has fewer and fewer moral codes, and has become so permissive, that social norms have become more than increasingly liberal. People have become obsessed with abominations, corruption, immodesty and filth – everything that destroys souls. As sexual freedom increases, the freedom to view violent and sexual material also increases, but the censorship of these and other things, like films, music, art and literature, decreases. As permissiveness spreads, so does the rates of separations, divorces, teenage pregnancies and abortion rise. When the allowing of behavior gets so bad that Middle Schools are looking into giving birth control pills to their students, things have gotten not only very bad, but shamefully out of hand, and even out of control.

> "But that doesn't mean that the law has lost its force. It is easier for heaven and earth to disappear than for the smallest point of God's law to be overturned." (Luke 16:17)

There is a difference between instantaneously allowing something to happen which is brought about abruptly, and the other form of permissiveness, of letting something happen gradually. One is sudden, and the other grows stronger and intensifies through time.

Permissiveness opens the flood gates to temptation, allowing access to all that was forbidden. Our culture has become the product of ongoing degradation that first started at the very beginning of our civilization. The momentum today has accelerated to the point of being almost impossible to stop.

Evil has spread with such velocity, that children have become victims of the laxity and permissiveness of parents and society. Immorality is overlooked. Sexuality is condoned. No real effort is being made to fight corruption in our schools, our governments and sad to say, in our homes. How do we attack this difficult course, this dilemma that has plagued this country and the world with liberalism, rationalism, humanism and all manners of fallacy? We should go back to the basics and search out the needed power and authority to start engaging the necessary steps towards a cleansing of our corrupt culture. The first and most effective place to start is in the home, by turning to the parents. The parents have got to overcome their laxity, and replace it with teaching the children about the value of self-discipline and to also adopt and show stern discipline. The most effective tool however is the proper example shown by the parents, guardians or teachers. The necessity of becoming a family unit is so important. The family that plays and prays together – stays together! Our government, as a nation, state or city has to establish guidelines to promote the return of decency and morality to our society, otherwise we will all be swimming against the current.

Permissiveness decreases moral values. It is allowed, and rests in a wrong conception of human freedom and behavior. Education is the predominant factor in the development of true freedom, and this only derives from the acceptance and teaching of better rules, laws, and regulations. Those that are responsible for teaching the young, have to be responsible, and expected to give them the appropriate and necessary instructions in respect to the truth that brings about the qualities of moral and spiritual dignity, which lead to a more joyful life and a well nourished soul.

DOUBT – FEAR

Doubt which in definition is quite similar to fear, differs in that it is more about the lack of certainty, distrust, indecision, hesitation in belief, to be unsure, to waiver in opinion, to question, to be inclined not to believe, to be apprehensive of, to suspect, dread, or to have unsettled suspicion.

> "If you must tell me your opinions tell me what you believe in.
> I have plenty of doubts of my own."
> – Johann von Goethe –

> "Doubts are more cruel than the worst of truths."
> – Jean Baptiste Moliere –

> "Our doubts are traitors and make us lose the good
> we oft might win by fearing to attempt."
> – William Shakespeare –

As earlier mentioned, doubt is one of the Devil's primary tools, which he utilized in tempting Eve in Eden. Some say, "Where there is confusion – there is the Devil." Satan loves to spread doubt and confusion. Although there are many things that might occur during our life's journey, the one thing that should never be *doubted*, is God's Love and His Word.

> "When doubts filled my mind, your comfort gave me renewed hope and cheer." (Ps 94:19)

Doubting comes to mind when we think of the story about Peter and the other disciples that had seen Jesus walking on the water towards them while they were in the boat. Peter not being sure it was Jesus, said to Him, that if it was really Him, to have Jesus tell him to walk towards Him on the water. Jesus told Peter that it was alright. So, Peter going over the side of the boat started walking towards Jesus. Once on the water, when Peter noticed the high waves around him, got terrified and began to sink and shouted to Jesus to help him. Jesus instantly reached out His hand to grab him. He then told Peter that he didn't have much faith, then asked him why he *doubted Him*.

An other occurrence concerning Jesus teaching about doubt, was after He caused the fig tree to wither-up.

"I assure you, if you have faith and don't doubt, you can do things like this and much more. You can even say to this mountain, 'May God lift you up and throw you into the sea.' and it will happen." (Mt 21:21)

Fear, unlike doubt, is more a distressing or irksome emotion marked by alarm; a disquiet or anxious concern; solicitude; a feeling of disturbance or anxiety caused by the expectation or the realization of danger or of the unknown. Fear is also used to express a reverence or awe, as in – the holy fear of God.

"The oldest and strongest emotion of mankind is fear, and the oldest and strongest kind of fear is fear of the unknown."
– H. P. Lovecraft –

There will come the time when He who made heaven and earth, the sea, and all the springs of water, will sit as *Judge*. This is why a voice from the Throne said, that all His servants, from the least to the greatest, all who *fear* God, should praise Him.

"Fools rush in where angels fear to tread."
– Alexander Pope –

"We should not let our fears hold us back from pursuing our hopes."
– John Fitzgerald Kennedy –

When we *fear* the LORD it avoids evil, and allows us to work towards complete purity. We then live according to His will, love Him with all our heart and soul, and obey His laws and commands.

"God is love, and all who live in love live in God, and

God lives in them. And as we live in God, our love grows more perfect. So we will not be afraid on the day of judgment, but we can face him with confidence because we are like Christ here in this world." (1 Jn 4:16,17)

The fear of the LORD is not only the beginning of wisdom, but it is true wisdom, and the knowledge of the Holy One results in real understanding, and renounces all evil.

When we find our way, our only and true way, through Christ, we have no more *doubts* or *fear*!

DISOBEDIENCE

Disobedience is the refusal, neglect or failure to obey, fulfill or follow a rule, order or a command. It could also be a *violation* of a command or prohibition. It is born by the glory of being vain.

The *first* sin came from our *first* parent. From the origination of that sin, sin was then transferred to mankind. This disobedience then brought about pride from which people would disobey. Therefore disobedience is related to every sin.

Disobedience plays an even bigger part in our everyday life, than the refusal of doing something. For instance, if we are uncharitable to our neighbors, and this charity is a requirement by God to obey His Commandments, the act becomes sinful because it is contrary to the love of God and our neighbor. Obstinacy or stubbornness makes the disobedience even more severe.

The slander of a person becomes a greater sin than a disobedience of a command. The gravity, seriousness or importance of a command will amount to the degree of disobedience. The more grievous the command – the greater the disobedience. The same applies to the disobedience of a higher or lower authority's command. The disobedience is greater by disobeying the higher authority.

> "Oh, what joy for those whose disobedience is forgiven, whose sins are put out of sight." (Ro 4:7)

God gets angry at us for our failure to obey or follow His rules. When we refuse to acknowledge or obey Him, He abandons us to our own evil minds and allows us to do anything we choose. Then we get involved in all kinds of deception, envy, fighting, gossip, greed, hate, malicious behavior, murder, sin and wickedness. So we also become arrogant, back stabbers, boastful, breakers of promises, heartless, insolent, or proud. We refuse to understand – becoming unforgiving, and haters of God.

We should be very much aware that there is a punishment for disobedience. Not only being aware of God's penalty for doing so, but in being indifferent, we *encourage* others to do the same.

> "So those who refuse to obey the laws of the land are refusing to obey God, and punishment will follow."
> (Ro 13:2)

DISHONESTY – DECEITFULNESS – HYPOCRISY

Dishonesty and deceitfulness have similar traits, features and characteristics, as both are about being fraudulent or deliberately misleading, false, corrupt, or lacking integrity in an act or statement. Dishonesty however seems to be more about lying and untruths, while *deceitfulness* would involve the use of trickery or deception.

> "Good people are guided by their honesty;
> treacherous people are destroyed by their dishonesty."
> (Pr 11:3)

Dishonesty brings about malicious behavior, and takes on additional, more inclusive, and a wider scope of meanings in our present society; from a little fib, an outright lie, or the whim or notion of just pretending, to including: blackmail, bribery, burglary, cheating, computer corruption, crime, exaggeration, fabrication, falsehoods, falsification, forgery, improbity, kiting, obstruction of justice, omission, perfidiousness, perjury, piracy, quackery, robbery, shoplifting, shrinkage, untruths and countless others.

> "We know we have rebelled against the LORD. We have turned our backs to God. We know how unfair and oppressive we have been, carefully planning our deceitful lies." (Isa 59:13)

Some additional usages of *deceitfulness* would include: cheating, crookedness, double-dealing, double-crossing, disloyalty, duping, duplicity, flattery, hypocrisy, insincerity, perversion, plotting, pretense, trickery, twisting, underhandedness, villainy, and many more could be grouped.

> "Neighbors lie to each other, speaking with flattering lips and insincere hearts." (Ps 12:2)

Hypocrisy is somewhat different than dishonesty and deceitfulness. Its display is more about the practice or art of professing virtues and beliefs that one does not possess. It involves a simulation, feigning to be what one is not, or playing the part. It is also said to be the false assumption of an appearance of virtue or religion, or to cant a simulation of goodness, or morality – the lack of sincerity. It is indeed, also considered to be, self-deception.

> "Such people are not serving Christ our Lord; they are serving their own personal interests. By smooth talk and glowing words they deceive innocent people." (Ro 16:18)

Jesus also warned his disciples against hypocrisy, when He told them to beware of the yeast of the Pharisees and their hypocrisy, that the time would come when everything will be revealed when all that is secret would be made public.

> "So get rid of all evil behavior. Be done with all deceit, hypocrisy, jealousy, and all unkind speech." (1 Pe 2:1)

The word hypocrisy actually comes from the Greek word *hypokrisis,* which means: *acting out*; an answer; dissembling; or feigning. A derivative of the word also meant, *judge*, because the performance would involve the text's interpretation by the actor.

So during those times, as Hypokrisis was being applied to public performance and rhetoric, *hypocrites* became the technical term for a stage actor and was not considered an appropriate role for a public figure. One of Athens' actor became a politician, and because of his previous skill at impersonating characters on stage it then made him an untrustworthy politician.

HATE

To hate is to feel intense aversion, animosity, hatred, repugnance or hostility toward someone or something; to abhor, abominate, despise, detest, loathe, or wish to avoid; to dislike exceedingly; utter intolerance or disgust. Hate is usually a *reaction* to something or someone. It can be unexpected, or be a feeling that has grown for a long period of time. It is usually brought about by some sort of fear.

Hate can intensify to various degrees. It can be implied more generally to, different ways of living, religion or politics. It could imply something happening by chance, accidentally, or a milder dislike, as not wanting to wear brown clothes. One can hate to clean a closet. But it can profoundly grow into more deliberate and extremely serious hatred, with intense dislike, repugnancy, aversion, antipathy, and can lead to enmity and malice, coupling with the feeling of wanting to hurt or harm someone. At which point the hate has become almost uncontrollable.

Other related forms of hate would be found in bigotry, condemnation or prejudices, especially hate crimes that involve race. It seems that in this day and age, people are so apt to bash others. Most of the time the purposeful abasement of others is not only to bring down another person, which is bad enough in itself, but because that is the only way that person decides to make himself look better or more superior. The same is true with people who have been ignored, abused or neglected. If a person has not been treated well by his parents, it is more likely that he will show abusiveness to others.

When it comes to spirituality, hate takes on a different meaning because it affects the soul. Jesus, being considered the light of the world, came to us from heaven, to enlighten the world by His many teachings, but people wanting to live in the darkness of the world, *hated* the light because it illuminated and exposed all the many evil and sinful things they preferred doing. Jesus also told us, that those that do what is right will gladly come to the light so they can see that what they are doing is what God wants. Jesus also said that if the world hates you, to remember that it hated Him and what He was doing. Those that belong to the world, are loved by the worldly.

"And everyone will hate you because of your allegiance to me.
But those who endure to the end will be saved."
(Mt 10:22)

The thought of loving our neighbor doesn't seem that difficult to do, but when God tells us to not hate our enemies, but to pray for them, and also to wish them well, this is where the real challenge comes in.

"And many will turn away from me
and betray and hate each other."
(Mt 24:10)

If we are to hate *something*, it should be hating a wrong or false way of life, or any evil that will turn our life away from God; and if we are to hate *someone*, it should be the hating of ourselves for the wrongs and evils we have done. If we hate, and continue to hate someone, we end up hating *our self* even more than the other person, because of what we are doing to our self, emotionally, physically, and spiritually.

THE SEVEN CAPITAL SINS

The Seven Capital Sins, sometimes called the Seven Deadly Sins, are: Pride, Avarice, Envy, Wrath, Lust, Gluttony, and Sloth. They are considered to be fatal to Spiritual Progress, and are also noted to deserve a more Capital Punishment.

It could be that one of the reasons that we don't hear much mentioned about these destructive tools, is that people are so busy utilizing them.

The reason they are called *Capital* Sins, is not only because they stand out from other sins, like when you capitalize a word by accenting the first letter, but because they *engender* other sins and vices.

PRIDE

Good pride – vs – *Evil* pride.

There is a very distinguishable difference, between the pride of, let's say, parents seeing their son or daughter graduate with honors, versus the type of pride that brings about self-flattery, conceit, and self-praising.

> "It is better to live humbly with the poor
> than to share plunder with the proud."
> (Pr 16:19)

The first example of pride would be defined as: a person or thing of which someone is proud, like for example, a noteworthy accomplishment of something that is considered good. The latter, would then be described as: perceiving a high opinion of one's self or having an excessive sense of dignity, value, or self-respect, bringing about conceit, and or, arrogance. For the sake of clarity, the ensuing pride that will be focused on, will be, the *Evil* pride.

> "I, the LORD, will punish the world for its evil and the wicked for their sin. I will crush the arrogance of the proud and the haughtiness of the mighty." (Isa 13:11)

Pride, the wrong use of interest, is a trait that enslaves the character, and is a reflection of a person's ego. Proud people haven't seen a mirror they didn't like! Pride is shown, as if it was expensive jewels. But the proud usually end up in humiliation and a hardened heart.

In our illusions we look upon what we as humans have accomplished, by measuring in terms of tall buildings, but our vanity has brought us to moral failure and regression.

> "Because of the sinful things they say, because of the evil that is on their lips, let them be captured by their pride, their curses, and their lies." (Ps 59:12)

God warned that when judgement comes, the proud, the arrogant, and the wicked will be burned up like a tree – roots and all.

AVARICE

Avarice is the immoderate desires for money, wealth or possessions that are unregulated, unrestrained or plainly excessive. It is also, to be: miserly, covetous, increasing, hoarding, amassing, or storing up something of value. These desires become a hindrance in the search for God and our real destiny.

> Where you find your treasures,
> there your heart and thoughts will also be.

If we look to the *richest* man that ever walked the face of the earth, Christ, we find that He never had *any* earthly possessions.

> "Those who are wise must finally die, just like the foolish and senseless, leaving all their wealth behind. The grave is their eternal home, where they will stay forever. They may name their estates after themselves, but they leave their wealth to others." (Ps 49:10,11)

When I was growing up, I remember that we would listen with my Mother, to a program on the radio. The ongoing weekly series, was about a man who lived on a farm with his family. His life-long ambition was the accumulation of money. He was so possessed in his miserly ways, that he was denying not only himself, but the necessities of life for his entire family. The story about his greedy ways of living, enraged with his arrogance, self-centered and self-fulfilling ways, was quite unbearable, even to listen to on radio.

> "Then he said, 'Beware! Don't be greedy for what you don't have. Real life is not measured by how much we own.'"
> (Lk 12:15)

It is for us to realize that there is no extreme, or to what extent that many will go to, in order to fulfill their accumulation and ownership of things or power, even to the degree of treachery, deceitfulness, and their never-satisfiable greed. Once caught up, being seduced and addicted, through either the hoarding or wagering process, and the false promise of that appeal – it becomes like having been bribed into sin. Affluence also brings false pride to many people – making some feel that they are more special than others.

> "Those who love money will never have enough. How

absurd to think that wealth brings true happiness! The more you have, the more people come to help you spend it. So what is the advantage of wealth – except perhaps to watch it run through your fingers!" (Ecc 5:10,11)

People who make greed their life-long ambition will be as naked getting out of this world, as they were when they were born.

– You can't take it with you! –

By having loosened the grasp on the earthly things that rightly belong to God, we are left with open hands to have Him fill them to overflowing.

"Yes, a person is a fool to store up earthly wealth but not have a rich relationship with God." (Lk 12:21)

The most important, realistic, and significant approach to the accumulation of wealth, and its only justification, is in the storing-up of eternal wealth – treasures in Heaven; the kind of wealth that will last forever, and be ever so pleasing to God.

"Honor the LORD with your wealth and with the best part of everything your land produces. Then he will fill your barns with grain, and your vats will overflow with the finest wine." (Pr 3:9,10)

ENVY

A sensitive awareness or consciousness of discontent, and or resentment, stirred up by observation of another's attractive possessions, achievement or qualities, and having a strong desire to acquire them for oneself.

Covetousness is a sin against charity and justice – it gives one the belief of losing to the success of others. So, instead of being happy for someone else, the want of happiness is instead for self. God, detesting envy, stated in one of His Ten Commandments, that we should not covet our neighbor's house, his wife, his servants, or anything else that the neighbor might own.

> "Once we, too, were foolish and disobedient. We were misled by others and became slaves to many wicked desires and evil pleasures. Our lives were full of evil and envy. We hated others, and they hated us." (Tit 3:3)

It was because of *envy* that Jesus was arrested by the Jewish leaders. The *envy* of others, only leads to harm.

> "Then I observed that most people are motivated to success by their envy of their neighbors. But this too, is meaningless, like chasing the wind." (Ecc 4:4)

WRATH

Wrath being emotionally caused, is bitter anger, or rage. A behavior or conduct brought about by anger, and acted upon, out of punishment or revenge. Especially in God's retribution towards sin.

> "I will not tolerate people who slander their neighbors. I will not endure conceit or pride." (Ps 101:5)

Anger, the forerunner of *wrath*, usually is a response, or an arousal, to an observed or detected threat, either real or imagined, of our self, or someone of importance to us. The threat could have happened some time ago, could be happening now, or could be something that might happen in the future. Quite often it is in reaction to an observation of threat, due to a competition or dispute, which could vary from, negligence, a wrong-doing, degradation, unfaithfulness, or even physical fighting. It can appear as either: *visual*, as resulting from a physical or verbal confrontation – going into a terribly violent rage, or fierce fury, or could also be a *silent* show of enmity, hatred, hostility, antagonism, or just plain sulking.

"Don't be quick tempered, for anger is the friend of fools."
(Ecc 7:9)

The occurrence of *anger* could be derived from many, or a combination of sources – even including physical pain, or just being tired, or having a mood-swing caused by either drugs, medicine or other reasons; some occurring changes in the body; or just being sexually frustrated. Any of these or other causes could bring about a certain degree of anger. The harshest or most severe degree of anger is *wrath*. The two of the strongest senses God gave us, is the ability to *love*, and the ability to *hate*. So, because we were created to *love* and respond to being *loved* – if the *love* or affection is not received, the lack of it, might trigger a reaction of anger. God, in dealing with the sinful nature of man, did not pour out his anger on us – a wrath that we justly deserved, but instead decided to save us through His Son Jesus.

"The God of peace is never glorified by human violence."
– Thomas Merton –

One way to turn away wrath, is with a gentle answer or response. Using harsh words will only stir it up. It is also very wise to not let it take control over you. It's best to remain silent and think about the situation – overnight.

"A fool gives full vent to anger, but a wise person quietly holds it back." (Pr 29:11)

LUST

An excessive, intense, or unrestrained inclination or desire for sexual pleasure. A sensuous craving with degradation, passion or obsession, usually in a sinful manner. Also, the craving, or lusting for the worldly life, and what it offers.

> "Don't let me lust for evil things; don't let me participate in acts of wickedness. Don't let me share in the delicacies of those who do evil." (Ps 141:4)

This decaying culture that we are living in, is so eager in the brandishing of its products and lust, that it has gone to the point, and even to the extreme of having lust and sex become the merchants' selling tools – for monetary gratification. There are so many ways that people are being exploited. Almost all of the conceivable forms of communication, even performers, are selfishly, unethically and without embarrassment, attempting to create attention to themselves through either sex or violence. What is even more degrading, is that a lot of this attention is directed to children. We shouldn't let this culture, that has been reduced to shame, tell us what is *acceptable* behavior.

It is bad enough to think of the growing problem of the illegal trafficking of drugs, but when so many countries are engaged in or exposed to, the dealings and trafficking of humans, *adults* and *children*, for the purpose of satisfying the pleasures of the wicked – sin and shame have plummeted to an outrageous and abominable dishonor, disrespect and disgrace.

It used to be that you could go out to enjoy a cup of coffee, or a meal at a restaurant, or have a meaningful conversation while you were having a haircut. Even these supposed innocent things have now become a haven for utilizing beauty and sex, in order to *sell*.

> "Don't lust for her beauty.
> Don't let her coyness seduce you."
> (Pr 6:25)

Our *falsely accepted* way of living has come to fruition because of the gradual *allowing* of one tiny step at a time. But the hazardous road that these individual and accumulated steps have led to, and keep on leading to, is to a society and culture of degeneration, which will keep on showing more and more signs of societal decay, from one generation to the next. What kind of picture are we painting of ourselves as a *supposed* civilized world? What are we leaving for those that will follow?

Sexual *lust* has existed since the beginning of time. But today, lust has been *liberalized* and *accepted*. Not only has it been liberalized and accepted all over the world, but it has become *the* money maker. It is utilized in practically every imagineable thing that can be seen, read, or listened to. It has infiltrated into sports, music, the theater, the Arts, the cinema, and almost every other conceivable or devised means of reaching the public. But it has now reached a point, in its diverseness and false way of living, where, if a person even questions that kind of immorality or its evil ways – that person, because of his not conforming and not accepting what is considered to be the *norm* or what's in *vogue*, is now the one being labeled as *not being with it*, or the one regarded as the *bad guy*. Things have changed – and not for the better.

The Scriptures tell us that we should stop loving and embracing this evil world and everything that it is offering. It is a matter of choice, of good over evil. *Lust* is not only a gift that our creator gave us for the legal and moral fulfillment of sexual pleasure, but becomes a different kind of lust when applied towards the *desiring* and *craving* for the worldly things that we seek, or for anything that will boost our pride or our possessions.

God wants us to live in holiness and honor, and keep clear of all sexual sin. If we live in the ignorance of God and his ways it will be in lustful passion as the pagans do.

> "So put to death the sinful, earthly things lurking within you. Have nothing to do with sexual sin, impurity, lust, and shameful desires. Don't be greedy for the good things of

this life, for that is idolatry." (Col 3:5)

Lust, being a form of coveting, usually turns to obsession or addiction, and has a very broad spectrum, such as: abduction, adultery, criminal assault, fornication, incest, pornography, rape, sodomy, trafficking, etc. It could also be manifested in other evil and sadistic ways.

GLUTTONY

Gluttony is the act of greedily eating, consuming, ingesting, or drinking; veraciousness; gormandizing; devouring; engulfing.

"So try to walk a middle course." (Ecc 7:18a)

According to Saint Thomas of Aquinas, an Early Church Elder, gluttony could be defined in different ways. Being too quick or anxious. Eating too elegantly, or too pricy foods. Eating in excess. Eating too enthusiastically or too exquisitely.

"But when the Holy Spirit controls our lives, he will produce this kind of fruit in us: love, joy, peace, patience, kindness, goodness, faithfulness, gentleness, and self-control." (Gal 5:22,23a)

Of things to be consumed, you have probably heard, or used the expressions:

Concerning Food – A Bucket. A Crate. A Full Rack. A Peck. A Treat. A Snack. A Wedge. An Appetizer. Any way you like! Baker's Dozen. Buffet. Can't eat another bite! Cup or Bowl? Cutting Down. Delicious. Diet. Doggie Bag? Double Size it! Eat it or it'll go to waste! Eating Contest. Extra Large! Extra Sauce! Fasting.

Finger Licking. Free Dessert. From Soup to Nuts. Gourmet. Hearty Appetite. How many Scoops? I'll have another! I'm full! Jumbo! Just a bite! King Size! Loaded! Love that taste! Munch. Nutritious. Palate Pleasing! Platter. Satisfying. Smorgasbord. Second Helping. Seven Course Meal. Side Order. Stuffed. There's plenty left! Three Quarter Pounder. Two for One.

Concerning Drink – A Bottle. A Case. A Cup. A Fifth. A Flask. A Gallon. A Glass. A Keg. A Liter. A Mug. A Pitcher. A Shot. A Sip. A Six-Pack. A Stein. A Swig. A Tankard. Beerfest. Cheers! Chug-a-lug! I'll Drink to That! Let's make a Toast! Make it a Double! One for the Road! Wine Tasting Party. With Cream and Four Sugars.

Overeating, overindulgence, or lack of temperance in consumption of food or drink, more than likely will result in obesity, and also often creates severe psychological, health, and obsessive or addictive problems. Temperance could then be looked at from *both* sides of the *scale*. It can be seen as, the *excess* of what is needed for human consumption, or the *deprivation* of what is needed, which in that case would lead to anorexia.

"People need more than bread for their life; they must feed on every word of God." (Mt 4:4)

One very important thing to consider about overeating, or eating more than is necessary for the maintaining of proper health and nourishment, is that the excess is actually wasted, because it is not needed by the body for it to function. In fact, it actually slows down the body's ability to heal itself, because the system's energy is being used to burn up the food. The wasted energy could then be utilized for better use, like applying it towards more exercise time, or using the extra energy to help someone in a task. This displaced desire for self-satisfaction in overindulging, causes such an unnecessary waste – an excess that could feed not only the needy and less fortunate, but also the destitute, desperate and those that are starving.

SLOTH

Sloth is of the unwillingness or lack of interest or ambition to be energetic; inclined to be disposed to idleness; slothful; habitually lazy; one who suggests a calm idleness and ease.

"Never be lazy in your work, but serve the Lord enthusiastically."
(Ro 12:11)

In learning how to work, we should take some lessons from God. He gave us some examples as to how He does things. He created the Angels, and the Universe, then He created Man to share in the joy of His work. He not only created everything else that was needed to support all forms of life, but He also made it beautiful – a Showpiece. Then He looked at what He had done and saw that it was good in every way. That meant that He was pleased with His work. He took six days to accomplish the creation of the earth, and He only rested for one. He is always helping us in every imaginable way. He came to live with us, not to *be* served, but *to* serve. Jesus worked as a carpenter. He walked devotedly in His mission to reach the many people that He loved so much, to give them hope through the Good News. He washed His Disciples' feet. He even worked at carrying His own Cross, on which He gave His life for us. Yes, we can learn from this Teacher. And one of the many things He taught us, is that we were all given talents. Talents we need to develop and use, for His work, to help others, and above all to satisfy *Him*, not ourselves.

If we are to utilize our talents, we must activate them.

When man was first created, God placed him in an environment of Utopia, filled with abundance of good and plenty, and offered him a life of pleasure and leisure. Upon sinning all this was taken away.

Sin brought drastic consequences to humanity. The pleasure and leisure had thus turned to sweat and struggle. From then on, and until their dying days, man would have to *labor* using *physical* and *mental* effort to sustain himself; and now adding to their burden, having to work through nature's hazards and the elements.

Work is not always a chore,
it usually is just something that needs to get done.

But *work* can be a *joy,* if only regarded as something that is being done for and offered to please God. Work is not thought of as being dreadful if it is something one enjoys doing. The sharing of duties is very motivating especially if the workers have the same interest and drive to accomplish their undertaking. Attitude plays a tremendous part in performing a task, whether it is done for the sake of duty, or for the satisfaction of having accomplished something, or better yet, something worthwhile. Depending on the attitude, the feeling could be either, 'I had to do it', or 'I'm so glad I did that'.

"Do what you love,
and you'll never have to work another day in your life."
— Author Unknown —

My Father was blessed with many talents, and utilized them well and to their fullest. He was a very good mechanic. He worked at his trade as a loom-fixer for many years. Many times he needed a special tool to perform a particular task, and if he couldn't find it in a store, or if the tool was too costly, or not yet available, he would either invent or create it. I remember him utilizing a gas burner from our kitchen stove to harden some metal to be used in making an odd-shaped wrench that he needed at his work. My dad never called a technician to do anything. He always found a way of taking care of the situation. He also took much pride in his work. His motto was, "Anything worth doing is worth doing well."

The Bible tells us that while we are fulfilling our existence, whatever we do, we should do well, because once we are in the grave there will be no more work, planning, knowledge or wisdom. The importance is not in the amount of time that we devote to doing something, but the true value lies in the accomplishment.

Some people regard themselves as clever for the wrong reason; and thus work so hard at relying on others to do their work for them, or take pride in the trickery of attempting to get out of doing things. In so doing, never realizing that they are robbing themselves of the benefit and satisfaction of the joy of accomplishment. We should never want to become lazy or have someone purposely do our work for us.

It is just amazing how quickly some young adults learn to drive a car, but do not understand the use of a vacuum cleaner, lawn mower or snow blower.

"Nothing is really work
unless you would rather be doing something else."
– J. M. Barrie –

It is good to keep a sense of balance in what we do. Going to one extreme would be to become a *workaholic*. The opposite extreme would be a *easeaholic*. The workaholic as we know would work in excess, while the easeaholic would not work enough. It is either working too much or too little. One of the traits of an easeaholic would be one that would be living his life solely to entertain or enjoy himself, or for his own fulfillment, and not caring, sharing or taking time to use his talents that God gave him to help others. God also want us to use temperance in the things that we do. Not to *over-do*, and not to *under-do*.

"Anything you do can get you fired, this includes doing nothing."
– Author Unknown –

When we hang up our hats for the last time, and we look back to see what we have accomplished during our very *brief* stay here on this side of the fence, will we be happy and content with the quantity and quality of work that we have done? Someone once, in amazement, remarked to Albert Einstein, how they appreciated his many and remarkable accomplishments – and in reply Einstein merely stated that most people go to their graves after having utilized but a fraction of their capabilities.

"Some people are so lazy
that they won't even lift a finger to feed themselves."
(Pr 19:24)

Chapter 5

HUMILITY

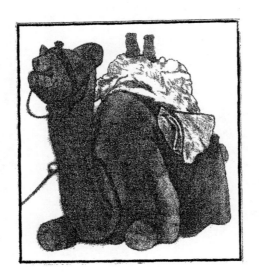

CAMEL
(Kneels to be loaded — a symbol of humility.)

"His clothes were woven from camel hair, and he wore a leather belt; his food was locusts and wild honey." (Mark 1:6)

HUMILITY

H onoring everyone, is the way to grace;

U ndoing the pride's power, with an embrace.

M indful of *their* ideals, or goals and feelings;

I mpassioned on *them,* receiving blessings.

L ike all loving Mothers, feeding their child first;

I nstead of satisfying, their own thirsts.

T is Love, that leads us to think, and act this way;

Y ahweh, does intend for us, this way to pray.

HUMILITY

H   harmonious, holiness, homage, honesty, honoring, hospitable.

U   unassuming, undeceiving, unifying, unworldly, useful.

M   mannered, meek, mindful, moderate, modest, moral, mournful, mystical.

I   innocence, inoffensive.

L   labouring, loving.

I   irradiative.

T   temperance, thankfulness, thoughtfulness, timidity, tolerance, tranquility, truthfulness, trustworthiness.

Y   yearning, yielding.

IN PRAISE OF HUMILITY

The previous chapter (Pride) consisted of the many tools that Satan efficiently and effectively utilizes in his quest to lure, destroy, gather and amass souls into his deceived and eternal fold. This chapter will be devoted to the tools available to us, not only to be used as a defense, but also to protect us from his attacks. The subjects will consist of, and contain words, that have been, sad to say, uncommon and even foreign to today's culture and society. Morality and virtues have somewhat been set aside, making way for the more popular, liberal, and accepted views that are demoralizing and degenerating people everywhere. In utilizing the following virtues, we find ourselves to be not only more powerful than Satan, but definitely and fittingly more superior. They are the tools desperately needed to change, our way of living, our society, and the cultures of the world.

"True humility is not an abject, groveling, self despising spirit;
it is a right estimate of ourselves as God sees us."
– Tryon Edwards –

Humilis is the Latin word for Humility, which means low, humble, and from the earth. Humility is the quality, state or condition of being humble in spirit, unpretentious and modest. It is the freedom from, or the lack of pride, and to not think of oneself as being better or more important than others. Humility shouldn't be confused with humiliation. Humiliation is entirely different and quite opposite, as it is the act of degrading or disgracing someone.

Humility is also an attribute or quality, that even while considering our own defects, that it gives a modest opinion of oneself. It allows us to be unpretentious and reserved, to submit, and show our humbled character to ourselves and to others, for God's sake. Humility is a way towards inner peace; it also builds bridges instead of building walls. In other words, being humble consists of not being selfish or trying to impress others, but to think of others as better than ourselves, and to not look for our own interests, but to take notice and be interested in others.

> "Now Moses was more humble than any other person on earth."
> (Num 12:13)

Humility consists of certain behaviors and attitudes which include: being submissive to God and any legitimate authority, being able to recognize the virtues and talents that others possess, especially those that surpass our own, giving due and proper honor, to give obedience when required, to be able to recognize the limits of one's ability, authority, or talents, and also, not reaching for that which is beyond one's reach.

> "Don't be humble. You're not that great."
> – Golda Meir –

Among some of the benefits of humility as described in Scripture, would be, honor, unity, wisdom, eternal life, and eternal rewards.

Humility being considered the first virtue, is inferior only to faith, because it takes away the obstacles leading to it. Humility also keeps us within our own boundaries, so that we don't reach above ourselves, and also allows to submit to our superior. It is also considered to be a promising part of temperance, because temperance deals with our desires and appetites. Humility along with patience in suffering were established as the foundation of the firmness of grace.

> "Be humble, be big in mind and soul, be kindly;
> you will like yourself that way and so will other people."
> – Norman Vincent Peale –

False humility is quite different than humility. False humility consists of purposely negating, or deprecating one's own accomplishments, gifts, sanctity or talents for the intention of getting approval or admiration from others.

Through subjugation, humbling occurs when someone is brought under dominion. When a person is dehumanized, he is deprived of human attributes, interests, qualities, or rendered mechanical or routine.

The practicing of virtues is the *means* by which to protect one against temptation from the Seven Deadly Sins. Humility is one of the Seven Holy Virtues, which are:

> *Chastity* – The opposition of lust; the boldness, courage and purity of willingly accepting moral well-being and attaining the purity of thought and action.
>
> *Abstinence* – Unchanging awareness of others and one's environment; the practicing of self-control, or to keep from doing something; using moderation.
>
> *Liberality* – Being generous and willing to give and share; having high morals and character in thought and action; having an openness of mind or attitude; tolerance.
>
> *Diligence* – To work and act with zeal and care; to apply good work ethics; efficiently and effectively utilizing one's time; guarding against laziness.
>
> *Patience* – The ability of enduring peacefully, and resolving situations of waiting or delay or provocation without being annoyed or upset; being able to forgive and show mercy, and to deal calmly with troublesome affairs.
>
> *Kindness* – The quality or state of being kind; a kind act; to show compassion, charity, sympathy, and not show prejudice.
>
> *Humility* – Behaving modestly and selflessly, and showing respect; not bringing attention to oneself, but giving others their due credit.

Other virtues would include, Valor, Prudence, Justice, Temperance, Fortitude, and the very popular, Faith, Hope, and Love, which is Charity.

Humility which is the confidence to be the person that God wants us to be, requires a lifetime's work, and when used will allow all to find their best before Him.

> "God sets himself against the proud, but he shows favor to the humble." (Jas 4:6b)

A humble person is unpretentious and reserved, has a modest opinion of himself, and doesn't think of being better than others. He is able to submit himself to God and to others, for God's sake. Humility is allowing others to be first in line, allowing others to have the best seats, allowing others to be first to eat, and allowing others to have more on their plates.

> "Action without humility or a realistic sense of human condition will always result in not being significant."
> – Author Unknown –

Evil and immoral behavior or action takes away the glamour of an extremely beautiful woman or a very stunning and handsome man. For this reason there is a lot of truth in the saying,

> "Beauty Is – As Beauty Does."

Beauty is at its greatest when it shines from within. One of the most attractive things a person can wear, is not to be found hanging in anyone's closet, but in the simple adornment of showing a *humble* smile. It is not the clothing, hairstyle, manicure, cosmetics, jewelry, perfumes, or other attention getters that really matter, or captures and gives that first stunning impression. Nothing will draw attention as much as a *genuine* smile. It will outdo all of the above mentioned vanities, and it will give not only a guarantee of feeling good about oneself for donning that smile, but it will naturally seize the hearts of others.

— The first sign of goodness is humility. —

Humility is found to be a greater and more expressed form in *self-abasement*. Self-abasement consists of not only being humble but to purposely lower oneself in rank, prestige or esteem.

One of the most renown signs of self-abasement came to us as a response from Mary the Mother of Jesus, when Elizabeth expressed to her that she had been blessed. Mary's *humble* response was:

The Magnificat – Mary's Song of Praise.

"Oh, how I praise the Lord.
How I rejoice in God my Savior!
For he took notice of his lowly servant girl,
and now generation after generation
will call me blessed.
For he, the Mighty One, is holy,
and he has done great things for me.
His mercy goes on from generation to generation,
to all who fear him.
His mighty arm does tremendous things!
How he scatters the proud and haughty ones!
He has taken princes from their thrones
and exalted the lowly.
He has satisfied the hungry with good things
and sent the rich away with empty hands.
And how he has helped his servant Israel!
He has not forgotten his promise to be merciful.
For he promised our ancestors – Abraham and his children –
to be merciful to them forever."

There are people that seem to standout amongst others. It could be their looks, their personality, their character, or just something about them that attracts your attention. They could either be drawn to you by something positive or negative. In this day and age of, *self,* being the importance, what stands out the most from everything else, all other attributes or appearances, is a person's *humility*.

When you meet, or if you know such a person, you are probably apt to find out that he or she likes helping others when asked, and if not asked, will undoubtedly volunteer or offer to help. You would surely find, if you started to converse with this person, that he or she would rather talk about things that would interest you, rather than drawing the attention to his or her self. Thus wanting to make you feel that your topics were more important and interesting to talk about. The fact is, that the person is probably very knowledgeable about many different subjects, but through the thoughtfulness and kindness of becoming a good listener, not only did it make you feel good to have someone be attentive to what was being said, but because of his or her humbleness, the listener learned something from the conversation. People need to be listened to – we should *learn* from one another.

> "Better to remain silent and be thought a fool,
> than to speak out and remove all doubt!"
> – Abraham Lincoln –

It is difficult for some to accept blame. Sharing or taking the blame when it is deserved, not only shows a sign of humility, but also avoids confrontations, arguments, heartaches, hurts, and miseries that could and probably would result.

Jesus explicitly explained this when He said,

> "All right, stone her. But let those who have never sinned throw the first stone." (Jn 8:7b)

Other signs of self-abasement would be:

- When John the Baptist chose to decrease his mission, so that Jesus could increase His.
- A humbling prayer at Church prior to receiving the Eucharist: "Lord, I am not worthy to receive you, but only

say the word, and I shall be healed."

A most inspiring, touching, ever popular, humble and self abasing prayer is the:

PRAYER OF ST. FRANCIS

Lord, make me an instrument of your peace,
Where there is hatred, let me sow love;
where there is injury, pardon;
where there is doubt, faith;
where there is despair, hope;
where there is darkness, light;
where there is sadness, joy.

O Divine Master, grant that I may not so much
seek to be consoled as to console;
to be understood as to understand;
to be loved as to love.

For it is in giving that we receive;
it is in pardoning that we are pardoned;
and it is in dying that we are born to eternal life.

---

*Humility is the true assessment of oneself
that makes prayer authentic.*

GOD'S HUMILITY

For us to understand, achieve the right attitude about, and learn to apply humility, we need to go to the original source of humility –

which is God Himself, our Supreme example.. The Almighty consisting of the Father, the Son and the Holy Spirit, a Trinity formed as *one* Godhead, *equally sharing* in a Divinity of Omnipotence. Christ said that if you saw Him, you saw the Father.

God humbly chose *Himself* as a redeeming source for our sins. *He* came on this earth to accomplish His Mission, that through Redemption, Christ would give us the way to, and the promise of salvation. Acts that show Supreme Humility.

One of the most humble events ever recorded, was when a room was denied at the Inn for our Savior's birth. A God-man was then born in a *manger* and was wrapped in *strips of cloth.*

Our God came to earth to spend some time with us – not to *be* served, but *to* serve. While He was with us He showed us many examples of humility.

He became *one of us*. Lived *among* us, teaching, guiding and caring for us. He was *obedient* to His parents. He didn't cling to His *rights* and *powers* as God. He came to us in *human* form, and was *rejected* by many. Christ took it upon Himself to do a *lowly* act of *washing* His Disciples' feet. He obeyed God the Father, and *humbling* Himself, suffered the unjust torture of the scourging, the crowning of thorns, being spat upon, carrying His own Cross, and experiencing His execution and dying a *criminal's* death.

> "He did not retaliate when he was insulted. When he suffered, he did not threaten to get even. He left his case in the hands of God, who always judges fairly." (1 Pe 2:23)

Christ did this because of His extreme love for us – paying the price for something He didn't do. It wasn't His sins! It was our sins! We were the ones deserving the crucifixion. Not too many would want to suffer and die for someone else's sins. How many would die for the wrong-doing of another?

> "Your attitude should be the same that Christ Jesus had. Though he was God, he did not demand and cling to his

rights as God. He made himself nothing; he took the humble position of a slave and appeared in human form. And in human form he obediently humbled himself even further by dying a criminal's death on a cross." (Php 2:5-8)

SELF - CONTROL

Self control is about the control, or the managing of oneself, our actions, our desires, our drives, our ambitions, our emotions and our thought process. It is usually accomplished through *will power*. It could be self-activated, it could be taught, or it could be in obedience.

It is understood or perceived in different ways. Philosophically, it could be defined as exerting one's own will on our actions, behavior or thought process. Much of this comes about as how a person sees oneself and is able to set for himself certain boundaries. A further understanding of self-control would range from, and including, abstinence, endurance, patience, perseverance, persistency, respect or will power. It requires one's ability to be centered in putting into effect or bringing to bear their strength and will over the habits or urges of the body or self. Simply speaking, self-control is self-regulation, or impulse control.

Self-control can be applied in physical, psychological, or moral and spiritual ways.

When *physical* self-control is utilized, it usually involves activity that requires conditioning or improvement, like body-building, exercising, or athletics.

> "All athletes practice strict self-control. They do it to win a prize that will fade away, but we do it for an eternal prize."
> (1Cor 9:25)

The *psychological* use of self-control would be in the form of resolutions to improve one's lifestyle. It could be through certain areas, like abstinence, getting rid of bad habits or creating good habits

– like New Year's resolutions.

When dealing with self-control in a *moral* manner, it takes on a spiritual meaning. Scripture tells us that we should utilize control and right conduct while living in this world filled with evil, so as to prevent our being enslaved by it.

In utilizing self-control it helps us to avoid temptations, wickedness, sinful desires, being cruel, unforgiving, unloving, or being slanderous of others. It will make us focus more on what is good and turn us towards God. When we let the Spirit control our lives, He will produce many wonderful fruits, like love, joy, peace, patience, goodness, faithfulness, and self-control.

> "A life of moral excellence leads to knowing God better. Knowing God leads to self-control. Self-control leads to patient endurance, and patient endurance leads to godliness...and finally you will grow to have genuine love for everyone." (2 Pe 1:5b,6,7b)

DISCIPLINE

Discipline is often referred to as a branch of knowledge involving learning or research. It is about instruction and training that corrects, molds, strengthens, modifies or perfects, in order to gain control of skill and behavior, by enforcing either, or a combination of: chastisement, methods, obedience, order, punishment, rule, system, or teaching, to affect conduct, development or action. It is usually applied, through books, creative ideas, punishment, tips, solutions, or through appropriate communication. Rewards are often used in order to inspire and motivate the process. Self-discipline requires a strong devotion.

> "People think I am disciplined. It is not discipline.
> It is devotion. There is a difference."
> – Luciano Pavarotti –

Because discipline involves the importance of consistency and persistency it almost always, involves much stress, and frustration.

"How I hated discipline! If only I had not demanded my own way! Oh, why didn't I listen to my teachers? Why didn't I pay attention to those who gave me instruction? (Pr 5:12,13)

Solomon who wrote the Proverbs, consisting of Thirty-One Chapters, which are found in the Old Testament, told us that the reason why he wrote the illustrations was to teach people wisdom and discipline, so they could understand the wise sayings, and through them, the people would receive the instructions needed for *discipline* – which are good-conduct, doing what is right, just and fair. He even added that they will make the simpleminded – clever.

"Discipline is the bridge between goals and accomplishments."
– Jim Rohn –

We are the children of God. Being a loving God, He did not give us a spirit of fear and timidity. He gave us a spirit of power, love, and self-discipline. He treats us as His children. As a loving Father, He wants to correct or punish us, when we do wrong, and we shouldn't be unhappy or discouraged about it. He disciplines because He cares very much so that we stay on the straight and narrow road. God knows what is good for us, better than we know what is good for ourselves. We become lenient. He is focused on the big and eternal picture. Punishment is certainly not enjoyable or pleasant while it is happening – it usually is very painful! But the result reaps a bountiful and lush harvest for those that have allowed themselves to be trained in this way, because we will not have become weak or lame, or stumble, but we will have strength.

"Discipline is the refining fire by which talent becomes ability."
– Roy L. Smith –

If we look at the strategy of someone running a race, either by foot, or other means, one of the most important things being done is to strip off as much weight as possible that could cause delay by slowing down the pace. We are also surrounded by a huge crowd, all witnesses to our fast paced movement towards our eternal goal. We must also remove anything that would interfere with our process – any sin or evil doing that might slow down our *spiritual* progress. God tells us that we should run with endurance, this race that He has set for us. We should do this by putting blinders on, and focusing on God on whom our faith depends, from start to finish.

"I've never known a man worth his salt who in long run, deep down in his heart, didn't appreciate the grind, the discipline."
– Vince Lombardi –

The disciplining of children takes on many different approaches, because of age, character, personality, temperament, and so many more involved reasons. Cause and blame is scattered in every direction, to parents, babysitters, care-givers, teachers, society, environment, exposure, peer-pressure, or because of authority or even for the lack of authority. Needless to say, child rearing in this entangled environment and society is quite difficult. Our culture is losing its sense of authenticity and dignity. Society is now celebrating aspiration rather talent or morals. There is nevertheless, much help available through different sources, such as books and special programs. Some seem to not only be quite helpful, but very beneficial. The first seven years are the most crucial in building and forming a child's foundation – giving the child good roots, from which will grow. character, personality, and spirituality.

Because so many children lack discipline today, the cause seems to be focused on the parents. Are the parents flunking in discipline? Do they need a Time-Out, or a Do-Over? Certainly a lot depends on the parents' wanting or caring to apply discipline. Knowing what method, or how much and when to apply it. Who ever heard of a child that had never been disciplined?

"And have you entirely forgotten the encouraging words God spoke to you, his children? He said, 'My child, don't ignore it when the Lord disciplines you, and don't be discouraged when he corrects you. For the Lord disciplines those he loves, and he punishes those he accepts as his children.'" (Heb 12:5,6)

The need for discipline is not only to remedy the situation for the moment, but because of the love that the parent has for the child, that the end result would consequentially be a mutual and lasting love between the parents and the child. If the discipline is applied properly and in time, the child will later thank the parent for his or her having been disciplined. Stress between the parents could lead to harsh, and an unfavorable type of discipline.

Discipline is actually *everything* that you put into children which influences how they turn out. A very effective tool in disciplining a child, is for the parent to discipline himself or herself in the attention being shown to the child. How much proper love is the child receiving? How much time, caring and attention? There is a closeness and a bonding occurring from reading to a child daily. Both the parent and the child get to look forward to it. Read to the child about things that promote the building of character, goodness, gentleness and the importance of good behavior. If this theory, in its importance, is not applied at an early age, the children will start to investigate or experiment on their own, as many are today. The explosive idea for youngsters to want to imitate some of the degenerate and immoral celebrities, is shameful to our culture. The idea that, even if something is wrong, if it is desired, it is acceptable – is shameful. Some children have been led to believe that it is acceptable for them to find their sexuality at such an early age.

"Happy are those whom you discipline, LORD,
and those whom you teach
from your law."
(Ps 94:12)

Listed are a few general hints concerning the disciplining of children:

- Do not keep changing your methods of how you discipline the child. This way the child will know and expect the proper consequences for his actions.
- In order to avoid a negative reaction, you should know ahead of time, what you're going to do or say, so that it will be clear and easy for the child to understand.
- The younger children should have an established procedure, knowing when things are going to happen, throughout each day – things like meal time, recreation or bedtime.
- Make sure that there are no hazards, leaving areas free to wander. Make sure that drawers, cabinets and doors are not accessible, by securing locks.
- Remember that as a parent, that you are in charge, and for your child's benefit, you will have him do something, or will avoid him from doing something. In dealing with younger children, even if the child cries, or has a fit of bad temper, because the child is not getting his or her way – this type of unruly behavior should probably be ignored.
- Try to be specific and positive about the rules, and not offer alternatives. Instead of asking the child if he wants to brush his teeth, it would be better to simply say, "It's now time to brush your teeth."
- By giving in to a child when he is behaving badly, crying, or having a fit of bad temper, will teach the child that this kind of demeanor is an acceptable way for him to get what he wants.
- Disregard the small stuff – the unimportant and harmless whims or notions. Don't make the child feel like he's being nagged.
- Make sure that the rewards or consequences are exercised right away, as it will be much more effective.

- If you ask something of your child and there is no response, then repeat the command one more time. If by then there is no reaction. Do not repeat the command again. Just follow through with the consequences.
- There shouldn't be any discussion or argument about the punishment at the time that it is to be carried out. There will be time to talk later.
- Be prepared! If you know that you are going to have a situation that might become difficult, have a plan ready ahead of time, about your expectations and the appropriate consequences.
- With adolescents and older children it is sometimes good to have their input in regards to the rules and how they will be enforced.
- The messages should not be demeaning or humiliating. In conversations, 'I' and 'We' should be used instead of 'You'. An accusatory statement can easily lead to an argument.
- Every attempt should be made to make sure that your child understands the rules and the outcome of misbehaving, but more importantly, an emphasis should also be made on what the *proper* behavior should have been.

Discipline Is Tough Love!

"If you refuse to discipline your children, it proves you don't love them; if you love your children, you will be prompt to discipline them." (Pr 13:24)

LOVE – CARING

Love is more than a zero score in tennis. Although the *zero* score would compassionately and fittingly apply in what Mother Teresa said regarding, and in relationship to the abandoned and the destitute, that the worst poverty is the *absence* of love.

> "If we want a love message to be heard, it has got to be sent out
> To keep a lamp burning we have to keep putting oil in it."
> – Mother Teresa –

Love can be applied to, or can be described, with many diverse and different meanings. It exists as an essential quality or characteristic in all humans in the result of intellectual development. Love is a disposition.

> "Love is wisdom of the fool and the folly of the wise."
> – Samuel Johnson –

Impersonal love, which is not between or towards persons, would be referring to, little or less pleasure, as that derived from an object such as a favorite recipe, a piece of jewelry, a vehicle, or a brand new golf club. It could also be of an object of engrossed interest, excitement, or enthusiasm – in loving sports, activities, music, food, literature, nature, money, power, fame, or other things of intimate value. Love can also be the expressing of a strong feeling towards a dedication or loyalty towards things like, a bonding friendship, loving one's country, loyalty, or patriotism.

A more intense feeling which is found in *interpersonal* love, would describe emotion or affection. Usually, and more ordinarily, love is most often referred to in regards to interpersonal love, love between human beings, for instance, between couples, friends or family members. In our social and cultural activities and differences it is difficult to explain the many varied applications about, or the many feelings of, love; as there are as many types of lovers as there are many types f love.

> "The only way of full knowledge lies in the act of love;
> this act transcends thought, it transcends words. It is the
> daring plunge into the experience of union. To love

somebody is not just a strong feeling – it is a decision, it is a judgement, it is a promise."
— Eric Forum —

In the interpersonal application, love is directed to either or the combination of emotions towards the soul, the mind, or the person. For this reason love themes are largely used in the arts. Interpersonally, love would be: a warm or strong feeling of personal attachment, or affection of varying degrees. It would consist of more than just liking a person. When love is not reciprocated, it is referred to as *unrequited* love. Interpersonal love however, usually describes a passionate and intense desire for one of the opposite sex; lending one's boundary or self-esteem to another; an ardent liking or fondness; a strong attraction; having a sweet heart; a puppy love; love at first sight; infatuation; or a crush. It could also be the affection of parents towards their children, or the children for their parents.

"Love is shown best in little ways."
— Linda Thomson —

In association with interpersonal love, there are many types of feelings:

Affection – feelings of loving gentleness, or physical desire.
Altruism – selfless concern for someone.
Attachment – attaining certain emotional needs.
Caring – responsible or watchful attachment.
Commitment – wishing to preserve love.
Emotional Intimacy – feelings of joy or sympathy.
Friendship – a bonding between friends.
Kinship – family attachments.
Passion – intense desire.
Physical Intimacy – showing physical closeness.
Service – helpful gesture.

Love

Love has many powers,
it can bring you to your knees,
can rip your heart like paper,
then mend it back with ease,
can draw out tears of sadness,
and also tears of joy,
can make us smile at someone
whose trying to annoy.
Love is all around us,
no matter where we turn;
love can be so simple,
yet hard for us to learn.
Love's a soothing feeling,
that helps us sleep at night;
love makes us grab a loved one,
and hug them oh so tight.
Love has many powers,
as I have said above;
the most important thing of all,
is remember, "God is love."

– George A Hellard Jr. –

Because of ethics, age, status, or morality, sexual intimacy in certain relationships, is considered either unacceptable, inappropriate, or undesirable. Other ways of showing love would be in the display of emotion or in finding enjoyment in each other's interests.

> "Pay all your debts, except the debt of love for others. You can never finish paying that! If you love your neighbor, you will fulfill all the requirements of God's law." (Ro 13:8)

The suitable and adaptable forms of love would include: *intimacy* which would be classified as: liking, friendship, romantic love, companionate love, and consummate love; *passion* would be about: infatuation, romantic love, or fatuous love; *commitment* could include, compassionate love, fatuous love, and consummate love.

> "Place me like a seal over your heart, or like a seal on your arm. For love is as strong as death, and its jealousy is as enduring as the grave. Love flashes like fire, the brightest kind of flame. Many waters cannot quench love, neither can rivers drown it. If a man tried to buy love with everything he owned, his offer would be utterly despised. (SS 8:6,7)

Psychologists regard love as an intuitive and compassionate phenomenon. Some consider love to have certain stages – going from attraction, lust, and attachment. Attachment being the only lasting and bonding one, as it involves commitment. So, love can fall into the categories of being romantic, passionate or committable. *Romantic* love is usually considered as an intimate, gentle and tender interpersonal relationship, and therefore *passionate* love as being more lustful. Usually romantic and passionate love are short lived, while *committable* love is considered as lasting.

There are different love styles or theories, each having its own meaning and intensity: Agape, Eros, Ludus, Mania, Pragma, and Storge.

"Gravitation is not responsible for people falling in love."
— Albert Einstein —

Some of the words that enhance and give added intensity to love are: Life, Mind, Principle, Soul, and Truth.

> "Love is patient and kind. Love is not jealous or boastful or proud or rude. Love does not demand its own way. Love is not irritable, and it keeps no record of when it has been wronged. It is never glad about injustice but rejoices whenever the truth wins out. Love never gives up, never loses faith, is always hopeful, and endures through every circumstance." (1 Co 13:4-7)

Love, because of its essentiality, importance, and significance in our lives, is mentioned over six hundred and fifty times in the Bible. Scriptures give us different meanings to love, as when Adam *knew* his wife and she conceived. The word *knowledge* was also used to describe a man's intimate relationship with his wife, and his personal relationship with God. It is also displayed in God's kindness and mercy to man, and man's devotional adoration to God. God however is the epitome of love in His actions, affection, and relationship to us. Scripture also tells us continue to love one another, because love comes from God – for God *is* love. He is the origin of love, and wants us to, and we should, imitate Him in our relationships, as He does in His relationship with us.

"To love someone is to see a miracle invisible to others."
— Francois Mauriac —

The Bible also mentions the physical devotion between husbands and wives, that the husband should not deprive his wife, nor the wife deprive the husband of sexual intimacy, giving each other authority to each other's body. The only exception being of mutual consent and agreement, and that it should only be for limited or specified amount of time, in order to give themselves more completely to prayer. They should afterward come together again, so that Satan will not tempt them because of their lack of self-control.

> "Your embraces alone give life to my heart."
> – Ancient Egyptian Saying –

The Bible also says that even though God has given us some meaningless days in this world, that we should live happily with the woman that we love. A wife being a reward for man's earthly toil.

> "Love is a fruit in season at all times."
> – Mother Teresa –

Love is not only finding the perfect person, but finding perfection in the person. Knowing a person's need is an indication of love; filling that need is an indication of even a greater love. Loving is caring – and loving is also a behavior!

Christ showed us how love is measured – by laying down His life for us; and how we should extend our love to our neighbors.

When we show love, we do no wrong to anyone, seek no revenge, and do not bear a grudge to anyone, because we are satisfying God's requirements. We find perfect harmony in the love that binds us. Love should then be our beginning, our course, and our goal. We must do *everything* in love, because our wholehearted love of God and neighbor is the way to eternal life. We can't love only those that love us, we have to love everybody.

> "Love one another – I mean really love. If you don't know the guy on the other side of the world, love him anyway because he's just like you."
> – Frank Sinatra –

We were told to *love* our enemies, to pray and be good to them, and that we should do to others what we would like them to do for us. The expression of love through action is not merely doing something to get it done, but by doing it with love, joy, excitement and enthusiasm.

"'Tis better to have loved and lost, than not to have loved at all."
– Lore Tennyson –

"There are three things that will endure – faith, hope, and love – and the greatest of these is love."
(1 Co 13:13)

Caring is an other form of love. It is an attentiveness, a feeling, interest, thoughtfulness, affection, or opinion in regards to an anxiousness, concern, support, or a sense of responsible, watchful or cautious attention, for someone's welfare; to feel, be attentive to, or exercise care.

When we think of caring, we often relate or associate it with Nannies, Nursing, Care-Givers and the like. Usually in any of these applications of personal care, a true and liberal amount of TLC is displayed. Tender Loving Care is sometimes as healing as the medicine, along with faith in the practitioner.

Our hats come off in appreciation to these *caring* individuals for the amount of care, attention, love, time, effort, persistency, patience, and devotion given to the many afflicted patients, especially those with Alzheimer, Dementia, or other disabling illnesses.

The Bible tells us that it is more important to care for our parents than to give money to God. Another instance of *caring* is in the story of the Good Samaritan that stopped to help and care for a man that had been robbed, stripped of his clothes and money, and left on the side of the road, half-dead. Not only did the Samaritan tend to his needs, but he made sure he had money to continue his travel. Caring should be as natural, as gentle and as devoted, as a mother feeding her child. We should be diligent and turn from our *indifference*.

There was a statement made, and it should be repeated often, that, "The road to *Auschwitz* was paved with *indifference*." Indifference is the opposite of caring. Because people didn't *care* to react more quickly to a situation, that at its start involved a single country, the calamity spread throughout an entire continent. We mustn't care only for our own needs, or what's going on in our home, or own backyard. We are one people sharing one world, we, in many ways affect one another. We have to turn indifference into – making a difference, a difference for the better for *everyone*. Indifference leads to a degenerating culture and decayed society, while caring brings peacefulness and unity.

If we were told by our Lord that we should love our neighbor as our self, then we should love our self enough to give the very best to our loved ones and to our neighbors.

Much care should also be given to the Care-Giver.

"A smile is the light in your window that tells others that there is a caring, sharing person inside."
– Denis Waitley –

"But anyone who does not love does not know God – for God is love."
(1 Jn 4:8)

FAITH – TRUST – BELIEF

Faith – The belief, trust and confidence in the principles of God. That which is believed, but not based on logical proof or material evidence; a divinely inspired form of positive belief; to believe without reason.

"What is faith? It is confident assurance that what we hope for is going to happen. It is the evidence of things we cannot yet see. God gave his approval to people in days of old because of their faith." (Heb 11:1,2)

Faith, Trust, and *Belief* are likely to be intertwined in their meanings, and sometimes used interchangeably. They seem to combine with each other; for when one has *faith*, there is usually trust and belief. Where there is *trust*, there is usually faith and belief, and where there is *belief* there is usually faith and trust. Some differentiation would be, that faith, in the Biblical sense, always suggests complete assurance in the one who agrees, even when there is no indication of proof, while trust and faith might not always.

> Where there is *faith* – there is God;
> where there is *doubt* – the devil.

We either have faith or we have doubt – because if we don't have complete faith, we are still doubtful. Jesus told His disciples, that they needed more faith, and He assured them that if they had enough faith, nothing would be impossible.

> "But we who live by the Spirit eagerly wait to receive everything promised to us who are right with God through faith." (Gal 5:5)

Faith was the basis for many occurrences since the beginning of time. Just to describe a few, it was by *faith* that:

– Abel brought a more acceptable offering to God than his brother Cain.
– Enoch was lifted up to heaven without dying.
– Noah built an ark to save his family from the flood.
– Abraham left his home to go to another land.
– Sara being barren, and Abraham being old, were still able to have a child.
– Abraham was willing to offer his son Isaac as a sacrifice.

- Moses' parents secluded him for three months.
- the people of Israel went through the Red Sea.
- a hemorrhaging woman was instantly healed when she touched the fringe of Jesus' robe.
- Jesus calmed the waves while his disciples were afraid in the boat.
- the blind man was restored his vision.
- a man was healed from leprosy.

The Virgin Mary, through faith in the message she received, became our Reparatrix by conceiving a child that would become our Savior.

> "Faith is not belief. Belief is passive. Faith is active."
> – Edith Hamilton –

It is not enough though to have good faith. Good faith should also be shown through good deeds. This is why all the above mentioned people took action to show their faith in God – to fulfill whatever He was asking of them to do. This is a way in which God puts us to the test, because when we go through trials we have a chance to grow spiritually thus gaining strength and even more faith.

> "Faith is the daring of the soul to go farther than it can see."
> – William Newton Clark –

Why should we be afraid or fear mortals, or anything of this world? Putting our faith in God should be one of the easiest things for us to do, simply for the reason of His unfailing love for us.

> "Such love has no fear because perfect love expels all fear. If we are afraid, it is for fear of judgment, and this shows that his love has not been perfect in us. We love each other as a result of his loving us first." (1 Jn 4:18,19)

Let Go – and – Let God!

Scriptures tell us that anyone who believes in the trustworthy message of the Word and the Truth, and is baptized, will be saved and have eternal life through Redemption and Salvation. Anyone who so refuses to believe, will not be saved, but be condemned.

> "Look at the proud! They trust in themselves and their lives are crooked; but the righteous will live by their faith."
> (Hab 2:4)

God knows how to take care of us, better than we can take care of ourselves. He not only knows and understands everything about us, but can fill our needs, and even some, that we are not aware of. The One who created the body, the mind and the soul, can certainly take care of, or repair the parts. Doctors have found that patients have been healed in miraculous ways. He will also heal the soul – if we allow Him.

> "God heals and the doctor sends the bill."
> – Benjamin Franklin –

He will take care of all of our needs day by day, if only we live for Him and make His Kingdom our primary concern. We were also warned about being sure that we don't cause little ones who trust in God, to lose their faith.

> "An everyday application to the state or the act of believing is that, God will be present, whether asked or not."
> – Latin Proverb –

Foremost and more importantly, the standard of personal conduct is that faith that comes to us from the message of the *Good News*, requires patience. We should then *rest* in our faith, because God's time is not our time. We should feel secure, justified and take pleasure in the joy, the confidence, the assurance and the peacefulness attained by our faith, that a loving and caring Father will take care of His children. Surveys show that having faith adds three years to our lives.

> "Sometimes when we're waiting for God to speak,
> He's waiting for us to listen."
> – Martha Bolton –

Trust – Having or placing assured confidence, hope or anticipation; relying on, depending on or counting on, the integrity, honesty, veracity, justice, or power of someone or something; being dependable or reliable; the placing in the care or keeping of another; to assume or entrust; a measure of belief – as it is a relationship of reliance.

> "Faith is not belief without proof,
> but trust without reservations."
> – Elton Trueblood –

In trusting, we have to rely on other than our own self or our own convictions. We have to place our faith and belief in something, or someone, with confidence and anticipation of being certain, and of knowing that we have made the right decision.

> "Self-conscious, uncertain, I'm showered by the dust.
> But the spirit enters into me and I submit to trust."
> – Peter Gabriel –

Trust is mentioned many times in the Bible. One that stands out, is that God could not trust even His angels, as some of them, in pride, turned against Him. How do we compare to the angels? Humankind has gotten to be so impure, corrupt and sinful, and has a thirst for wickedness.

> "Jesus shouted to the crowds,
> 'If you trust me, you are really trusting God who sent me.'"
> (Jn 12:44)

This is why we must not put trust in ourselves or other mere fellowmen who are as frail as breath. How would they be able to help anyone? Man's wisdom is not God's wisdom.

> "To be trusted is a greater compliment than to be loved."
> – George MacDonald –

Instead of being afraid of anything, we should rejoice in our trust in God. He told us to come to Him with trust, in time of trouble and that He would rescue us. Because He loves us, has given us so much, and thus worthy of our trust – we should trust that He will take care of us. We should offer sacrifices to Him, praise Him, show Him appreciation, and put our trust in Him, and in Him alone – in good times, and in troubled times.

> "Trust me in your times of trouble,
> and I will rescue you, and you will give me glory."
> (Ps 50:15)

> "Watch out! Don't let me find you living in careless ease
> and drunkenness, and filled with the worries of this life."
> (Lk 21:34a)

Faith is a journey towards *trust* and hope.

Belief – The psychological state, or state of mind, act, or condition of an individual in which there is a conviction to the validity or the truth of a proposition or premise, without the necessity of being able to properly prove that contention. It is also the trust or confidence in someone or something. Having a mental acceptance or supposition of what is right, true or real. The conviction of the truth or validity of something proposed or promised, and to accept it as true, without being able to adequately prove the main contention. To have faith in someone or something, truth, or value without validating reason, especially in religious or spiritual convictions. It is to accept one's opinion or conviction as true; to deem; to believe without seeing.

> "A belief is not merely an idea the mind possesses;
> it is an idea that possesses the mind."
> – Robert Bolton –

Every Sunday, after the church service, our pastor has a little humorous story to read to us, in order to help put a smile on our faces. In case you haven't heard this one about the Atheist who went hunting, it *bears* repeating:

It seems the Atheist had been in the woods for a good part of the day. Not having had any luck at sighting something, in discuss, he started to leave, and call it a day. – when suddenly, he heard some movement behind him. Turning around, hoping it was a deer, he instead saw a gigantic bear. His first thought was not to frighten the bear, but to walk away as quietly as he could. Looking back again, he saw that the bear was gaining ground on him. He then hastened his pace in order to escape the situation, and in trying to check the improvement of his escape, he once more looked back, this time not only seeing, but feeling the bear's paw on his shoulder. Frightened, he exclaimed, "Oh God!" And at that moment, time was at a stand-still. Everything stopped – the Atheist, the bear – there wasn't any movement of any kind, nor was there a sound heard. The Atheist heard a voice say, "Yes!" In his amazement the Atheist asked, "Is that you God?" God then replied, "Yes! What is it that you want?" The Atheist addressed God and said, "I'm having a problem right now, and if you are really God, maybe you can help." God answered him, "All these years you have denied me, and now that you are in distress, you call out to me. What is your request?" The Atheist replied, "What I'm asking, is not for myself, but for the bear!" So God said, "I will grant you your wish! How do you want me to help?" The Atheist asked, "Can you make a Christian out of that bear?" Then God replied, "Yes!"

At that moment everything started up again. There was movement – the birds could be heard singing, and in amazement the Atheist saw the bear kneeling on the ground, and putting his paws together, saying, "Bless this meal that I am about to receive!"

Living in such a liberal society which has become so doubtful of so many things, it should make us even more aware that we have to embrace our belief in the truth of God, rather than the lies that our culture is throwing at us. Satan has blinded the minds of those that don't believe, making them unable to see the glorious light of God's goodness that is radiating and beaming upon us.

> "Man makes holy what he believes,
> as he makes beautiful what he loves."
> – Ernest Renan –

There was a time when the people didn't believe Moses, nor the promise, that God would bring them to the promised land. In order for God to show the people, that they should believe in His authenticity and power, God had Moses throw his staff on the ground, and it turned into a snake. Then God sent a second sign by instantly causing Moses' hand to have leprosy, and to instantly heal it again.

> "'But you are my witness, O Israel!' says the Lord. 'And you are my servant. You have been chosen to know me, believe in me, and understand that I alone am God. There is no other God; there never has been and never will be.'"
> (Isa 43:10)

It is from believing in our hearts, and confessing with our mouths, that we are made right with God, and are saved through Jesus Christ our Redeemer. That through Him, and believing in Him we should have life. We must live a disciplined and devout life, with strong and steadfast belief in the message that we were taught, and we should also encourage others to do the same.

Our Creator has given each and every one of us much talents, and the ability to utilize them. We must then believe in ourselves, that we can accomplish anything that we set our minds to do. The Bible tells us that we can do any, and all things, in which Christ strengthens us. For everything else beyond our capabilities, we then turn with belief to our loving , merciful, and generous God – a God of gentleness, righteousness, and faithfulness.

"If you believe you will receive anything you ask for in prayer."
(Mt 21:22)

FAITHFULNESS

Faithfulness could be defined as an allegiance, loyalty, or devotion with constancy, and reliance to: a person, a cause, an obligation, duties, idea, to which one is bound, especially as a member of a religious group; a staunch or loyal follower; one that would be full of faith, firm in adherence, resolute, steadfast, steady, supportive, true, or a liege; fealty; fidelity. Faithfulness generally refers to a disposed belief to God and His character.

We get our faithfulness from God's faithfulness. For the reason that He is rich in faithfulness, we can have faith in Him. He shows us His faithfulness in His unfailing love.

Faithfulness is nearing extinction in our degenerating society and culture. Faithfulness used to be a prized characteristic of our way of life. It has now become acceptable to see businesses, friendships, and marriages dissolve. Honor and faithfulness has to return to marriage, and our way of life. Churches are not being attended as much as they used to be, forcing some to close. The amount of time that people are giving to their religious or spiritual side of life, has become more than shameful. People are making, or finding time for whatever else interests them. Spending hours at the enjoyment of favorite programs, sport presentations, and yet finding it difficult to take a few minutes to attend a church service. How do we relate to these choices?

Fewer people are entering the clergy, causing a real hardship in bringing God's Word to the people. If we don't go to church, or bring our children to church, how will we, or our children perpetuate the ideals of faithfulness. What will that teach the children, and what impact and influence will that have on all other children in the world. As we are one body in Christ, we belong to each other, and each one of us needs all the others.

What ever happened to the steadfast manners and principles with which we lived with: commitment, integrity, loyalty, or reliability. They don't seem to be of as much concern or importance, or as essential anymore.

There are shows on television that devote their entire time to gossip and slander. The tongue can be a flame of fire, full of wickedness and can abruptly ruin many lives. Its destructiveness is set by hell itself. It is easier to tame an animal than to tame the uncontrollable tongue. At one moment it can be praising God, and in the next moment it can break in curses against those that have been made into the image of God. Is it then right to see blessing and slander coming out of the same mouth? How *faithful* are we to God and our neighbor when we talk badly about others, our friends, or anybody else.

When we start controlling our lives the Spirit will produce this kind of fruit in us: *faithfulness*, gentleness, goodness, joy, kindness, patience, peace, and self-control.

HOPE

To expect, wish, entertain, trust, desire, rely on, or look forward to accompanied with confidence, trust, or expectation of acquiring or obtaining something or a promise; or believing that it is obtainable; a thing or reason that gives reason for hope; to expect or entertain hope.

"Hope equals desire accompanied by expectation."
– James Nichols III –

Hope is not a physical emotion, it is a spiritual grace. It is believing with perseverance, and that a positive outcome of a certain event or circumstance is going to come about, even though there is no proof of its possibility, and even if there are circumstances indicating to the contrary. Hope is usually charged with faith. Hope is considered as a spiritual grace, while faith is a belief which is divinely inspired.

*The promised **reward** is the real focus and object of hope. It is what leads us to the intended purposeful goal.*

"If you do not hope, you will not find what is beyond your hopes."
– St. Clement of Alexandra –

Hopefulness, resulting from faith – which is a belief in a positive outcome, demands some patience and perseverance. It is the believing and removing of all doubt. Hope, being an emotional state, it differs from optimism which is the result of a thought process which leads to a positive attitude. While hope can take the form of a wish or prayer, or show action as a plan or idea, it shows an awareness of spiritual truth. In Catholic theology, hope is one of the three virtues that are gifts from God: faith, hope and charity.

"Let your unfailing love surround us LORD, for our hope is in you alone." (Ps 33:22)

Each new generation should renew its *hope* in God by remembering His wondrous deeds, attesting his faithfulness, and by obeying His commands.

> "Everything passes away – suffering, pain, blood, hunger, pestilence. The sword will pass away too, but the stars will still remain when the shadows of our presence and our deeds have vanished from the earth. There is no man who does not know that. Why, then, will we not turn our eyes towards the sky? Why?
> – Mikhail Bulgakov –

In its extended and broad belief in something, hope is the desiring with the expectation of obtaining something. Spiritually, when it has God for its object, it is a theological virtue.

> "Through Christ you have come to trust in God. And because God raised Christ from the dead and gave him great glory, your faith and hope can be placed confidently in God." (1 Pe 1:21)

Because Jesus was God's chosen servant, He said that His name would be the *hope* of all the world.

> "A leader is a dealer in hope."
> – Napoleon Bonaparte –

We should praise the Spirit of God for the guaranteed hope that He would give us everything He promised. The Good News is our hope through Redemption and Salvation. So if we live by the words of God, and in a world *with* God, we live in a world of hope, which gives us life and joy.

> "We must accept finite disappointment, but we must never lose infinite hope."
> – Martin Luther King –

We must however live properly, *patiently* and confidently until our final reward, the everlasting joys of heaven. Our hope should lie solely in the Lord – nothing else will ever achieve such a recompense. All other kinds of hope are for earthly desires, to obtain worldly pleasure – none of which will, or could, ever compare to what is divinely waiting for us when we place our hope in God.

"All human wisdom is summed up in two words – wait and hope."
– Alexander Dumas –

If we keep up our courage and remain confident in our hope in Christ, we become part of God's household.

"Every area of trouble gives out a ray of hope;
and the one unchangeable certainty
is that nothing is certain or unchangeable."
– John Fitzgerald Kennedy –

We obtain our confident assurance that what we hope for is going to happen, because our faith is the evidence of things we cannot yet see.

"Don't envy sinners, but always continue to fear the LORD. For surely you have a future ahead of you; your hope will not be disappointed." (Pr 23:17,18)

COURAGE

A quality of mind or spirit that enables one to meet or face danger or difficulties, with confidence, resolution and with firm control of oneself as with valor. To have spirit, tenacity; mettle; to be brave; or have fortitude.

Courage is one of the Four Cardinal Virtues which also include, Justice, Prudence and Temperament.

"Without courage you cannot practice any of the other virtues."
– Maya Angelou –

> "Everything passes away – suffering, pain, blood, hunger, pestilence. The sword will pass away too, but the stars will still remain when the shadows of our presence and our deeds have vanished from the earth. There is no man who does not know that. Why, then, will we not turn our eyes towards the sky? Why?
> – Mikhail Bulgakov –

In its extended and broad belief in something, hope is the desiring with the expectation of obtaining something. Spiritually, when it has God for its object, it is a theological virtue.

> "Through Christ you have come to trust in God. And because God raised Christ from the dead and gave him great glory, your faith and hope can be placed confidently in God." (1 Pe 1:21)

Because Jesus was God's chosen servant, He said that His name would be the *hope* of all the world.

> "A leader is a dealer in hope."
> – Napoleon Bonaparte –

We should praise the Spirit of God for the guaranteed hope that He would give us everything He promised. The Good News is our hope through Redemption and Salvation. So if we live by the words of God, and in a world *with* God, we live in a world of hope, which gives us life and joy.

> "We must accept finite disappointment, but we must never lose infinite hope."
> – Martin Luther King –

We must however live properly, *patiently* and confidently until our final reward, the everlasting joys of heaven. Our hope should lie solely in the Lord – nothing else will ever achieve such a recompense. All other kinds of hope are for earthly desires, to obtain worldly pleasure – none of which will, or could, ever compare to what is divinely waiting for us when we place our hope in God.

"All human wisdom is summed up in two words – wait and hope."
– Alexander Dumas –

If we keep up our courage and remain confident in our hope in Christ, we become part of God's household.

"Every area of trouble gives out a ray of hope;
and the one unchangeable certainty
is that nothing is certain or unchangeable."
– John Fitzgerald Kennedy –

We obtain our confident assurance that what we hope for is going to happen, because our faith is the evidence of things we cannot yet see.

"Don't envy sinners, but always continue to fear the LORD. For surely you have a future ahead of you; your hope will not be disappointed." (Pr 23:17,18)

COURAGE

A quality of mind or spirit that enables one to meet or face danger or difficulties, with confidence, resolution and with firm control of oneself as with valor. To have spirit, tenacity; mettle; to be brave; or have fortitude.
Courage is one of the Four Cardinal Virtues which also include, Justice, Prudence and Temperament.

"Without courage you cannot practice any of the other virtues."
– Maya Angelou –

One of the ways that courage can be described is by the different abilities or techniques needed to practice it. It must be as a reaction or response to an exposure to harm or danger without the thought of withdrawal. Utilizing the ability effectively to deal with a grave situation. Being able to follow directions and orders when faced with a dangerous situation. Having self-assurance and confidence that one will succeed if faced with adversity or an adversary.

"To face despair and not give in to it, that's courage."
– Ted Koppell –

There is *moral* courage when it relates to a spiritual application. It becomes *physical* courage when it is implied or applied with strength.

"You, too, must be patient. And take courage, for the coming of the Lord is near." (Jas 5:8)

Courage varies in degree and intensity depending on the situation. It could be defined as the lacking of fear in a situation that might accelerate it. The contrasting view would be, to say that you must have fear in order to overcome it.

"What is more mortifying than to feel that you have missed the plum for want of courage to shake the tree."
(Author Unknown)

God tells us that we should never be *discouraged*, because He is always there for us to turn to. He wants us to take courage as we fulfill our duties, and that if we do, then He will be with us, helping us. The reason we have courage is because we have hope – a protective hope that allows us to rest safely, while the wicked will lose hope, and have no escape because their lack of hope becomes despair. The Bible also tells us that the courage of many will falter because of the fearful fate they see coming upon the earth, which will be unbearable to them because of their lack of faith and hope.

> "We must pray to God for courage.
> No future is totally dark and hopeless if we have faith."
> – Rev. Paul Osumi –

CHARITY – SHARING

Charity in its simplest form, is the goodwill and brotherly love towards others, but in its most profound meaning, it is the giving of attention, love, care, or things to help one survive.

> "With malice towards none, with charity for all."
> – Abraham Lincoln –

It is described as a kind of generous act; tolerance and leniency in judging others; a feeling of affection; good will to the poor and suffering; help or relief from an individual, group, institution, fund, or an eleemosynary foundation, established to help society, the needy, a cause, or humanity. It is also the act of loving all men. The modern meaning of charity is about giving time or something to those in need. It is usually performed to assist others in need and not to gain profit or recognition.

> "Charity sees the need not the cause." – German Proverb –

The saying, "Charity begins at home." – implies the giving to those related to us, above and beyond providing.

Charity being an expression of *love*, is one of the three theological virtues, which also include, faith and hope.

Charity is often called Christian Love, or defines the Divine love for man. It is also the act of loving all men as brothers because they are sons of God.

> "Be charitable before wealth makes you covetous."
> – Sir Thomas Browne –

Being charitable could be as either an *act or service,* or *objects* given:

- *of performing an act or service* – acceptance, altruism, being forgiving, compassionate, benignity, charitableness, clemency, goodwill, grace, kindheartedness, leniency, philanthropy, tolerance, and showing interest. (In the writings of Matthew, he gives us examples of acts of charity: burying the dead, clothing the naked, feeding the hungry, giving drink to the thirsty, sheltering the homeless, visiting the sick and the prisoners.)
- *of something given* – alms, a gift, benefaction, a contribution, a donation, a handout, an offering, a pledge.

Some of the charitable acts we can do, would be in visiting the homebound, hospitalized and the incarcerated. It could be in the act of educating, giving care, food, clothing, or tending to the needs of the helpless. One of the best examples of being charitable, was found in the humble nature of Mother Teresa. She devoted her entire life to charity, giving herself unselfishly to the *cause* for the love of God. It is true when they say that, "The gift always points to the Giver."

> "In charity there is no excess."
> – Sir Francis Bacon –

Jesus gave an explanation of being charitable:

> "'When you put on a luncheon or dinner,' he said, 'Don't invite your friends, brothers, relatives, and rich neighbors. For they will repay you by inviting you back. Instead, invite the poor, the crippled, the lame, and the blind. Then at the resurrection of the godly, God will reward you for inviting those who could not repay you.'" (Lk 14:12b-14)

Saint Francis included in his prayer that, it is in *giving* that we receive – and Jesus told us that we are more *blessed* when we give than when we receive.

> "Give generously, for your gifts will return to you later."
> (Ecc 11:1)

Many people don't attend church, thus not helping the church in its many dire needs. They are not participating in uniting as a people, nor are they helping the church financially. The expression of, "giving 'til it hurts," seems to relate to the giving to *self*. If a poor widow can drop in two pennies, we can certainly do our appropriate share. Each should decide as to the amount given – but *all* should be giving. If you plant a garden, plant an extra row to be given to the needy.

> "The best thing to give to your enemy is forgiveness; to an opponent, tolerance; to a friend, your heart; to your child, a good example; to a father, difference; to your mother, conduct that will make her proud of you; to yourself, respect; to all men, charity."
> – Francis Maitland Balfour –

We as sinners are justified and made righteous in the sight of God when we accept freely the unearned gift of faith and we respond to it by acts of *charity*, and doing good works that are performed out of love for God and our neighbor.

> "The charity that happens to proclaim its good deeds, ceases to be charity, and is only pride and ostentation."
> – William Hutton –

Sharing is the joint or alternating use of existing and essential resources, as to apportion, divide, have a share, to experience or enjoy with others, or the granting of a privilege or right, such as information. It can also be in the form of a gift. Sharing is another form of showing love and charity. We can do these wonderful acts by use of time or different means and resources. We can participate and share in common, many things and responsibilities.

"Three keys to more abundant living:
caring about others, daring for others, sharing with others."
– William A. Ward –

Sharing can simply mean, to not hurry in eating our meal, but sharing that bonding time with others.

"When we share – that is poetry in the prose of life."
– Sigmund Freud –

Because of our faith, trust, and belief, the most exciting thing that we can confidently and joyfully look forward to, is the highest privilege, of being able to *share* in God's glory.

*It is possible to give without loving,
but if you are to love, you have to give.*

HONOR – RESPECT – DIGNITY

Honor is how a person is highly regarded, manifested, specially respected or evaluated in regards to his social status, trustworthiness, reputation or good name. Honor is sometimes based on someone's espousals or actions. It is a cause or source of credit or distinction; showing an inner sense of what is right, moral or ethical; integrity; esteem which is paid or due to worth; excellence of character. It is also a sense of what is right and true. It can vary in its applications, such as: the honor given for an accomplishment, a cause, a person or a nation.

Good character is what some conceive as honor. It is usually a sign that reflects fairness, integrity, fairness or honesty. Based on a code of honor, actions and general social acceptance, people are assigned a certain worth or stature. In men the measure for honor is integrity and uprightness. In women, it is purity and chastity. It is as real to the human condition, as love.

"No amount of ability is of the slightest avail without honor."
— Andrew Carnegie —

The state of affairs of this world have become so unruly and so extremely chaotic. One of the things the Bible tells us about honor, is that we shouldn't try to dishonor or speak evil of *anyone* who rules over us. There is such a need to reestablish a sense of decency, integrity, peace and happiness. We have to be selective as to who we honor, because we tend to imitate them. A person is not honored by what he's *received*, but what he has *given*.

"Let's honor our mistakes by allowing them to teach us. Let's consider our failings to be gifts and share them humbly with others. Let the cracks in our perfect facades let in light and air so that new life can grow through them."
— Molly Gordon —

To solve a problem, any problem, it is easier to go back to the source of the problem, back to the basics. Peace and happiness, which is everyone's right, has to start, at the very beginning, within the family. The family unit has its own little society, with rules, regulations and values; the teaching of which promotes and encourages honor, and respect for one another. The honor should be given to the parents – not the other way around. The switch in honor has become acceptable in many families. The honoring of parents meant so much to God, that He commanded us in obedience to it. Honoring our parents is like saying, "Wow! This is my father!" or, "Wow! This is my mother!" It should resonate and show an excitement and an expression of pride, like *rooting* for your favorite team. Parents in return have to *love* their children. One of best gifts you can give to your child is the *present* of *being* present – **time**. Wrapped or unwrapped, that present can be given *freely* and *abundantly*. This is a gift that anyone can afford to give, and it should be given at the *present* – not later.

Children will forget about toys, clothing, and material things, but they will not soon forget the good times that they shared with their parents, nor the heartwarming things that were done and accomplished together.

> "The greatest way to live with honor in this world
> is to be what we pretend to be."
> – Socrates –

In order to achieve peace in families, nations, or the world, we have to learn to not only discipline ourselves, but to *love* disciplining ourselves, because of its intrinsic values. This is where the change of attitude comes in. The parents must first engage in honoring themselves as husband and wife, and in self-discipline, then teach their children by example. The children in return, and in honor, also have to learn why they must love to be disciplined, and to also want and care about disciplining themselves – because the end result is the appreciation and the gaining of good values, morals, respect, ethics, integrity and the learning of what is right. They, the children, in turn will be the ones to teach their own children what *they* have learned. This is how character is built and transported to the next generation. Nothing works better than starting at the source! Imagine how peaceful, loving and joyful the world would become if all families would practice this kind of behavior.

> "Dignity does not consist in possessing honors,
> but in deserving them."
> – Aristotle –

Being haughty or prideful brings in destruction, while humbling ourselves brings honor. Avoiding confrontations is a sign of honor.

"Yes, an ounce of foolishness can outweigh a pound of wisdom and honor." (Ecc 10:1b)

Respect is the condition or the act of showing consideration, deferential or high regard, or being esteemed; concern or favor; to consider; to be worthy of esteem; deem.

"Probably no greater honor can come to any man than the respect of his colleagues."
— Cary Grant —

The necessary amounts of certain traits such as integrity, manners, moral values, politeness, trust and skills, could be pointed towards an other person or oneself to determine the qualification for respect, which is essential for people to get along with each other.

"I had to fight hard against loneliness, abuse, and the knowledge that any mistakes I made would be magnified because I was the only black man out there...I never cared about acceptance as much as I cared about respect."
— Jackie Robinson —

People from different backgrounds or cultures have different ways of showing respect, especially in greeting one another. It can vary from a hand shake to a bow of the head, and for women it might be a curtsy. In some Asian countries, the bow would be from the waist.

"Love and respect are the most important aspects of parenting, and of all relationships."
— Jodie Foster —

The Bible tells us that if we *respect* our earthly fathers who have disciplines us, we should all the more, submit to our heavenly Father, and in doing so, we will live forever. We are also told to stand up in the presence of elderly people and show *respect* for the aged. It is difficult for some to respect and take the advice of others, but those that do will succeed.

> "If one doesn't respect oneself
> one can have neither love nor respect for others."
> – Ayn Rand –

Dignity is the condition of being esteemed, worthy, respected, or honorable; having an important position or station; having nobility, excellence, formal reserve of manner, aspect or style; elevation of character or intrinsic worth; a degree of estimation; stateliness.

It is of earning or expecting personal esteem or respect. Other forms of dignity would be: righteous indignation, pride, self-concept, or self-respect. Still other areas would include: being prestigious, honorable, having a good name, reputation, status or high standing.

> She is clothed with strength and dignity, and she laughs with no fear of the future." (Pr 31:25)

It is so important to uphold the dignity of others as well as our own. It should be defended at all costs.

Being created in the image of God, every single life, and each person's dignity must be respected. From an unborn child in a mother's womb, every person, whatever their status in life, whatever their worth or accomplishments, or the lack of such, whether sickly or dying, whether a criminal – every human life is sacred and must have dignity from conception, to a natural death.

> "Pray this way for kings and all others who are in authority, so that we can live in peace and quietness, in godliness and dignity." (1 Ti 2:2)

The reputation and honor of our neighbor is destroyed through detraction and calumny. Human dignity comes from being honored socially. We have a natural right to the honor of our name, our respect, and our reputation. When we dishonor or discredit someone, we break the law of charity and justice, because it is an act of dehumanizing, and robbing someone of their credibility.

> "A good reputation is more valuable than the most expensive perfume." (Ecc 7:1a)

INTEGRITY

Integrity is considered to be of strict and personal honesty, or moral soundness, and independence. Or the state or quality of being unimpaired, unbroken or undivided; uprightness; to have honesty or purity; completeness; entirety; unity.

> "Integrity is not something that grownups have and adolescents can aspire to. Integrity is something that all of us, at all ages, are constantly striving for."
> – Harold Kushner –

It is a characteristic that is usually found in people that are self-actualized. When a person knows oneself it intensifies the degree of integrity. It is a stature that is difficult to obtain, and it takes a long time to achieve. It is fed by self-confidence and consistency, ever maintaining the same idealistic core of values, with a certain outcome in mind.

> "I know, my God, that you examine our hearts and rejoice when you find integrity there." (1 Ch 29:17)

When we pray to God, we should ask Him for the gift of mercy and the strength to live our lives with the utmost integrity and honesty, knowing that He would then rise us up, and restore our lives. It is integrity that gives us firm footing, and keeps us on the right paths, so that we won't slip and fall into the pits of the world.

HELPFULNESS – KINDNESS

Helpfulness is the act of furnishing or providing useful help or assistance; assisting or being useful; showing a kindly or helpful disposition.

Being helpful is the opposite of being indifferent. Helpfulness and assistance to someone is an act that comes from the heart. It usually comes about as an expression of love and generosity.

> "There is no exercise better for the heart
> than reaching down and lifting people up."
> – John Andrew Holmes –

The display of helping others would indeed come more from a person with integrity, than a person who is an egotist. Some can offer to help at a time when it is noticeably needed, while others will want to plan to assist, before the need arrives. Help is given to others for many different reasons, but generally, it is simply to assist in the outcome of another. When God commanded us to love our neighbor, that obviously included helping him.

> "The kind of man who thinks that helping with the dishes is beneath him will also think that helping with the baby is beneath him, and then he certainly is not going to be a very successful father."   – Eleanor Roosevelt –

There is a lot to be said about some people's indifference towards others. Sometimes their unwillingness to help in time of dire need, can be disastrous, and sometimes could result as fatal. If a person chooses not to help others, and basically lives to please himself, he is not adding much value to his life. One of the greatest cures for depression, or to boost up self-esteem, is to *help others*.

> "Learned helplessness is the giving-up reaction, the quitting response that follows from the belief that whatever you do doesn't matter." – Arnold Schwarzenegger –

Our society could be broken down into three distinctive kinds of people. In life you will find: *givers, receivers,* and *takers.*

- *Givers* are the ones who are helpful, who give to others in the form of their time, their support, material things, as a show of affection, or because of need.
- *Receivers* are those that think that everything should be coming their way, or given to them. They often rely on the generosity of others.
- *Takers* are the ones that take more than their share or will attain what they want through deceit, or unlawfully take it from others.

> "For though I do my work with wisdom, knowledge and skill, I must leave everything I gain to people who haven't worked to earn it." (Ecc 2:21)

There are so many ways that people can get involved. They can join an organization such as the Jaycees, the Elks, the Lions, the Rotary, Church functions, or many other social activities, engineered to help the community or mankind. In serving in these organizations, one gets so much satisfaction by satisfying the needs of many. Everyone needs some type of help at one time or other.

> "Ask not what your country can do for you;
> ask what you can do for your country."
> – John Fitzgerald Kennedy –

Our words, can even be such a help and encouragement to many, in helping them through certain heart-wrenching or devastating situations.

> "Help your brother's boat across, and Lo!
> Thine own has reached the shore."
> – Hindu Proverb –

Another way of helping is by showing or teaching others how to help themselves. Some people never got the opportunity to learn how to take care of themselves. By taking time to help others through certain procedures, they can become self-sufficient, self-reliant, and feel so much better about themselves. There is nothing more depressing to someone as the feeling of incompetency.

> "You need to be aware of what others are doing, applaud their efforts, acknowledge their successes, and encourage them in their pursuits. When we all help one another, everybody wins."
> – Jim Stovall –

Good people seem to speak words that are helpful, while the wicked tend to say things that will hurt or corrupt.

> "God has given gifts to each of you from his great variety of spiritual gifts. Manage them well so that God's generosity can flow through you." (1Pe 4:10)

Kindness is the quality or state of charitable behavior or being kind; having affection or kind feeling; doing a kind act or an act of good will; good deeds.

> "No act of kindness, however small, is ever wasted."
> – Aesop –

Kindness being one of the Seven Virtues, is not only a valued virtue but is also one of the Seven Contrary Virtues. Kindness is contrary to the sin of envy, and it is often referred to as *loving-kindness* – as kindness is an act of love.

"I expect to pass through this world but once; any good thing therefore that I can do, or any kindness that I can show to any fellow creature, let me do it now; let me not defer or neglect it, for I shall not pass this way again."
– Etienne De Grellet –

The Scriptures tell us that we will be judged, not only by our faith, but by our deeds as well. We also must judge others fairly and honestly by showing mercy and kindness to everyone. Deeds of kindness are signs of someone's faithfulness, because faith is empty without deeds, just as the body is dead without the spirit. When Jesus comes back with His angels, all people will be judged according to their belief and their deeds.

"Sometimes when we are generous in small, barely detectable ways it can change someone's life forever."
– Margaret Cho –

True kindness doesn't seek or demand anything in return. It is not to benefit the giver in any way, but solely intended to be helpful to someone. It is also the most desired trait in relationships.

"That best portion of a good man's life, His title, nameless acts of kindness and of love."
– William Wordsworth –

Acts of good deeds or kindness are easily given to our loved ones or those close to us, but the real application of kindness is when it includes everyone.

"Yet do I fear thy nature; It is too full o' the milk of human kindness."
– William Shakespeare –

Kindness is produced and delivered from a good heart, while evil is produced and spread from an evil heart. It is through God's kindness that we are called to His eternal glory by means of His Son who became our Redeemer.

> "If you want others to be happy, practice compassion.
> If you want to be happy, practice compassion."
> – The Dalai Lama –

GOODNESS

Goodness is the state, quality, feeling or condition of being generous, upright, good or virtuous; a sign of moral excellence of worth or workmanship; what is perceived as the best part of something; having integrity, honesty, and virtue.

> "What a strange illusion it is to suppose that beauty is goodness."
> – Leo Tolstoy –

In order to gain the approval and esteem of others for possessing goodness, one has to attain, possess and maintain the required qualities of character morality and conduct. If a person maintains the quality of goodness, he is then considered as being virtuous. Goodness also comes from humility.

> "It seemed the world was divided into good and bad people. The good ones slept better...while the bad ones seemed to enjoy the waking hours much more."
> – Woody Allen –

In order to become virtuous, we not only have to be good, but be consistent. God has called us to receive His own glory and goodness, and by the same power He gave us His generous promises. He tells us to live a life of *steady* goodness, so that only good deeds will pour forth, and that we shouldn't brag about our doings.

"We must use time wisely and forever realize that the time
is always ripe to do right." – Nelson Mendela –

It is important that we all plant seeds of goodness. In planting seeds, they get multiplied through the harvest. For this reason we have to live in the way of goodness that will influence our society and the world, by setting profoundly good examples. Our present, allowed cultures, have not only become an accepted way of life, but are stripping away the innocence from our children.

"Each person has inside a basic decency and goodness. If
he listens to it, and acts on it, he is giving a great deal of
what it is the world needs most. It is not complicated but it
takes courage. It takes courage for a person to listen to his
own goodness and act on it."
– Pablo Casals –

Goodness can be used as a reference to God or as euphemisms for God, such as: "Goodness Gracious!" or "For Goodness Sake!" As the result of being surprised: "Goodness, you gave me a scare!."

"After the verb 'to Love,'
'to Help' is the most beautiful verb in the world."
– Bertha von Suttner –

We cannot count on our own goodness, or obeying the laws to be saved, but instead we must count on the belief that Christ is our Salvation. The Kingdom of God has been defined in the Bible as living a life of goodness – and in His goodness He called us to be His children; and out of all creation we became His choice possession.

"What makes saintliness in my view, as distinguished
from ordinary goodness, is a certain quality of magnanimity
and greatness of soul that brings life within the circle of the
heroic."   – Harriet Beecher Stowe –

CONSIDERATION

Consideration is the act or process of giving careful thought or consideration; having thoughtful or sympathetic regard or notice; to attain or arrive at a matured decision or opinion.

"Politeness and consideration for others is like investing pennies and getting dollars back." – Thomas Sowel –

It can also be a result of having reflected, considered, or having attentive respect; appreciative regard; a claim to notice; the tendency to consider others.

"Did blind chance know that there was light and what was its refraction, and fit the eyes of all creatures after the most curious manner to make use of it? These and other suchlike considerations, always have, and always will prevail with mankind, to believe that there is a Being who made all things, who has all these things in his power, and who is therefore to be feared." – Isaac Newton –

To consider in good conscience, is not only to come up with one's own opinion but to also take into balance the opinions and considerations of others; as the consideration of others implies one's humility, respect and kindness.

"Though force can protect in emergency, only justice, fairness, consideration and cooperation can finally lead men to the dawn of eternal peace." – Dwight D. Eisenhower –

Once we identify with an opinion, we weigh and balance it with reasoning, then tend to bend all other thoughts toward that one objective. Once we have considered, we then take the risk.

"Yes, each of us will have to give a personal account to

God. So don't condemn each other anymore."
(Ro 14:12,13a)

COOPERATION – UNSELFISHNESS

Cooperation is joint action, assistance or support amongst people. It is the collective willingness to agree or cooperate for common benefit.

In the application of cooperation, certain goals can be met more efficiently because of the common and mutual supportive efforts and methods towards a specific goal. Cooperation is basically and fundamentally applied towards the basis of harmony. While cooperating with something else, everything works better.

> "It is probably not love that makes the world go around, but rather those mutually supportive alliances through which partners recognize their dependency on each other for the achievement of shared and private goals."– Fred A. Allen –

Cooperation can be voluntary, freely chosen, and agreed upon, or it can forced, demanded, commanded or coerced, thus forcing submission.

> "Pleasure usually takes the form of me and now; joy is us and always."   – Marion J. Ashton –

Mary cooperated with the message given to her by the angel, and bore for us the Son God. Jesus in turn cooperated with His Father and became our Redeemer and Salvation. Why then shouldn't we cooperate with what is asked of us, to live a life in the way that Our Creator intended for us to live?

> "We confess that we have been unfaithful to our God."
> "We will obey the law of God. Take courage, for it is your

duty to tell us how to proceed in setting things straight, and we will cooperate fully." (Esr 10:2b,3c,4)

Unselfishness is the state or quality of being generous, greathearted, magnanimous, unsparing, munificent, or openhanded. Not always thinking or looking out for oneself, but wanting to share with others.

Unselfishness is a virtue making up Four Absolutes, which also include: Honesty, Love, and Purity. One of the best meanings of unselfishness is, the importance and morality of placing others before ourselves, and doing it with care and love.

> "Magnanimous people have no vanity, they have no jealousy, they have no reserves, and they feed on the true and solid wherever they find it. And what is more, they find it everywhere."   – Van Wyck Brooks –

When asked in surveys, the most given reason for a long married relationship that lasted with so much happiness for over sixty or seventy years, was the blend of *unselfishness.*

The perfection of all virtues lies in unselfish love. The more we forget about self, the more we move towards sinless moral excellence.

The Bible tells us that we should let everyone see that we are unselfish and considerate in all that we do. True love is not self-seeking, it is selfless. God in His divine generosity and unselfishness wanted us to be like unto Himself, which was promoted by His abundant love for us.

> "He died for everyone so that those who receive his new life will no longer live to please themselves. Instead, they will live to please Christ, who died and was raised for them." (2 Co 5:15)

FRIENDLINESS

Friendliness is the act of befitting a friend; being affectionate, amiable, benevolent, chummy, comforting, companionable, congenial, cordial; favorably or well disposed; genial; gracious; helpful; kindly; neighborly; propitious; warm-hearted.

"Some people think that friendliness is a sign of weakness,
when in reality it is a sign of strength."
– Wolfgang Singer –

It is also found in a warm and comforting gesture. To possess the amicable presence of friendliness, one must appreciate and give to the need of another.

"Vitality of relationships is not in the enjoyment of similarities
but in the honoring of differences."
"A friend is someone who knows the song in your heart,
and can sing it back to you when you've forgotten the words."
"Friends never betray you,
only people you thought were your friends."
– T. Mike Runger –

The way to a friend's house is *never long*, because of being anxious to get there. The time spent together is so full of excitement, that the time seems to fly by. The distance is not an issue when the occasion is needed to talk, visit, seek advice, or offer a helping hand. The amount of travel is well worth it.

"Don't you realize
that friendliness with this world
makes you an enemy of God?
I say it again, that if your aim is to enjoy this world,
you can't be a friend of God."
(Jas 4:4b)

GENTLENESS

Gentleness is considered to be the consideration in disposition; easily managed or handled; having softness in manners or the quality and value in one's character; chivalrous; mollified; tamed; graceful; soft hearted; tenderhearted; well-born.

"Only the weak are cruel. Gentleness can only be expected from the strong." – Leo Buscaglia –

Being a refining of character, gentleness is usually used in situations that are sometimes difficult, and can through its approach of being thoughtful, serve as a fine example for others. It might keep one from hurting another, unintentionally.

"When you encounter difficulties and contradictions, do not try to break them, but bend them with gentleness and time." – Saint Francis de Sales –

"True gentleness is founded on a sense of what we owe to him who made us and to the common nature which we all share. It arises from reflection on our own failings and wants, and from just views of the condition and duty of man. It is native feeling heightened and improved by principle."
– Hugh Blair –

Gentleness is a virtue within a group considered to be fruits of the Holy Spirit, all of which lead us to a godlier way of life.

"Since God chose you to be holy people whom he loves, you must clothe yourselves with tenderhearted mercy, kindness, humility, gentleness, and patience." (Col 3:12)

"Should I come with punishment and scolding, or should I come with quiet love and gentleness?" (1 Co 4:21b,c)

JOY

Joy is a condition, state, or feeling of happiness or great pleasure; a manifestation or expression of delight or satisfaction; rejoicing; gladness; to be excited by the expectation or acquisition of something good; exhibition of joy; extreme cheerfulness; having ecstatic or exultant happiness; rejoicing; bliss.

> "Joy is prayer – Joy is strength – Joy is Love –
> Joy is a net of love by which you can catch souls."
> – Mother Teresa –

It is also the showing of high spirits, elation, and the lightness of heart. The source of a positive stimulus, delight, or happiness provided by someone or something.

> "Joy is not in things; it is in us."
> – Richard Wagner –

Joy is one of the twelve fruits of the Holy Spirit. When we come to know Christ as an ultimate experience, we then experience extreme exultant happiness and pleasure. The joy from this closeness becomes a completion to happiness, only to be even more magnified in heaven.

> "There is no greater joy nor greater reward than to
> make a fundamental difference in someone's life."
> – Sister Mary Rose McGeady –

There are different degrees and expressions of joy ranging from mild to extreme: from showing enthusiasm, exuberance; being cheerful and lively; exhilaration or excitement – to showing extreme joy, exultation or jubilation.

> "Things won are done; joy's soul lies in the doing."
> – William Shakespeare –

Some have a different way of explaining or expressing joy, such as to: be glad, be on cloud nine, cheer up, experience, exult, rejoice, walk on air. One of the best ways to *spread* joy, is to bring sunshine with us wherever we go.

> "Grief can take care of itself, but to get the full value of joy you must have somebody to divide it with."
> – Mark Twain –

> "May your walls know joy; May every room hold laughter and every window open to great possibility."
> – Maryanne Radmacher Hershey –

The following are just a few of the *joyful expressions* found in the Bible: be radiant with joy, clap your hands for joy, dance for joy, everlasting joy, festivals of joy, filled with joy, jump for joy, leaping with joy, oil of joy, overcome with joy, pride and joy, ray of joy, shout for joy, sing for joy, sounds of joy, tears of joy, thrill with joy, and, What joy!

> "This is the true joy in life, the being used for a purpose recognized by yourself as a mighty one; the being thoroughly worn out before you are thrown on the scrap heap; the being a force of Nature instead of a feverish selfish little clod of ailments and grievances complaining that the world will not devote itself to making you happy."
> – George Bernard Shaw –

What a joy we should also feel, when God chastises us for our wrongdoings. Joy is not always from some delight received because of worldly pleasure, but it can come in many forms, like when a beneficial outcome is shown from having been tested through trials and tribulations. We should regard these as opportunities for joy, because when we are tested, our endurance has a chance to grow. By letting our endurance grow we then become strong in character and have the strength to be ready for anything. We should also find that same joy when our disobedience is forgiven and God puts our sins out of sight.

"But let the godly rejoice, Let them be glad in God's presence. Let them be filed with joy." (Ps 68:3)

"Hope deferred makes the heart sick, but when dreams come true, there is life and joy." (Pr 13:12)

PEACEFULNESS

Peacefulness is the state or the act of possessing calmness; placidity; quietude; serenity; being pacific; enjoying or marked by peace; tranquility; silence; a hush; a lull; a quietness; stillness; untroubledness.

"First find peace within yourself, then you can also bring peace to others."   — Thomas a Kempis —

It is the absence of anxiety, hostility, mental stress, disputes, and motion of disturbance, or a state of non-violence. It is when justice, peace and respect characterizes a relationship between two parties. Mother Teresa said that peace begins with a smile.

"There is no way to peace. Peace is the way." — A. J. Muste —

It is generally described as having *inner peace*, or being *at peace* — indicating a calmness, serenity or equilibrium with oneself. Possessing a tranquil state of mind, body or soul; having found and enjoying a calmness within oneself.

"Let us not be justices of the peace, but angels of peace."
— St Theresa of Lisieux —

> "I am leaving you with a gift — peace of mind and heart.
> And the peace I give isn't like the peace the world gives."
> (Jn 14:27a,b,c)

The peace that Christ left us, is threefold. The peace *with* God. The peace *of* God. The peace with our *fellow man.*

Peacefulness is not something that is dependent on people, place, time or situation. A person can experience peace amidst difficulties and tragedies. Because peace, being a state of mind, and also of spirituality, it gives oneself the strength in time of difficulties and stress.

> "We shall find peace. We shall hear the angels, we shall see the sky sparkling with diamonds." — Anton Chekhov —

In order to seek peace, happiness and freedom, we must find a suitable peaceful living area, or work to make the area peacefully suitable. Peacefulness is an individual development which brings happiness – *happiness is a decision.*

> "He lets me rest in green meadows; he leads me beside peaceful streams." (Ps 23:2)

We should be so thankful for the song that is enjoyed by so many, by Sy Miller and Jill Jackson, the writers of the music and lyrics, "Let There Be Peace On Earth." It is not only enjoyable to listen to, but it has brought to so many, the reality that peace is not something that should be waited for until someone makes it available to us, but that it should start within everyone of us.

TOLERANCE

Tolerance is the act, capacity for, or the practice, or quality of recognizing and respecting the behavior, belief, habits, opinions, or practices of others, even when being different from one's own. It is also the capacity to be able to endure pain and hardship.

> "The wiser you are, the more you believe in equality because the difference between what the most and the least learned people know is inexpressibly trivial in relation to all that is unknown."   – Albert Einstein –

It is also being able to allow for differences or error in certain attitudes, beliefs, religions, situations, or ways, even if they are not accepted by the majority.

> "The American ideal is not that we all agree with each other, or even like each other, every minute of the day. It is rather that we will respect each other's right, especially the right to be different..."   – Arthur J. Kropp –

True tolerance becomes a virtue and necessary when it is applied towards the errors of others, and not so much because of the accepting of differences and views.

> "I ask you to uphold the values of America and remember why so many have come here. We're in a fight for our principles, and our first responsibility is to live by them. No one should be singled out for unfair treatment or unkind words because of their ethnic background or religious faith."
> – George W. Bush –

There is no reason to expect God to tolerate our wrongdoings.
Wrong is Wrong!

> "O God, you take no pleasure in wickedness;
> you cannot tolerate the slightest sin."
> (Ps 5:4)

RESPONSIBILITY

Responsibility is the condition, fact, quality or state of being responsible or accountable; a person or thing that one is responsible for.

"You cannot escape the responsibility of tomorrow by evading it today."   – Abraham Lincoln –

It could be the accountability or responsibility towards a burden, duty, job, obligation or project. It is a role in one's attitude towards shaping their experiences. Responsibility is also attributed to the amount of mental capacity a person thinks he possesses or cares to give to a certain situation.

"Character – the willingness to accept responsibility for one's own life – is the source from which self respect springs."   – Joan Didion –

Responsibility could be from a legal, moral, social, or spiritual command, demand or obligation. We have to be careful not to disregard, avoid, shun, lessen, or stay away from our actions or obligations, or to classify work, responsibilities or accountability, as something that doesn't necessarily have to be done, or that we shouldn't be the one to perform it, only to find that *somebody else* has do it for us. The lack of responsibility can result in hurt feelings, negative situations or consequences.

We should in turn, take these opportunities to turn these responsibilities, which are all individual tests that God is sending our way, into a satisfaction of obedience, as an accomplishment, and of building for ourselves a better self-worth and character.

"I believe in recovery, and I believe that as a role model I have the responsibility to let young people know that you can make a mistake and come back from it."   – Ann Richards –

Applications of responsibility would be, as in the line of duty, a requirement, or a demand. These applications can be displayed through accountability, dependability or trustworthiness.

"We are at the very beginning of time for the human race. It is not unreasonable that we grapple with problem. But there are tens of thousands of years in the future. Our responsibility is to do what we can, learn what we can, improve the solutions and pass them on."
– Richard Feynman –

The acceptance of responsibility is usually rewarded by either praise or other forms of approval. When responsibility is not adhered to, the result can come in either blame, shame or can have very serious consequences.

"If God has given you leadership ability, take the responsibility seriously, And if you have a gift for showing kindness to others, do it gladly." (Ro 12:8)

"Don't try to avoid responsibility by saying you didn't know about it. For God knows all hearts, and he sees you. He keeps watch over your soul, and he knows you knew! And he will judge all people according to what they have done." (Pr 24:12)

"Who is a faithful, sensible servant, to whom the master can give the responsibility of managing his household and feeding his family?" (Mt 24:45)

HONESTY

Honesty is the quality or state of being honest; the state of being truthful; freedom from fraud; chastity; honor; integrity; sincerity;

rectitude. Honesty can also be in a form of a pledge.

> "The best measure of a man's honesty isn't his income tax return. It's the zero adjust on his bathroom scale."
> – Arthur C. Clark –

It is a quality of being able to act or communicate sincerely in regards to truth and value, whether while speaking or listening. It is the sincerity of stating our facts, information or views according to what we truly believe them to be, either to our self or to another.

> "Honesty pays, but it doesn't seem to pay enough to suit some people." – Kin Hubbard –

Above all, it is the refusal to deceive, lie or steal in any way. It consists of holding fast to the allegiance of one's calling, position or profession, to the point of being incapable of being false to a trust.

> "Where is there dignity unless there is honesty."
> – Cicero –

We can't pretend to just love or care for someone. God doesn't expect a pretension from us in obeying His laws; if we are to love others, we truly have to love them. That is, being honest to them, and to ourselves. The same applies with pretension about what is wrong.

> "The very spring and root of honesty and virtue lie in good education." – Plutarch –

> "Honesty is a question of right or wrong, not a matter of policy." – Author Unknown –

Everything we do should be genuine. If we show affection – it should be genuine. If we stand for what is good – that should be genuine as well.

"Underlying the whole scheme of civilization is the confidence men have in each other, confidence in their integrity, confidence in their honesty, confidence in their future."   – Bourke Cockran –

It is very difficult for people to admit that they have been dishonest, but the mark of good and moral character comes from a frank and helpful admission, as a solution to clear given circumstances.

"But you desire honesty from the heart, so you can teach me to be wise in my inmost being." (Ps 51:6)

"May integrity and honesty protect me, for I put my hope in you." (Ps 25:21)

"Yes, what joy for those whose record the LORD has cleared of sin, whose lives are lived in complete honesty." (Ps 32:2)

"The godly are directed by their honesty; the wicked fall beneath their load of sin." (Pr 11:5)

JUSTICE

Justice is the principle of absolute or moral rightness; the conformity or quality of what is just, either in action or attitude; or the upholding of what is just; equity; fairness; honorableness; morality; righteousness; upholding justly; validity.

"It is the spirit and not the form of law that keeps justice alive."
– Earl Warren –

As it applies to a person: one who is duly commissioned to establish fairness; one who administers justice or decides over controversies;

or one who holds courts in the capacity of a judge or magistrate, according to the rules and procedures of law or equity. Justice can also be applied as meaning: a mutual agreement; and authoritative command, or a divine command.

> "Next in importance to freedom and justice is popular education, without which neither freedom nor justice can be permanently maintained."   – James Garfield –

It can also be regarded as: treating someone fairly; a due punishment for a wrongdoing; a justifiable or merited reward for something deserved. In either case it could be in accordance with honor, the law, or certain standards. It is the effect of what is just or due. Simply speaking – giving people what they justly deserve.

> "In the part of this universe that we know there is great injustice, and often the good suffer, and often the wicked prosper, and one hardly knows which of those is the more annoying."   – Bertrand Russell –

Justice can also be recognized with fairness and impartiality, but generally it is in reference to the maintenance, procedure and the administration of law. That which is fully appreciated, adequately and fairly treated, as to adhering to moral principles.

> "I have always found that mercy bears richer fruits than strict justice."   – Abraham Lincoln –

> "Justice does not come from the outside. It comes from inner peace."   – Barbara Hall –

It is also in its conformity, the just dealing of men towards each other in principles of rectitude, fact, sound reason, truth or integrity. It is considered as a natural law, but its main purpose is to establish and keep order concerning things and people. It has been debated legally, psychologically and theologically throughout history.

Justice is the most important of the four Cardinal Virtues, which also include Prudence, Fortitude and Temperance. Justice, being a moral quality, inclines the will to render to everyone what belongs to them. Intertwined with Charity, it promotes man's relation to each other. While Charity leads us to *help* our neighbor and his needs, justice teaches us to give to others what *belongs* to them. Justice causes dread and apprehension to the evildoers, but brings joy to those that are good.

> "You (God) have not commanded continence, that is, from what things we are to retrain our love, but also justice, that is, on what we are to bestow our love."–St Augustine–

When speaking of Divine Justice, it is justification of the adherence to the laws of God, which are eternal and perfectly true. God does not tailor justice to our demands, but that we should live on the principles of love and justice, with confident dependence on Him.

> "God is not on the side of any nation, yet we know He is on the side of justice. Our finest moments (as a nation) have come when we faithfully served the cause of justice for our own citizens, and for the people of other lands."
> – George W. Bush –

Justice can also be tainted through liberalism. Some laws are now protecting those that break them. Scriptures tell us that we are not to pass along false reports, nor cooperate with evil doers by telling lies on the witness stand. It also says that we are sometimes quicker to tithe even the tiniest part of our income, but ignore the important things of faith, justice, mercy, or the law.

> "For he has set a day for judging the world with justice by the man he has appointed, and he proved to everyone who this is by raising him from the dead." (Ac 17:31)

Some people become quite judgmental, and tend to judge others by outward appearances and according to personal influence.

> "The law has become paralyzed and useless, and there is no justice given in the courts. The wicked far outnumber the righteous, and justice is perverted with bribes and trickery." (Hab 1:4)

PURITY – PRUDENCE

Purity is the quality or condition of making, becoming or being pure; the degree of purity by which something is measured; being free from sin or guilt; the abstinence of anything that would be corrupting, or inappropriate to goodness; to clear away from material defiling impurities, or moral blemish; charity; innocence.

> "Purity and simplicity are two wings
> with which man sores above the earth and all temporary nature."
> – Thomas a Kempis –

Purity is one of the Four Absolutes that also include: Honesty, Love, and Unselfishness. In the family of purity, the virtue Chastity is the most unpopular of the Christian values. The reason it is so unpopular, is because our society gives us almost no support to its adherence in moral living, or to live chastely. Our accepted culture seems instead, so determined to ridicule and mock those that are chaste, or support chastity. Very few people would choose to, or want to, delay self-gratification.

> "He who loves with purity
> considers not the gift of the lover but the love of the giver."
> – Thomas a Kempis –

Purifying the heart demands the use of prayer and the practice of chastity and to purify our perceptions and intentions. For the reason that it is so important to our Divine Creator that we purify ourselves before we can be in his presence, we should look upon the disciplining of ourselves as not only a prerequisite but a preconditioning before we can see Him.

When we work at purifying ourselves, it enables us to see things in a more godly manner, because purity lets us love with upright and wholesome heart.

> "A life of peace, purity, and refinement leads to a calm and untroubled old age."   – Cicero –

In the act of purifying our souls, body, and sexual-self, to God's vision of how human sexuality should be applied, we need to let Scripture show us how it lays it out. The cleansing process deals with the disciplining of our imagination and feelings, in refusing thoughts of impurity or appearances that lead to arousal.. As fire tests the purity of gold, we must let God test our hearts.

> "It is astonishing what force, purity, and wisdom it requires for a human being to keep clear of falsehoods."
> – Margaret Fuller –

The Sixth Beatitude tells us that the pure in heart, not only will be blessed, but that they will see God. The purity of heart refers to those who have focused themselves through their choices and intellect, to what God's Holiness is demanding from us in our application of chastity, charity and sexual behavior.

> "Treat the older women as you would your mother, and treat the younger women with all purity as your own sister."
> (1 Ti 5:2)

> "Because we have these promises, dear fiends, let us cleanse ourselves from everything that can defile our body

or spirit. And let us work toward complete purity because we fear God. (2 Co 7:1)

Prudence is the condition, fact, quality, or state of being prudent; using careful management; caution; taking precaution; utilizing common sense, frugality, judgment and wisdom in the way of caution and provision; carefulness; circumspection; discretion; economical.

"Genius always gives its best at first, prudence, at last."
– Lucius Anneous Seneca –

"Rashness belongs to youth; prudence to old age."
– Marcus Tullius Cicero –

It is the ability to self-regulate and discipline oneself through the exercise of reason. It can also be described as the capacity of management or the skillful or provident use of resources.

"One column of truth cannot hold an institution of ideas from falling into ignorance. It is wiser that a person of prudence and purpose save his strength for battles that can be won." – Bryant H. McGill –

Prudence is a Cardinal Virtue along with Courage, Justice and Temperance. Being different from the other virtues, it perfects the intellect and inclines the prudent man to act in all things according to the right reasons.

"These proverbs will make the simpleminded clever.
They will give knowledge and purpose to young people."
(Pr 1:4)

"It is dangerous to make a rash promise to God before counting the cost." (Pr 20:25)

DECENCY – MODESTY

Decency is the condition, quality, service, or state of being decent; conformity to prevailing standards of modesty; decorous or respectable behavior; the condition of being chaste; of which is becoming or proper; grace; seemliness.

> "Decency is the least of all laws,
> but yet it is the law which is most strictly observed."
> – Francois De La Rochefoucauld –

It is the adequate conforming principles pertaining to social or moral properties. It could be for either services or surroundings which are found to be necessary for a certain acceptable standard of living.

> "In every country, we should be teaching our children the scientific method and the reasons for a Bill of Rights. With it comes a certain decency, humility and community spirit. In the demon-haunted world that we inhabit by virtue of being human, this may be all that stands between us and the enveloping darkness."   – Carl Sagan –

The term 'social actions and decency' has lost most of its meaning throughout the ages. Whether in language used, means of advertising, or any other cultural applications, decency has been put on a back burner, or in the closet, while other now more accepted things, are out of the closet. There is a need for a reversal in our values and acceptance.

> "And I want women to be modest in their appearance. They should wear decent and appropriate clothing and not draw attention to themselves by the way they fix their hair or by wearing gold or pearls or expensive clothes. For women who claim to be devoted to God should make

themselves attractive by the good things they do.
(1 Ti 2:9,10)

Decency being a sense of propriety or righteousness, is based on conscience and what is right or wrong, and therefor it shouldn't be based on what the majority deems acceptable because of liberalism.

"Conversation should be pleasant without scurrility,
witty without affection, free without indecency,
learned without conceitedness, novel without falsehood."
– William Shakespeare –

"We should be decent and true in everything we do,
so that everyone can approve of our behavior."
(Ro 13:13)

Modesty is the condition, quality, or state of being modest; to have propriety in behavior, dress or speech; moral or chaste conduct in the display of the body.

"Modesty is the conscience of the body."
– Honore De Balzac –

It is the absence of arrogance, presumption, or self-assertion. It is composed of, or consists of preset religiously or culturally determined values, that relate to, or regulate the presentation of oneself to others; the keeping of one's appearance within measure.

"Modesty is a shining light, it prepares the mind
to receive knowledge, and the heart for truth."
– Madam, Guizot –

In the displaying of modesty in action, appearance or behavior one would use *moderation*, while the show of modesty in regards to accomplishments, would be *downplayed*. Moderation was the original signification of modesty, as Cicero stated as being the 'golden mean of living.'

> "Modesty is the citadel of beauty."
> – Demades –

The immoral display of the body does not conform to what the rest of society deems as acceptable behavior, as well as of ethical and religious traditions. The perceptive reasoning is that the body should not be flaunted as a sexual object.

> "Thoughtfulness for others, generosity, modesty, and self-respect are the qualities which makes a real gentleman or lady," – Thomas H. Huxley –

The *Islamic* religion requires women to cover everything except their hands and face. The face and hands can be covered voluntarily.

The *Jewish* religion requires men to wear a head covering in the form of a *yarmulke* or a *kipo*, which is a physical reminder of God, and also to instill humility. In many countries many Jewish women covered their heads while at home, and in public, would wear a larger covering called a *redheedh* that covered the back and sides of the neck and the sides of the face.

While many *Christians* consider modesty as being very important, there are many existing discussions regarding its requirements and purposes. In 1917, Our Lady of Fatima said that, "Certain fashions will be introduced which will offend my Son (Jesus) very much." Traditionally minded Christians find modesty quite important, despite the lack of specific guidelines.

Modesty is decency in appearance, and purity requires modesty, which is a constituent part of temperance. Modesty not only protects the intimacy of a person, but it refuses to unveil what should be left hidden. It serves as a guide as to how one is perceived or behaves in conformation with dignity. Modesty also creates a sense of mystery, and helps in the encouragement of patience and moderation in relationships. It is not only the choice of clothing, but also of discretion, to avoid undesirable curiosity.

> "Modesty is the chastity of merit, the virginity of noble souls."
> – Madame de Girardin –

> "Modesty forbids what the law does not." – Seneca –

The media plays a gigantic and oppressive role in exploiting immorality through as many ways that can be imagined, and even more through their advertising, that go beyond the reasonable exhibition of intimate things or actions. The immodest displays tend to inspire a way of life, that makes it alluring through fashions and the pressures of certain ideologies. It is only in teaching our children and adolescents that modesty is an institution of the spiritual dignity of man, that we can awake them to respect and have dignity for the human person.

> "And the parts we regard as less honorable are those we clothe with the greatest care. So we carefully protect from the eyes of others those parts that should not be seen, while other parts do not require this special care. So God has put the body together in such a way that extra honor and care are given to those parts that have less dignity." (1 Co 12:23,24)

ABSTINENCE – TEMPERANCE

Abstinence is the voluntary forbearance, especially from the indulgence of appetite, or from eating certain foods; constant abstaining from intoxicating beverages; abstention; voluntary restraint from indulging a desire or appetite for certain bodily activities; abstaining from alcohol, food or sexual activity.

It can also be called *total abstinence* if it is concerning ongoing abstinence. People that have had an addiction to a certain substance sometimes decide to give up the addiction indefinitely.

> "Abstinence is the great strengthener and cleaner of reason."
> – Robert South –

> "A rich man cannot enjoy a sound mind nor a sound body without exercise and abstinence; and yet these are truly the worst ingredients of poverty."   – Henry Home –

Abstinence can be either voluntary, recommended or demanded; from moral prohibitions or from practical considerations. It can refer to partial or temporary abstinence from food, as one would do in fasting. It is generally chosen freely as an enhancement to one's health. Some find it helpful in spiritual discipline, as it elevates beyond the normal life of desire, in the following of a path of renunciation. Abstinence is then opposed to such vices as gluttony and drunkenness.

> "They help people develop inner strength, help them take charge of their lives, and redirect their energies into healthy and productive choices. While the evidence is still being collected, we are seeing the benefits of a strong abstinence message."   – Wade Horn –

From the dawn of Christianity. Friday has been signaled out as a day of abstinence. For many years Catholics considered the eating of meat on Friday as being sinful, although many still keep to the tradition as a way of either, atonement, or sacrifice. During Lent it is customary to give up either certain activities, foods or habits, in remembrance of what our Savior did for us.

> "We teach abstinence first. If you don't do anything, you can't get anything."   – William Burney –

Abstinence is also found as applying to habits or actions. The abstaining of sexual activity before marriage is regarded upon by many as being irresponsible or inhumane. Whatever the arguments, it is still morally wrong, so is the idea of experimentation. Just because something is desired doesn't make it right. God tells us that no temptation is greater than the strength to resist it. The strength is there if you choose to ask for it. As St. Paul told the people of Philippi,

> "For I can do everything with the help of Christ who gives me the strength I need." (Php 4:13)

> "You and your descendants must never drink wine or any other alcoholic drink before going into the Tabernacle." (Lev 10:9)

> "David begged God to spare the child. He went without food an lay all night on the bare ground." (2 Sa 12:16)

> "All that time I had eaten no rich food or meat, had drunk no wine, and had used no fragrant oils." (Da 10:3)

Temperance

Temperance is the condition of being temperate; the moderation of, or a specific moderation, in the indulgence of the passions or appetites; total abstinence from alcoholic beverages or the use of intoxicants; moderation; restraint.

Temperance comes from the Greek word *engkrateia,* which means self-control and discipline.

> "Temperance and labor are the two best virtues.
> Labor whets the appetite, temperance curbs it."
> – Author Unknown –

Being one of the Four Cardinal Virtues, that include Prudence

Justice and Fortitude, Temperance is considered to be vital, central and pivotal to Christian behavior, and many religions. It is also one of the Precepts of Buddhism.

> "Perfect wisdom has four parts, viz, wisdom, the principle of doing a right; justice, the principle of doing things equally in public and private; fortitude, the principle of not fleeing danger, but meeting it; and temperance, the principle of subduing desires and living moderately."   – Plato –

Temperance is a moral self-regarding virtue that governs or moderates the natural attraction or appetite for the pleasures of the senses within the bounds and norm of reason. It provides a balance in the utilization of created goods. It enables the will to master over instincts, to sustain desire within the limits of what is considered as honorable or moral. It controls our longing for delights and pleasures which attract the human heart so powerfully. Because temperance gives the ability to control oneself, therefore the other virtues can be realized or sustained.

"Joy, Temperance and repose slam the door on the doctor's nose."
– Henry Wadsworth Longfellow –

The other virtues that derive from the virtue of Temperance are, Abstinence, Charity and Modesty, because Temperance controls the practices that relate to food, drink, of sexual relations, and the restraint of vanity.

> "Temperance is a tree which has for its root
> very little contentment and for its fruit calm and peace."
> – Hindu Prince Siddharta –

Temperance is believed to be a fruit, a special grace as evidence of the influence of the Holy Spirit in one's life. It is a demonstrating characteristic of a believer who is continually living his life for God.

"Temperance is simply a disposition of mind which binds the passions." – St Thomas Aquinas –

"To live well is nothing other than to love God with all one's heart; from this it comes about that love is kept whole and uncorrupted. No misfortune can disturb it. It obeys only, and is careful in discerning things, so as not to be surprised by deceit or trickery." – St Augustine –

We should live in this evil world with self-control, right conduct, and devotion to God." (Tit 2:12)

PATIENCE

Patience is the ability, fact, power, quality or state of being patient; the capacity to have endurance through hardship, trials, tribulation or trouble. The capacity to bear, delay, strain or stress.

"Patience is the art of hoping." – Marquis de Vauvemarques –

"Endurance is patience concentrated." – Thomas Carlyle –

It is the ability to endure; being tolerant and understanding, through delay, provocation or wait, without annoyance, being upset, complaining, or getting angry, but being able to persevere serenely when faced with adversities or difficulties.

"Adapt the pace of nature, her secret is patience."
– Ralph Waldo Emerson –

Patience is found to be one of the most valuable virtues in Christian religions. It is one of the seven virtues, though it isn't one of the traditional biblical three theological virtues, nor is it one of the traditional cardinal virtues. When a Christian has accepted the gift of

Salvation, the growth of patience is considered as the work of the Holy Spirit.

> "Patience and perseverance have a magical effect before which difficulties vanish."   – John Quincy Adams –

There are many things that we can learn from others, and so much more also that we can learn from children, like how much patience we really have, and how much patience we show them.

> "The chemist who can extract from his heart's elements, compassion, respect, longing, patience, regret, surprise, and forgiveness, and compound them into one, can create that atom which is called love."   – Kahlil Gibran –

We live in a very impatient society. Not only do we revolve in a world of; *fast* food, *fast* cars and *fast* computers, but we want them *high speed.*

We want, what we want, when we want it. We don't take time to go shopping – it's faster *on-line.* We don't take time to *write* a letter we send an e-mail. We don't go to the library – we *search* the web.

We want fast service ; we don't like to: wait for a taxi, sit through the commercials while watching a favorite show or sports presentation, wait for a table at a restaurant, wait for our merchandise to be rung-up at the register while shopping. Most people consider all of this as wasted time. Which in a way it is. But in an other way, it is valuable time, because this is when God is testing us. It is not so much the trials He sends us, but how we handle them.

> "Patience is something you admire in the driver behind you, but not in one ahead."   – Bill Glashen –

Evidence of high value viewed about patience is found in many Bible references. The tradition of the church lists twelve different fruits of the Spirit, which are gifts of perfection, that are formed in us as the first fruits of eternal glory: charity, chastity, faithfulness, generosity, gentleness, goodness, joy, kindness, modesty, *patience,* peace, and self-control. The more we say *no* to ourselves, the more we say *yes* to the Spirit.

"Patient endurance is what you need now, so you will continue to do God's will." (Heb 10:36a)

"Consider the farmers who eagerly look for the rains in the fall and in the spring. They patiently wait for the precious harvest to ripen." (Jas 5:7)

"But if we look forward to something we don't have yet, we must wait patiently and confidently." (Ro 8:25)

"Then you will not become spiritually dull and indifferent. Instead you will follow the example of those who are going to inherit God's promises because of their faith and patience." (Heb 6:12)

ENDURANCE – FORTITUDE

Endurance is the fact, power, or strength of withstanding hardship, such as pain, stress, strain or use. The capacity, condition, fact, or state of lasting, persevering, in continuing survival; act or power of suffering; to continue under hardship or pain without being overcome; having duration or stamina.

It is also the ability to go through extended exertion from either exercise or work for a long period of time despite fatigue or other adverse condition. The length of time varying with the type of exertion.

Endurance is also the withstanding or continuing through trials and troubling times. Being able to persevere in adverse emotional, mental or psychological conditions or situations.

"A man may die, nations may rise and fall, but an idea lives on. Ideas have endured without death."
– John Fitzgerald Kennedy –

"Few people know how to take a walk. The qualifications are endurance, plain clothes, old shoes, an eye for nature, good humor, vast curiosity, good speech, good silence and nothing too much."   – Ralph Waldo Emerson –

The Bible tells us that endurance develops in us a strength of character, and the character in turn strengthens our confident expectation of salvation.

In extreme conditions, it would be the ability to withstand conditions to the extent of surviving or staying alive.

"And let us run with endurance the race that God has set before us." (Heb 12:1b)

"In everything we do we try to show that we are true ministers of God. We patiently endure troubles and hardships and calamities of every kind." (2 Co 6:4)

Fortitude is the strength of mind that allows one to endure pain or adversity with courage; firmness of mind in meeting danger or adversity; impregnability; resolute endurance.

"Whether it be to failure or success; the first need of being is endurance – to endure with gladness if we can, with fortitude in any event."   – Bill Carman –

Fortitude can be of emotional or mental strength when courageously facing adversity, danger, difficulty, pain or danger. It can also have different meanings such as:

• *backbone* – the ability to stand up to one's objectives and

principles, in the face of opposition.
- *grit* – not letting oneself be downed by hardship or difficulties.
- *guts* – having the essential stamina which might frighten one, when facing or putting up with certain duties or difficulties.
- *pluck* – having vigor and being game when fighting, especially against odds.
- *sand* – similar to grit, but not necessarily triumphing over obstacles; moments of duration or time.

Fortitude is one of the Cardinal Virtues. It is the virtue of a man when confronted with the danger of death, encounters the occasion with fearless meekness. The highest virtue of intellect however, is the knowledge of God.

> "The necessity of times, more than ever, calls for our utmost circumspection, deliberation, fortitude, and perseverance." – Samuel Adams –

Aristotle did not consider fortitude as being the highest virtue, but he selected it first as the treatment in describing moral virtues.

> "A modest conduct, a standard of courage, discipline, fortitude and integrity can do a great deal to make a woman beautiful." – Jacqueline Bisset –

St Thomas saw fortitude, as a gift from the Holy Spirit, and as the specific supernatural virtue, the one that braves the greatest dangers which meets the risk of life and death. He painstakingly mentioned that fortitude ranked third in the cardinal virtues. It is the virtue, that we as Christians, should always have in mind in order to make our actions acceptable for eternal life, because it is from that virtue's natural principles that grace is built. It enables us to attain good even when we are suffering and when help is needed, especially when dealing with temptations, as it is a self-regarding virtue, it controls the irascible passions. It is through it's strength that we can combat the forces that are thrown to us in these evil times, in dealing with disrespect, dishonesty and a degenerating society and culture. It takes fortitude and courage to be a Christian, as it does to rise up from poverty.

> "Perfect love is rare indeed – for to be a lover will require that you continually have the subtlety of the very wise, the flexibility of the child, the sensitivity of the artist, the understanding of the philosopher, the acceptance of the saint, the tolerance of the scholar and the fortitude of the certain." – Leo Buscaglia –

SUFFERING – AFFLICTION

Suffering is the act, experience, condition or state of one who suffers; physical or mental pain or distress.

> "Although the world is full of suffering, it is full also of the overcoming of it." – Helen Keller –

It is the experiencing of pain or suffering as an unpleasant effect of harm or the possibility of being harmed. It could be physical if it is inevitable or concerns the body, such as breathlessness or nausea; or mental if it is optional or concerns the mind, as anxiety, boredom, grief or hatred.

> "You desire the act of living, my friend? It is contained in one phrase; make use of suffering." –Henri Frederic Amiel–

Suffering can vary in different ways. It can derive from cultural, personal or social behaviors. The amount or intensity of suffering can be from mild to unbearable. Other factors to consider would be the frequency of occurrence and duration.

> "Whenever evil befalls us, we ought to ask ourselves, after the first suffering, how we can turn it into good. So shall we take occasion, from one bitter root, to raise perhaps many flowers." — Leigh Hunt —

One's tolerance or attitude is also a determining factor according as to how severe one deems it to be. Some claim suffering as being optional, while pain is inevitable. Its acceptance is usually measured by its severity, usefulness, whether it is deserving, chosen, or wanted.

> "The truth that many people never understand, until it is too late, is that the more you try to avoid suffering the more you suffer because smaller and more insignificant things begin to torture you in proportion to your fear of being hurt." — Thomas Merton —

In a religious sense, suffering is a consequence of the original sin. It could be applied as a self-accepting form of exerting oneself to exercising things like penance or self-deprivation, so as to grow spiritually. A wonderful explanation to suffering is found in the Bible's Book of Job, as he persevered through his many trials, and thus remained faithful to the Lord.

> "But penance need not be paid in suffering. It can be paid in forward motion. Correcting the mistakes is a positive move; a nurturing move." — Barbara Hall —

A meaning that revolves around the notion of redemptive suffering is that simplicity, moderation, and discipline, as well as a spirit of sacrifice, must become a part of everyday life, otherwise all will suffer the negative consequences of the careless habits of a few.

The greatest form of suffering was by our Savior. He sacrificed Himself and accepted the pains and torture that came about by His

Crucifixion. Christ asked us to follow Him. We then should also show Him that we can endure our sufferings for Him. God doesn't always use His Divine power to stop suffering – but always to heal and help us in our distress. Suffering can make us either *bitter*, or it can make us *better*, but suffering becomes our true relief in mortal life.

"This suffering is all part of what God has called you to, Christ who suffered for you, is your example. Follow in his steps." (1Pe 2:21)

"Yet we suffer now is nothing to the glory he will give us later. For all creation is waiting eagerly for that day when God will reveal who his children really are." (Ro 8:18,19)

"Are any among you suffering? They should keep on praying about it." (Jas 5:13)

"He gives prosperity to the poor and humble, and he takes sufferers to safety." (Job 5:11)

"Suffering gladly borne for others convert more souls than sermons."   – St Theresa of the Child Jesus –

Prayers for the Suffering.

For the love of you Dear Jesus,
I offer my pain and suffering for the salvation of souls.

Dear Lord, I come to You to plead and offer my suffering
for the soul of a brother or sister,
united to me through our Lord the creator of us all.
Although their sins may be grievous,
their souls are precious and I pray to free them from
the grasp of Satan, and beg for Your mercy on their souls.

Affliction is a condition of continued pain or distress which causes emotional, mental or physical suffering; a state of being afflicted; a cause of pain or suffering; a grievous calamity; catastrophe; distress; a cross; disaster; grief; illness; losses; mishap; persecution; trial; tribulation; trouble.

Affliction is not only a serious misfortune but it suggests also an emotional effect, such as in, loss of hearing, loss of speech or loss of sight.

"Let your heart feel for the affliction and distress of everyone, and let your hand give in proportion to your purse."
– George Washington –

Adversity and misfortune along with affliction pertain to an occurrence, situation or circumstance that is difficult to endure or sustain.

"Difficult as it is really to listen to someone in affliction, it is just as difficult for him to know that compassion is listening to him." – Simone Well –

If the distress is in regard to something that takes place which is unfavorable or adverse, it would be considered as a misfortune. Distress or a calamity would imply, adversity. Trial would signify one's character being tested while going through trouble.

"It is said an eastern monarch once charged his wise men to invent a sentence, to be ever in view, and which should be true and appropriate in all times and situations. They presented him with the words, 'And this too shall pass away.' How much it expresses! How chastening in the hour of pride! How consoling in the depths of affliction."
– Abraham Lincoln –

There is an Irish Proverb which reads, "Without sorrow, the heart would never learn the meaning of joy. Without tears, our eyes would never see what we hold inside. Without darkness, we would have no reason to look to the light of heaven."

"Affliction comes to us all, not to make us sad, but sober; not to make us sorry, but to make us wise; not to make us despondent, but by its darkness to refresh us as the night refreshes the day; not to impoverish, but to enrich us."
– Henry Ward Beecher –

God allows us to go through difficulties, some much more serious than others for different reasons. One would be, because He wants to see how we will handle the situations. Secondly, it is a way for us to take advantage of the situation in order to grow in character. It is also a refining process, as you refine metal of its impurities, and, to test our integrity and loyalty to Him, as Job's was tested.

"I have refined you but not in the way silver is refined.
Rather I have refined you in the furnace of suffering."
(Isa 48:10)

The Bible tells us that the way of life is – The Way of the Cross, and that if we choose to go that way, we will encounter many tribulations, but then enter and live in the Kingdom of God. Sometimes when we experience either disaster, evil, injustice, suffering, and even death, it can lead to questioning one's faith, or tempt one to go against it. Christ has told us that while we are here on earth, we will have many sorrows, but because He has overcome the world, we should take heart. The passage to remember is:

"Since I know it is all for Christ's good,
I am quite content with my weakness
and with insults, hardships, persecutions, and calamities.
For when I am weak, then I am strong."
(2 Co 12:10)

"Come to me, all of you who are weary and carry heavy burdens, and I will give you rest." (Mt 11:28)

"Though the Lord gave you adversity for food and affliction for drink, he will still be with you to teach you." (Isa 30:20)

"We can rejoice, too, when we run into problems and trials for we know that they are good for us – they help us learn to endure." (Ro 5:3)

"I have told you this so that you may have peace in me. Here on earth you will have many trials and sorrows. But take heart because I have overcome the world." (Jn 16:33)

FORGIVENESS

Forgiveness is the mental or physical act of ending the feeling of anger, indignation or resentment of having been hurt or offended by someone; to excuse an offense, injury or fault; ending the demand of punishment or restitution; the ceasing of a feeling of resentment or anger; to absolve from debt of payment; to forgive one's enemies; pardon.

"Love is an act of endless forgiveness, a tender look which becomes habit."   – Peter Ustinov –

It relates to the forgiver, as well to the one being forgiven. It frees the one forgiving and the one being forgiven from the feelings of resentment or anger. Some demand restitution when forgiving.

Forgiveness is a relief of anger, tension, resentment, or hatred, and is good for the soul. Holding on to resentment makes a person smaller and is a sign of weakness – it takes strength to be forgiving, but it allows you to grow in character. It can also be the forgiveness of oneself for an action, occurrence or situation which one deems to have been inappropriate. Life is then an unusual experience of forgiveness.

> "It really doesn't matter if the person who hurt you deserves to be forgiven. Forgiveness is a gift you give yourself. You have things to do and want to move on."
> – Real Live Preacher –

> Forgiveness is almost a selfish act because of its immense benefits to the one who forgives." – Lawana Blackwell –

Hate will end up hurting you more than the person that has offended you, so it is one's benefit to forgive. God tells us that if we forgive one another, that He will forgive us. And the Bible also tells us that the number of times that we must forgive someone is seventy times seven. Jesus also left us with The Lord's Prayer, which includes forgiveness.

> "Holding on to anger, resentment and hurt only gives you tense muscles, a headache and a sore jaw from clenching your teeth. Forgiveness gives you back the laughter and the lightness in your life." – John Lunden –

We are guilty of many sins, and we find consolation in knowing that we have a God who is merciful, and generous with His forgiveness. Adam's sin led to condemnation, but Christ brought us forgiveness through God's bountiful gift. While Adam's sin caused death to rule over us, our accepting God's gracious gift of righteousness brings us a triumphant life over sin and death through His Son who shed His blood for us. There would have been no forgiveness of sins, if His blood had not been shed. One of the most momentous signs of forgiveness is found in Jesus asking His Father to forgive those who were crucifying Him, because they did not know what they were doing. Many people sin against us because they do not know what they are doing, and we sin against someone because we do not know what we are doing. But there must be forgiveness.

> "Sometimes the measure of friendship isn't your ability to not harm, but your capacity to forgive the things done to you, and ask for forgiveness for your own mistakes."
> – Randy K. Milholland –

The Roman Catholic church, and the Orthodox Christian churches, unlike other Christian denominations, teach that forgiveness from God is mediated through the church. Forgiveness is attained through an individual act of contrite confession of one's sins to an ordained priest and obtaining from him absolution, which is an expression of God's forgiveness. The Scriptural support for the mediation comes from Jesus telling His disciples,

> "If you forgive anyone's sins, they are forgiven.
> If you refuse to forgive them, they are unforgiven."
> (Jn 20:23)

Other denominations ask for forgiveness directly to God through an expression of sincere repentance, with the belief that they also must forgive others.

> "Then they will receive forgiveness for their sins
> and be given a place among God's people,
> who are set apart by faith in me."
> (Ac 26:18)

> "Without the shedding of blood, there is no forgiveness of sin."
> (Heb 9:22)

> "Even if he wrongs you seven times a day
> and each time turns again and asks forgiveness, forgive him."
> (Lk 17:4)

APPRECIATION – THANKFULNESS

Appreciation is the recognition of the importance, magnitude, quality, significance or worth of people or things; the action of appreciating; a favorable estimate; an awareness or perception of something of value; an expression of gratitude; gratefulness; gratitude.

> "Appreciation is a wonderful thing. It makes what is excellent in others belong to us as well." – Voltaire –

> "At times our own light goes out and is rekindled by a spark from another person. Each of us has cause to think with deep gratitude of those who have lighted the flame within us." – Albert Schweitzer –

It is a favorable judgment or opinion; an awareness of something perceived delicately, especially in the appearance of values or qualities; to show a liking or approval, as an admiration.

> "Courtesies of a small and trivial character are the ones which strike deepest in the grateful and appreciating heart."
> – Henry Clay –

> "Gratitude is not only the greatest of values, but the parent of others." – Cicero –

It can also be defined as the understanding of something's nature, as gratitude or enjoyment.

> "Enjoy yourself – it's later than you think."
> – Guy Lombardo –

It is through our loyalty and devotion to God that we show Him our appreciation for His ever loving kindness.

It is not the failure of others to appreciate your abilities that should trouble you, but rather your failure to appreciate theirs." – Confucius –

"Appreciation can make a day, even change a life. Your willingness to put it into words is all that is necessary."
– Margaret Cousins –

Thankfulness is the showing or feeling of gratitude; the expression of thanks; friendly and warm feelings of gratitude; being grateful; appreciativeness; gratefulness.

Before we can even begin to be thankful, we must first recognize the things we have received. We receive graces from God everyday and in every imaginable way. We have to understand and appreciate that we have a righteous God – everything He does is right. Only through the knowledge that God is righteous can we have thankfulness.

"Feeling of gratitude and not expressing it...
Is like wrapping a present and not giving it."
– William Arthur Ward –

Some of the things that come our way during our journey, can either make us very happy, give us mixed feelings, or sometimes make us very sad. Many of the things that we receive are sometimes not looked upon as a gift, but maybe more of a trial, and might even seem unfair. That's where the gratitude becomes difficult.

"If the only prayer you ever say in your life is 'thank you,' that would suffice."   – Meister Eckart –

We have to thank God for not only our *abilities*, but also for our *disabilities*. How, and what, do we teach ourselves and to others with our abilities? How, and what, do we teach ourselves and to others because of our disabilities? It is by the way that we *react* or *not react* to either type, that we will be judged according to our deeds. Some of the richest gifts that we receive, come to us through, or from something made memorable to us – for which we should say, *"Thanks For The Memory!"*

> "Life without thankfulness is devoid of love and passion.
> Hope without thankfulness is lacking in fine perception.
> Faith without thankfulness lacks strength and fortitude.
> Every virtue divorced from thankfulness is mimed and limps along the spiritual road."   – John Henry Jowett –

God showers us with His gifts. He is a generous God! The way we perceive these gifts, our attitudes, our acceptance and faith, play an important part in our feeling of gratitude. It is easier to thank God for something that brings us joy, than it is for something that might be burdensome. The cup is either half-full or half-empty. If you've worked in a garden, you've had to deal with weeds. You can be very grateful to God for all the bountiful results that resulted from your special attention of ridding your garden of all the unwanted plants. On the other hand, one might be very content in allowing things to grow more *naturally*, and even finding joy in seeing the birds getting nourishment from some of the weeds that grew amidst the beautiful flowers.

The Holy Spirit is the One who distributes the gifts. He is the one who decides what each individual will receive. These gifts vary from the ability to: be wise; have special knowledge; have faith; have power to heal the sick; have the power to perform miracles; have the ability to prophesy; know if it is really the Spirit of God that is speaking; speak in unknown languages; interpret what is being said in unknown languages. Every gift comes from God, even if it might seem to come from our self, or from another source.

> "No longer forward nor behind I look in hope and fear;
> But, grateful, take the good I find, The best of now and here."
>   – John Grennleaf Whittier –

The more you can share your thankfulness with others, the more thankful you will become. One of the best ways of uniting in thankfulness is through worshiping together.

If we are to be *forever* thankful,
then we should thank God, *at least* often.

It is not only on the day of Thanksgiving that we should show our gratitude. Showing our appreciation to others should be a way of life. Showing our gratitude to God for His Love, Caring and Generosity should be happening many times throughout the day. At the end of each day, as we go through all of the occurred events, we should thank Him for every single one, however bountiful or difficult it was.

Thank God for the trials and tribulation of life.
For it is *easy* to thank Him
for all the wonderful things that He gives us.

If you can't be thankful for what you've received,
be thankful for what you've escaped.

"Give thanks to the LORD and proclaim his greatness.
Let the whole world know what he has done."
(1 Ch 16:8)

RECIPROCITY

Reciprocity is a condition or relationship which is reciprocal; an interchange or exchange of favors which is mutual; making a return for something that is given or done; returning a compliment; mutual exchange; to return in degree or in kind; to repay in a positive or negative response.

Reciprocity could also be as a recompense for an act or something received. The most generally used form of reciprocity is the rendering, "You're Welcome!" after someone says, "Thank You!" Like the old saying goes, "One good thing deserves another."

> "There is no duty more obligatory than the repayment of kindness."   – Cicero –

One of the nicest displays of reciprocity I can remember from childhood, comes from an uncle and aunt that lived in a nearby state. They not only had a cottage on the shore in our state, which they utilized every weekend seasonally, but also visited us very often, and wouldn't miss any of the holidays. Not only did they bring us all a gift at Christmas time, but they also brought with them, something else that I always cherished, and which was so special about them – a genuine fondness and love for each other. My uncle didn't consider himself in anyway better than my aunt, and she likewise felt the same way toward him. There was a radiance and presence about them, that enhanced the environment, because of their smile and shared happiness.

> "Recompense injury with justice,
> and recompense kindness with kindness.
> – Confucius –

Happiness is never generated from the quest of control in a relationship, but by mutual self-abasement. In any relationship, there has to be a reciprocal positive and loving interchange – one can't do it alone. We will be treated as we treat others. We will be judged as we judged others. We have to love our neighbor as ourselves. Parents have to show love to their children, and the children have to show love to the parents. A true love relationship consists of not only receiving – but giving.

When it comes to spousal relationships, most women do no like to hear what the Bible says about the woman being, submissive to the man, as you do the Lord. If only that one verse had been read, it would be understakable that women would feel that way. The next verse however, brings a different light to the subject. It says that the husband is the *head of his wife as Christ is the head of the church,* for which He gave His life. Christ *served* His church – the husband then, has to serve his wife. It is quite easy to believe that the Bible was simply showing us an example of reciprocity. Not one better than the other, not one having more control or importance than the other, but living a life of mutual respect and self-abasement. The more authority you have been given, the more you should serve. If the men have been given more authority – then they should become servants.

"Do for others what you would like them to do for you."
(Mt 7:12)

If our God humbled Himself to come and serve us, we should take His example, to not dominate in our relationships, but to humble ourselves into them. Domination certainly doesn't make one loveable.

One morning at breakfast time, the newly wed husband was stating that it was the wife's duty to brew the coffee. His wife gently stated that there's a Book in the Bible that says He brews.

"Live happily with the woman you love through all the meaningless days of life that God has given you in this world. The wife God gives you is your reward for all your earthly toil." (Ecc 9:9)

"Most important of all continue to show deep love for each other, for love covers a multitude of sins." (1 Pe 4:8)

CLOSE RELATIONSHIP WITH GOD

God allows us freedom, a free will – our most precious gift. It is of our choosing to have a relationship with Him. Not only is He our best friend, but He wants to have a *close* relationship with each and every one of us.

He is not only our God, but He's the very best listener you'll ever find. He has a special love for each of us. That means that He wants to have a *personal* relationship with every single person now living; wanted the same with all those that lived; and with all those who are yet to come. He is the Father of many. He has a very big family, but He loves and cares for us individually, distinctly, and wants to identify with each of our personalities and characters. As the Prodigal Son was loved by his father, and accepted *as he was*, so does God love us and accepts us as we are, but sees us as how He would like us to be. His presence is available to us at all times. He is always there for us to talk to, twenty-four seven.

"Friendship with the LORD is reserved for those who fear him."
(Ps 25:14)

We find it quite easy to talk to a best friend because we know a lot about each other, and enjoy many of the same things. God is not only our *best* friend, but He knows *everything* about us. He wants to be part of our lives; so by finding out more about Him, we can be part of His life.

Just as the sun rises every morning,
God can brighten your heart every day.

In every relationship we try to better ourselves in order to enhance the mutual love. God doesn't need to better Himself as He is righteous in everything He does. We in turn must allow Him to work in us, so that we may experience and appreciate a closeness to Him. Life is getting more and more complicated, but the closer we get to God, the *more simple* life becomes. What does it require to have a close relationship with God? One of the requirements is that we fear Him, and live according to His will, and to love Him, worship Him with all our heart and soul, and to obey His commands and laws that

He gave us for our own good. He is our *God*, and He is worthy of our praise. Living a life of moral excellence leads us to know God better.

> God is at work in you. God is at work in me.
> God is at work in each and every one of us.

God asks us to love Him with *all* our hearts, *all* our souls, and with *all* our spirits; which means that we should be loving Him *always* – all the time. Some people might say that loving God in this manner, all the time, makes one a fanatic. But in understanding, and complying with *His* command, that we should forever be showing our love to Him, then there is no such thing as fanaticism. So nothing should be in the way of His being loved, continuously. We can never love Him enough, or too much. How do we want to be judged? How much effort do we want to, or care to devote to this relation with the Almighty One who will have the final say in regards to justly condemning or rewarding us according to our earthly performance, or lack thereof? The authenticity of our love of God has to include the element of fear. Jean Pierre Camus wrote, "We must fear God through love, not love through fear." Fearing the Lord serves as a motivator to the one searching. Pope St. Gregory the Great also said, "To fear God is never to pass over any good thing that ought to be done.

> "I cried out to the LORD in my suffering, and he heard
> me. He set me free from all my fears." (Ps 34:6)

What excuse do we use for not getting close to Him? Lack of Time? Lack of Trust? Lack of Faith? Afraid to talk to Him? Afraid to talk about Him? Who would we rather have a relationship with? Do we put it off because we don't want to let go of something or somebody? What is it in our life that we would have to give up, that we are now finding more desirable than the life that could be attained and enjoyed with Him? How would we feel suddenly standing face to face in front of Him? God tells us that He will search to find His sheep. We must allow Him to find us, not hide from Him; but expose ourselves to Him, and let Him know that we want that relationship with Him more than anything else. This new, true relationship with God only comes by faith, and a decision. Any true relationship is never for self-gratification.

God gave us spiritual nourishment through the body and blood of Christ. There could never be a more bonding relationship. In return we should humble ourselves as His little children and show Him our appreciation and loyalty by getting close to Him, telling Him how much we love Him, by loving each other, as He loves us, and respect all that He has created. When God gives His riches and graces, it doesn't take away from His infinite amount He has to give. The only thing that keeps us from His gifts and graces, is sin.

"Out of God's gifts, then, we make gifts to God." – St Augustine –

We could have read the whole Bible cover to cover; have studied about religion and the church; but if we can't apply this knowledge to a close relationship with God, it is all wasted. God invites everyone. It is a privilege, that He wants us to like Him and share in His kingdom. We should humbly realize who we are, who we are having a relationship with, and why. We should be loving God *in* all things, and *above* all things, and remember that He loved us first, and to His death.

> "O righteous Father, the world doesn't know you, but I do; and these disciples know you sent me. And I have revealed you to them and will keep on revealing you. I will do this that your love for me may be in them and I in them."
> (Jn 17:25,26)

> "For I know every thought that comes into your minds."
> (Eze 11:5b)

> "Draw close to God, and God will draw close to you."
> (Jas 4:8)

THE LOVE TRIANGLE

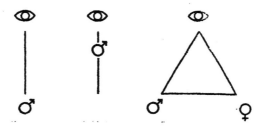

A true Love Triangle has to include God, who Himself is LOVE. If it is a personal relationship with God, then the closer you put God in your life, the more love will be in your life, — *No God, No Love,* — *Know God, Know Love.* If the relationship is between you and another person, then to attain *real* love, God has to be part of, and the focus of the Triangle.

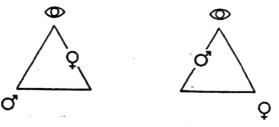

If the relationship is between two people, then if only one gets closer to God, then there is no *real-love-closeness* to each other.

But, when both get closer to God, the closer they get to *each other*.

Marriage Takes Three

Marriage takes three to be complete;

it's not enough for two to meet.

They must be united in love

by love's Creator, God above.

A marriage that follows God's plan

takes more than a woman and a man.

It needs a oneness that can be

only from Christ – marriage takes three.

– Beth Stuckwisch –

He Loves Me

He loves me! He loves me!
He loves as I am, Oh yes, He loves me!
Yes, He loved me yesterday,
And yes, He'll love me still tomorrow,
For He loves me just today, the way I am.
            He loves me! He loves me!
            And all He asks is that I let Him love me!
            Let Him love as He chooses,
            With no thoughts for wins or loses,
            Let Him love me as I am is all He asks!
He knows me! He knows me!
Better than I know myself, Oh yes, He knows me!
Who I was the other day,
And who I will become tomorrow,
But He loves me just the same the way I am!
            He calls me! He calls me!
            He calls me the way I am to spread His love!
            Knowing well who I have been,
            Who I will be, who I am,
            Yet He calls me just the same to spread His love!
He frees me! He frees me!
He frees me to say YES whenever He calls me!
Showing me His own compassion,
Love and care and understanding,
He frees me to say my YES when He calls me!
            He loves me! He loves me!
            He loves me as I am, Oh yes He loves me!
            Finding me wherever I am,
            He gently guides me by the hand,
            For He loves me as I am, oh He loves me!
            For He loves me as I am, oh, He loves me!

(A song given to Brother Patrick A Martin, F. I. C., April 14, 1977)

"Not only did God create us in His likeness, but He gave us the Spirit that we may understand what He has freely given us."
(1Co 2:12b)

"I know all the things you do – your love, your faith, your service, and your patient endurance." (Rev 2:19a)

"See how very much our heavenly Father loves us, for he allows us to be called his children, and we really are! But the people who belong to this world don't know God, so they don't understand that we are his children." (1 Jn 3:1)

GOD'S MERCY

When we think of God's mercy, we rightfully think of Him sending His Son to us because of our sinfulness, so that we could be made right in His sight. We were restored to God's friendship by the blood that Christ shed for us, which delivered us from eternal punishment. What Jesus did, made us friends of God, and we can now rejoice in a wonderful relationship with Him.

When Jesus told us that He was returning to His Father in Heaven, He said He would send us the Spirit to guide us, to give us strength, and to fill our hearts with His love.

Everything that we have, and everything around us comes from Him. Everything created was by His power and intended for His glory. He also calls us to share an eternal life with Him. An eternal life only made possible by the belief that His Son paid the price for our Salvation.

"A Deliverer will come from Jerusalem,
and he will turn Israel from all ungodliness.
And then I will keep my covenant with them
and take away their sins."
(Ro 11:26b,27)

As we go through our mortal life we can be confident that as we share our suffering, we will also share His comfort. We should also have confident dependence on Him, and act on the principles of love and justice.

Jesus used the Beatitudes to teach us about God' mercy. He said that God had blessings for:
- whoever realizes their need for Him – they would receive the Kingdom of Heaven.
- whoever mourns – they will receive comfort.
- whoever is gentle and lowly – the whole earth will be theirs.
- whoever is merciful – they also will be shown mercy.
- those with pure hearts – they will see God.
- those that are persecuted because they choose to live for God – they will receive the Kingdom of Heaven.

"God blesses you when you are mocked and persecuted and lied about because you are my followers." (Mt 5:11)

We have to look towards God's mercy, as Moses did when he interceded for the people and pleaded with the Lord, to please pardon their sins because of His magnificent and unfailing love. God had passed in front of Moses and said,

"I am the LORD, I am the LORD, the merciful and gracious God. I am slow to anger and rich in unfailing love and faithfulness." (Ex 34:6)

"I will praise you forever, O God, for what you have done. I will wait for your mercies, in the presence of your people." (Ps 52:9)

"...heaven will be happier over one lost sinner who returns to God than over ninety-nine others who are righteous and haven't strayed away." (Lk 15:7b)

Chapter 6

WISDOM

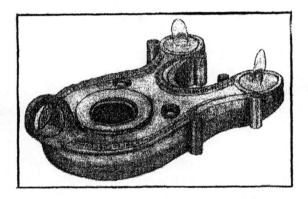

LAMP OF KNOWLEDGE

"For these commands and this teaching are a lamp to light the way ahead of you." (Pr 6:23)

WISDOM

W ise is the one who understands what is true;

I ncreasing knowledge, for its lifelong value.

S cholarly learning, without all the pretense;

D oing, with good judgement, and some common sense.

O penly applying, in ways upstanding;

M aintaining all that is good, right, and lasting.

WHO ARE WE ?

Besides being human beings, mortals, individuals, we are either, a combination of: a brother, a sister, a father, a mother, a cousin, an aunt or uncle, a grandfather or grandmother, a democrat, an independent, a republican, and have a religious preference. But aside from all the designations, we actually are an accumulation of many different traits. Many things have combined to form us, and make us who we are.

Whoever we are, we have one thing in common, we are all different.

Some of the things that give us distinctive features and help mold or form our personality, character, knowledge, and even our spiritual and moral well-being, come from:

- what we read or study.
- what we enjoy through the media.
- what we enjoy as entertainment.
- what we like to hear.
- what people we want to listen to.
- what people we associate with.
- what talents we develop.
- what we like to wear.
- what work we do.
- what we get involved in.
- what we like and want to own.
- what we buy.
- what we know.
- what we want to learn.
- what we think.
- what choices we make.
- what we do in our spare time.
- what we do when we are alone.

There might be so many more building blocks that could be added to the list, but this gives us a general idea as to what shapes us.

The examination of ourselves is not only so important but necessary. It is the accounting of, or taking inventory of, who we really are. Through this inspection we are able to put into perspective what formed and shaped us, and how it affected the way we live. But deeply looking into our inner self, our heart, our soul or better yet, our conscience, brings out much unearthing, and much realization of so many things that either have been set aside, not to be dealt with, or purposely dormant – maybe deliberately delayed, to be dealt with at a later time.

Whatever is found through the inspection is helpful in so many productive ways. Admitting to ourselves that we have done something, good or bad, not only helps us to feel better about ourselves, but it would at times, be very helpful in overcoming some denial, and bring a sense of truthfulness to the matter. Most psychologists say that being open or *confessing* about something, especially overtly to someone, is not only good psychologically, but it also helps one to feel better emotionally, spiritually and physically. Seeing that we are a combination of a physical being, a psychological being, and a spiritual being, we have to keep all of these *beings* in balance. By having *opened -up* to someone, not only has the matter been brought out openly, but it has become a *shared* burden, making it less heavy to carry. When we can't find someone to trust and confide in – God is always there.

We express our emotions in so many different ways – through:

> Acceptance, affection, alertness, ambivalence, anger, angst, anticipation, anxiety, apathy, bitterness, boredom, calmness, compassion, comprehension, confusion, contempt, depression, despair, disappointment, disgust, doubt, ecstacy, embarrassment, empathy, emptiness, enmity, enthusiasm, envy, epiphany, excitement, fanaticism, fear, frustration, gratification, gratitude, grief, guilt, happiness, hate, homesickness, hope, horror, hostility, humiliation,

jealousy, loneliness, love, lust, melancholia, mirth, panic, patience, pity, pride, rage, regret, remorse, repentance, righteous-indignation, sadness, self-pity, serenity, shame, shyness, suffering, surprise, sympathy.

It is no wonder that there are situations where we have *mixed* emotions, or that our emotions can suddenly run from one end of the spectrum to the other – having difficulty to bring out either tears or laughter.

This is why when it comes to making decisions, it is usually easier to seek *wisdom*, than to put our trust and faith only in our own judgment.

We are also, *mortals*. We are en-route, on our way, wayfarers. We entered and we will exit. Our existence is but temporary, incarnate, interim, itinerant. Throughout our journey, we are moved by either what excites us, or entices us. We must constantly struggle for self-improvement.

We are what we have been,
but we can be whatever we want to be.

Whatever way we choose to live our lives, what should be considered is that *laughter* will add several years to our lives, *singing* will add even more, but by adding *godliness* to our soul, will make it live in eternal happiness.

"It is not God's function to create or uncreate the circumstances of your life, God created you in the image and likeness of God. You have created the rest."
– Neale Donald Walsch –

The body, mind, and soul were so beautifully, intricately, masterfully, and purposely crafted in His image, to sustain life; not only in this life but more importantly for eternity. Yet during our mortal life we abuse the body and corrupt the mind and soul. For what we have been given, what are we to give back?

> "Since Christ lives within you, even though your body will die because of sin, your spirit is alive because you have been made right with God." (Ro 8:10)

God doesn't make *junk*! He gave us quite a container! He created our body to be used in so many different ways. Every part that forms us, either internally or externally has been arranged with such care and precision, each playing an important part for the overall functioning of the body. The container, though, is not as important as the soul, the spiritual entity that gives it life. Most people pay more attention to the container, than they do about what it contains. So, what good is a Castle to live in, if our own body hasn't been made as a Castle for God to live in?

> "You made all the delicate, inner parts of my body and knit me together in my mother's womb. Thank you for making me so wonderfully complex." (Ps 139:13,14a,b)

Jesus said that we are the salt of the earth, and the light of the world. But if salt has lost its flavor, then it has also lost its usefulness. We must also let our light shine through our good deeds in order to have everyone praise our Heavenly Father.

We are simply a creature of God. God made us, and He connects everything to himself, because everything is part of Him. If we see ourselves as being separated from God, then this is just an illusion. We must make it a purpose to see past the illusion and experience our connectedness to God. The only thing that separates us from God, is sin.

There is a little saying that comes from the *Old French* language, "Honi Soit Que Mal Y Pense! (Author Unknown) The translated meaning would be, "We are what evil we think!"

There is quite a lot being said in this very short verse. In that we are indeed drawn by our thinking to either act on, or ponder on, certain thoughts or subjects that would inevitably lead us into subsequent choices. Whether the choices are good or bad, much depends on choosing the good or bad side of our conscience at the time.

We try to customize our lives by giving ourselves whatever it is we *think* might satisfy our wants, desires or needs; while most of the time, neglecting the joy derived through the everyday more simple gifts that God gives us. The valuable ones that should mean the most to us.

> "Don't be impressed with your own wisdom. Instead fear the LORD and turn your back on evil. Then you will gain renewed health and vitality." (Pr 3:7,8)

> "Happy is the person who finds wisdom and gains understanding. For the profit of wisdom is better than silver, and her wages better than gold." (Pr 3:13,14)

WHAT IS WISDOM ?

Wisdom is said to be the quality of being wise; the understanding of what is lasting, right, and true; the ability to soundly judge; the ability to handle facts sagaciously as they relate to conduct or life; good judgment; common sense; discernment; knowledge; learning; sagacity; scholarly learning.

It could also imply, the accumulated learning of the philosophical or scientific realm. Being able to discern inner relationships and qualities. The acceptance of general beliefs. Having or acting on a wise belief, attitude or course of action. The teaching or knowledge of ancient wise men.

> "It requires wisdom to understand wisdom; the music is nothing if the audience is deaf." – Walter Lippman –

More than knowledge, commonsense, or good-judgment, *wisdom* is not so much of what is taught or learned, but *what has been experienced.* It is the principles and ideals that govern all actions and decisions. In practical matters it involves prudence.

> "Wise men talk because they have something to say, fools, because they have to say something."   – Plato –

Wisdom however can be identified in two categories. The first being the *human* or *materialistic,* earthly, worldly wisdom which basically consists of the accumulation of knowledge, as it relates to being smart, clever or intellectual, or to the extent of being regarded as a 'know it all'. The second being *spiritual* wisdom, which consists of two things: knowing goodness or righteousness (a godly way of living), and applying it. Having read and studied Scripture is not enough to make a person wise, although the necessary knowledge must be gained. Wisdom comes from being guided by, the knowledge of righteousness, and its application as an everyday godly way of living. It has to be put into action. It is a combination of the knowledge of goodness and its constant practice and application that forms wisdom. This power gained through either human or spiritual knowledge should be applied and utilized for good.

> "I will destroy human wisdom and discard their most brilliant ideas." (1 Co 1:19b)

> "But the wisdom that comes from heaven is first of all pure.
> It is also peace loving, gentle at all times,
> and willing to yield to others."
> (Jas 3:17a)

Spiritual wisdom has a different connotation from the usage of being a genius, brilliant, bright or educated. A person can be educated but not be smart, nor have common sense in certain things. Or be smart, but not be wise.

"When I was a boy of fourteen, my father was so ignorant I could hardly stand to have the old man around. But when I got to be twenty one I was astonished at how much the old man had learned in seven years."   – Mark Twain –

Together with Understanding, Counsel, Fortitude, Knowledge, Piety, and Fear of the Lord, Wisdom forms the seven gifts of the Holy Spirit. These virtues belong in their fulness to Christ and make the faithful more obedient to divine inspirations.

We should then live our lives depending on God's grace, and not on our own earthly wisdom, as wisdom is shown to be right by the way of life of those that follow it. Anyone who listens to and obeys the teachings of Jesus, our *source* of wisdom, will become wise. The Bible tells us that if we think we are wise by this world's standards, that we will have to become a fool so we can become spiritually wise by God's standards. Because the wisdom of this world is foolishness to Him.

"All I know is that I know nothing."
– Socrates –

"For from within, out of a person's heart, come evil thoughts, sexual immorality, theft, murder, adultery, greed, wickedness, deceit, eagerness for lustful pleasure, envy, slander, pride, and foolishness. All these vile things come from within; they are what defile you and make you unacceptable to God." (Mk 7:21-23)

"The cave you fear to enter
holds the treasure you seek."
– Joseph Campbell –

"Reverence in the LORD is the foundation of true wisdom. The rewards of wisdom come to all who obey him."
(Ps 111:10)

Many years ago I came upon this wonderful letter, that a very wise man wrote to his Grandchildren. As I was getting ready to write this chapter, it somehow just emerged. Having been given special permission from one of the grandchildren, I would like to share it with you:

"If I had the choice at giving each of you a large fortune OR, the gift of Wisdom, I would choose the latter without hesitation.

I now ask you to look into your dictionary to see the difference between Wisdom, and Learning, and Knowledge, and Education, and Intellect, and other similar words. (Find more as you explore this thought.)

You have, of course, heard that many humans become Educated beyond their intelligence. This comes when a person acquires book knowledge that outruns his or her Common Sense. I have a great respect for Book Knowledge, of course; I still indulge fervently in pursuing the same, still pursuing more information, adding to what has already been acquired. In other words, I remain a Student, regardless of my age. I like to refer to this as Intellectual Curiosity.

Despite what any "moderns" hold, human nature has NOT changed in thousands of years. Those who hold otherwise are either ignorant, or are pursuing special aims that go contrary to the common good in favor of personal goals of some kind of expense of the generality of people.

That human nature has NOT changed in a least 2,000 years, is well illustrated by the Fables of Aesop. If you will study these famous "Fables", which are not fairy stories but are the applications of age-old experience of mankind, you will save yourself many mistakes, and many regrets, and many heartaches.

PURSUE WISDOM; and good luck to you in its lifetime application."

I have never met this fine and wonderful gentleman, but I recognize him as a very special and kind person, that wanted to share his love, priorities, desires and wisdom with his beloved grandchildren.

WHERE TO FIND WISDOM

It is important to learn as much as we can in order to attain the necessary knowledge so that we can faithfully apply, wisdom. *When* we start learning is very crucial, because the sooner we can establish roots the quicker we can rejoice of the fruits. This is why it is so essential to teach the children about spiritual knowledge as soon as possible, so that they will enjoy their life filled with wisdom's peace. Scriptures have been given to us for that purpose; for the enrichment of our lives through the guidance towards a godly way of living. Why a *godly* way of living? Because, God wants us to be like Him. He wants us to imitate Him. So if we are to be like Him and imitate Him, then we must learn what is needed to achieve that state or quality that He desires from us.

> "The only wisdom we can hope to acquire
> is the wisdom of humility: Humility is endless."
> – Eliot –

Christ came to us from heaven for that very purpose of teaching us all about wisdom. All the treasures of wisdom and knowledge lie hidden in Him. He can be reached in many different and available ways; be it by the given Words of the Holy Bible, a close relationship with Him, or through prayer. Christ also told us that He would send us a Counselor, His Representative, the Holy Spirit, who would continue to teach and remind us of everything that Christ, himself told us. Through this Divine Power we must let God be at work in us. Truth, happiness, peace, contentment, and the real enjoyment of this life can only be found through *wisdom*.
The journey towards self, starts from within.

"We ought to be more prompt to find good...."
– St Ignatius of Loyola –

Another way of gaining wisdom is through humility. It strengthens us in being able to live for God, and what He desires from us, rather than to satisfy our own desires. By focusing on what He desires for us we gain the knowledge, that we should rely on Him, His teachings, and His Righteousness to become what He wants us to be. We can not forget still another area from which we gather wisdom – for the Bible tells us that understanding and wisdom comes from the aged who have lived many years. Not only will they teach you about wisdom, but also about the wisdom of past generations.

> "God surely knows where it can be found, for he looks throughout the whole earth, under all the heavens. He made the winds blow and determined how much rain should fall. He made the laws of the rain and prepared a path for the lightning. Then, when he had done all this, he saw wisdom and measured it. He established it and examined it thoroughly. And this is what he says to all humanity: 'The fear of the Lord is true wisdom; to forsake evil is real understanding.'" (Job 28:23-28)

The wisdom that comes from heaven is pure, and not defiled like earthly wisdom. It teaches us peace, love and gentleness that we should apply at all times, and the willingness to yield to others. It shows us that we should be merciful and full of good deeds; that we should show no partiality and always be sincere in what we do or say. It helps us to become peacemakers, and plants seeds of peace by which grows goodness. This is how wisdom comes about.

> "But you shouldn't be so concerned about perishable things like food. Spend your energy seeking the eternal life that I, the Son of Man, can give you. For God the Father has sent me for that very purpose." (Jn 6:27)

How many books have we read in our lifetime? How many of these books were related to finding wisdom, true *spiritual* wisdom? How many times have we read or referred to the Bible? The Proverbs found in the Bible were given to us, for that very purpose of gaining, not only wisdom, but discipline; and also to help us understand the wise sayings. It is through these Proverbs that we receive the instructions on good conduct, discipline, and thus doing what is fair, just, and what is right. But the beginning of knowledge is the fear of the Lord.

"May you have the foresight to know where you're going
and the insight to know when you're going too far."
– Irish Blessing –

Gaining wisdom is like walking out from darkness and experiencing light. When light appears, things become visible. It makes us able to see where we are, and what's around us. Only then can we look at things the way they really are, and choose to take the necessary steps towards the right path. Sometimes the longest journey that we experience is only eighteen inches long – the distance that separates our mind and our heart.

"In the darkness of water the sun never penetrates. Or is it that it
penetrates just enough to make that darkness visible."
– Author Unknown –

Wisdom is also found through the church. Religions were established in order to give us guidelines, direction, in the way to live our lives. It gives us needed reminders on how we should apply ourselves. Not only to better our own lives, but also to help others in their needs. Church gives us a sense of belonging and togetherness, making us realize that we are not walking alone on this journey, but there are others that are also walking with us. We become One Body.

Learn from the past and dream for tomorrow.

>Live *today* in a way that pleases God,
>so that *tomorrow* you'll rejoice in what you did *yesterday*.

It is a shame that our school systems have declined in, and even prohibited the teaching of spiritual wisdom, from which could be learned so many inspiring things about values and morality. What is more important, the education that will benefit the mind, or the education that will benefit the soul?

Still the best source of finding wisdom is the Bible, containing all the essential words that come from The Word Himself.

> "But words are things, and a small drop of ink falling like dew upon a thought, produces that which makes thousands, perhaps millions think."   – Sir Aubrey De Vere –

> "Remember, dear brothers and sisters, that few of you were wise in the world's eyes, or powerful, or wealthy when God called you. Instead, God deliberately chose things the world considers foolish in order to shame those who think they are wise. And he chose those who are powerless to shame those who are powerful. God chose things despised by the world, things counted as nothing at all, and used them to bring to nothing what the world considers important, so that no one can ever boast in the presence of God.
> (1 Co 1:26-29)

APPLYING WISDOM

We go to doctors, physicians, chiropractors, dentists, even psychiatrists, and whoever else we think can help us to improve our health. We go there to ask for their advice or service in seeking some cure for what ails us. We are anxious to take any medication or remedy prescribed to relieve any pain or affliction. We'll sometimes make several trips to follow-up on the progress or results of the medication or treatment. Why not do the same for the treatment of our spiritual needs – for our soul? Why not go to the source that can heal all afflictions? By turning to God, or to His Word, the Bible, or to prayer, we find the necessary help needed to give us spiritual medicine to heal any troubled or ailing soul. Our souls need and deserve greater attention than our bodies do. The soul will live forever, while the body is but temporary.

"You made me; you created me. Now give me the sense to follow your commands." (Ps 119:73)

If we can treat our bodies, and get them used to a regimen that is beneficial for special functions to promote and enjoy a healthier way of life, we should also treat our souls to become enriched and healthy – for the soul is far more important than the body.

"Being wise is as good as being rich; in fact better."
(Ecc 7:11)

Where do we find this Healer that will take care of all our needs? How about going to the source of creation – if He made the body and the soul – He can certainly repair the parts. *Faith* is the answer.

F ind
A nswers
I n
T he
H ealer

We should remember that New Year's resolutions are also spiritually necessary, and it's never too late to start a *new year* and a *new life*. In life we train ourselves to remember the things we *want* to remember. We have to learn from the mistakes of others; we can't live long enough to make all of them ourselves. We are always in need of change and renewal. And it's never too late to start, and in this case it's better to start before it's too late. *"Anything worth doing is worth doing well!"* Taking care of our soul is not only worth doing, it is the most important thing we can and must do concerning our existence. We only have one lifetime, one shot at it. We can't come back and redo it. They don't make erasures that big! There's no *second chance!* We've been given all the necessary tools to work with, and all the Words to explain to us how to use them. The decision is then up to us, to renew ourselves into new and better beings. Jesus said,

> "I assure you, unless you are born again, you can never see the Kingdom of God. The truth is, no one can enter the Kingdom of God without being born of water and Spirit. Humans can reproduce only human life, but the Holy Spirit gives new life from heaven. So don't be surprised at my statement that you must be born again. Just as you can hear the wind but can't tell where it comes from or where it is going, so you can't explain how people are born of the Spirit." (Jn 3:3,5-8)

How much of our lifetime will be devoted to our spouse, our children, our families, our friends, our work, or our activities? Focusing on some, and maybe neglecting others. In this spreading of devotion, we have to align things in order of importance. Our foremost devotion is to God, and to applying wisdom to create for ourselves and for others, a spiritual, purposeful and meaningful way of life. In applying wisdom – we either use it, or we lose it.

> "This reminded me that no one can discover everything God has created in our world, no matter how hard they work at it. Not even the wisest people know everything, even if they say they do." (Ecc 8:17)

Looking back at our accomplishments in life – what did we achieve? How were we successful? Why, How, and for Whom did we do anything? How well were these things done? What kind of child, person, mother, father, sister, brother, aunt, uncle, niece, nephew, grandson, granddaughter, grandfather, grandmother, friend or worker were we? How could all of these relationships have been changed by the application of wisdom? How much are we willing to give of ourselves for God's Kingdom? Life can only be understood going *backwards*, but must be lived going *forward.* If you don't understand history, you are condemned to repeat it.

> "Wisdom is not a question of learning facts with the mind;
> it can only be acquired through perfection of living."
> – N. Sri Ram –

When we examine our lives, and see how well we are taking care of ourselves, it makes us realize the attention we must also be giving to others. If we care for others, we will have taken care of ourselves. We shouldn't be overly concerned with our own well-being or weaknesses. God tells us that if we admit our weaknesses to ourselves and to Him, that He will turn those weaknesses into strength. If there is a hole in your heart, or in your life – nothing in *this world* will fill it – only the *Lord* can.

> "After starting your Christian lives in the Spirit, why are you now
> trying to become perfect by your own human effort?"
> (Gal 3:3b)

We shouldn't rely on God to do everything for us, nor should we attempt or try to do everything on our own. God expects us to do whatever we can according to our limitations, *then* leaving the rest to Him through faith and trust. The Bible tells us to let heaven fill our thoughts, and not to think or be controlled by things here on earth.

> "What man really seeks is not perfection which is in the future,
> but fulfilment which is ever in the present."
> – N. Sri Ram –

In applying wisdom we must be creative! God took dust, and from it, crafted man. He wants us to imitate Him in our creativity. Not only can we turn some boards into a cabinet, or cloth into a dress, yarn into mittens, or words into a letter, notes into a song, but more importantly, our talents can be utilized and enhanced by the application of wisdom – in helping the needy, the homeless, the desperate, the afflicted, and the hungry. Standing up for what is *right* in the world. Making a difference in our families, our communities, our country, and our world. We should use our human and worldly resources to benefit others, by being helpful and friendly in any way we can. Albert Einstein said before his death, that people go to their graves after having utilized but a mere percentage of their capabilities.

"Our hearts ache, but we always have joy.
We are poor, but we give spiritual riches to others.
We own nothing, and yet we have everything."
(2Co 6:10)

If you were given a brand new vehicle, along with all of the related details and instructions on how to use and care for it, along with the documentation of its performance, but never took it for a ride – how would you ever find out what the vehicle can do? The same relates to the application of wisdom. We can read all the Scriptures, and many interesting books about righteousness, but if we don't put it into practice in our daily lives, then we will never find its usefulness, or direct it on our journey and travel on our earthly roads.

"Yesterday is but a memory. Tomorrow an uncharted course.
So live today so it will be a memory without remorse."
– Author Unknown –

We must be logical! Logic is the act of thinking and reasoning in strict accordance with the limitations and incapacities of the human understanding. One of the most logical things we can do is to follow the Golden Rule by treating others as we would like to be treated.

> May our behavioral sciences be such,
> that in the future we can count them as blessings.

Children can learn a musical instrument at a very young age. Their minds absorb like sponges; they are so quick to learn new things. They can accomplish things as infants, that amaze many adults. People are astonished at the wonder of achievements of these youngsters' knowledge and abilities. What if it would be, instead of a musical instrument, the achievement of spiritual knowledge, that would intensify the greatness of their souls? Would the people be in awe of their accomplishments? Would the flourishing of their soul be regarded with as much value and appreciation? God certainly would!

> "Change your thought – and you can change the world."
> – Norman Vincent Peale –

We spend our whole youth to obtain wealth, and our whole wealth to obtain youth. We should find it more valuable to pass on our values to our loved ones, rather than our assets. Our deeds, good or bad, have a ripple-effect, like a pebble tossed in the water, affecting others as well. This is why it is so important to find, and to stay on, a straight and narrow path, so that those that follow us will not stumble and fall but will become strong and have good guidance and direction. This way no one will be hindered in finding the Lord by the way we act. It takes wisdom to learn from our experiences, and to make changes to better our lives accordingly. Change for good is invigorating. We should never be afraid to try some new venture even though we are not professionals. Amateurs built the ark, and professionals built the Titanic.

> "Trusting oneself is foolish, but those who walk in wisdom are safe." (Pr 28:26)

PURPOSE

Purpose is the anticipated aim, goal, object or reason, which guides life's action; something to be attained; the result or effect of an intended need or desire; a practical result; determination; goal; intention; objective; resolution; an end.

For everything there's a reason. A reason for the season. A reason for the clouds, the rain. A reason for animals. A reason for man, and a reason for woman. Not only is there a reason for everything, but God had an intended purpose for everything He created, even before He created them.

"The LORD has made everything for his own purposes."
(Pr 16:4a)

According to Albert Einstein's theory, everything is somehow related. Everything created has its own purpose, and its purpose is related to all other created things.

"The only true happiness comes from squandering ourselves for a purpose." – William Cowper –

Even God's purpose is shown to us through His wisdom. He created us in His image and wants us to imitate Him. In imitating Him we should rely on *Him* and *His* wisdom to guide us toward our intended purpose, or purposes during our earthly life. Whatever that might be, we should be open to it. No purpose for living could be as difficult to accept or accomplish as what Christ's intended purpose was. But whatever it is that God is calling us to do, we can rest assured that anything is possible through the strength that Christ gives us. We have to remember that it is not only what God has in mind *for* us to accomplish, but also the many things that He can accomplish *through* us.

"'For I know the plans I have for you.' says the LORD.

> 'They are plans for good and not for disaster,
> to give you a future and a hope.'"
> (Jer 29:11a)

By having a close-relationship with God, He will let you know what He had intended for you, show how to accomplish it, and He will also show you to be worthy of the life to which He called you.

> "Strong lives are motivated by dynamic purposes."
> – Kenneth Hildebrand –

It is good to reflect on what we have done; to think, ponder, or examine what has happened to form our lives, and to look at what kind of meaning, goals, reasons, and for what purpose we have conducted our lives; about the way we are living now, and the way we want to choose to live, as to pursue and achieve the intended goal of our existence, and for the purpose and reason of having been created. Has it been what we thought or hoped it would have been? Has it been what God would have wanted it to be? Is our main purpose in life, short lived, or one that will last forever? Are we electing and determining this decision by ourselves, or are we relying on God to guide us? Sometimes the answers don't come right away. But when we endure patiently, and rely on His judgement, we will enjoy whatever it is we are intended to do, at His designated time. By being patient, resolute, and trusting in God, He will let us know His purpose for each of our lives.

> "For everything comes from him, everything exists by his power and is intended for his glory." (Ro 11:36)

Every created being that ever was, is now, and is yet to come, had, has, or will have a definite purpose. Each and everyone of us is assigned a special ability to do certain things well, a specific talent, and a specific individualistic distinct purpose. It might involve serving others, teaching others, encouraging others, or sharing with others. If He has called us to be a leader, then we should take the responsibility seriously. If it is the gift or ability of showing kindness to others, we should do it gladly. Whatever it is, we should ask God to help us to accomplish these purposes of our journey. We want to go through life utilizing our abilities, talents, and our strength for a realistic, well-planned, well-executed purpose. It would be a shame to waste a lifetime with no specific accomplishment, or for the wrong purpose.

> "We are all parts of his body, and each of us has a different work to do. And since we are all one body in Christ, we belong to each other, and each of us needs all the others." (Ro 12:15b-e)

Christ was born to be, among other things, a teacher. He was born to bring truth to the world, to bring us Salvation, and to show us a life to be imitated. He told us that the smallest details of God's law will remain until its purpose is achieved. He asked us to be His followers, to live like He did, and for the same purpose that He did. His journey and purpose was more than difficult, but He pleased His Father by obeying and fulfilling His Father's will. So too, should we please the Father by loving each other, becoming of one mind, being united in thought and purpose so that we will all live in harmony.

> "Many persons have a wrong idea of what constitutes true happiness. It is not attained through self-gratification but through fidelity to a worthy purpose.
> – Helen Keller –

What we decide to do with our lives should end up in practical results, something that will create treasures, not only for ourselves, but for as many as possible. Treasures that can be stored eternally. In order to achieve this, God's plan for us has to be activated. *What value has success if it isn't worthwhile?* We have little time – it has to be used to the best advantage.

"And we know that God causes everything to work together for the good of those who love God and are called according to his purpose for them. For God knew his people in advance, and he chose them to become like his Son."
(Ro 8:28,29a)

CHARACTER

Character is an aggregate, or a combination of distinguishing attributes, features, qualities or traits that forms a person, group or thing that makes it different from another; a person's, or group's combined moral or ethical strength or structure; integrity; fortitude; reputation.

Character is an accumulation of qualities and values formed by the impressions from faith, nature, education or habits, which are then strengthened by self-discipline. Values are more easily displayed than taught.

"Between ourselves and our real natures we interpose that wax figure of idealizations and selections which we call our character." – Walter Lip Mann –

Moral character is built upon a variety of attributes such as courage, fortitude, honesty, integrity, loyalty, good behavior and good habits.

"Sow a thought and you reap an action; sow an act and you reap a habit; sow a habit and you reap a character; sow a character and you reap a destiny." – Author Unknown –

"Fame is a vapor, popularity an accident, riches take wing, and only character endures." – Horace Greeley –

Our character is shown through our behavior, the way we show our integrity – as when we act or react with a cheerful readiness or promptitude or briskness to any given occasion. It determines the way we live our lives. A good test of our character is shown by what we do when we know that no one is looking.

> "The discipline you learn and character you build from setting and achieving a goal can be more valuable than the achievement of the goal itself."   – Bo Bennett –

> "Character is what angels say about you before the throne of God."   – Author Unknown –

In order to set children on the right paths, parents must become more *conservative* and less *liberal* with their methods. The building of character takes effort and discipline, for the parent as well as the child. Parents have to set boundaries of what is acceptable behavior. Children learn consistently better through proper example shown by the parents, but the final forming of their character lies in their own attitudes and convictions.

> "Discipline your children while there is hope. If you don't, you will ruin their lives." (Pr 19:18)

God Himself revealed His character by the many things He did through Moses and His deeds to the people of Israel. He also tested and humbled them to let them prove their character, and to see if they would obey His commands.

Jesus even told us about the devil's character,

> "If God were your Father, you would love me, because I have come to you from God. I am not here on my own, but he sent me. Why can't you understand what I am saying? It is because you are unable to do so! For you are the children of your father the Devil, and you love to do the evil things he does. He was a murderer from the beginning and

has always hated the truth. There is not truth in him. When he lies, it is consistent with his character; for he is a liar and the father of lies." (Jn 8:42-44)

"For the kingdom of God is not a matter of what we eat or drink, but of living a life of goodness and peace and joy in the Holy Spirit. If you serve Christ with this attitude, you will please God. And other people will approve of you, too." (Ro 14:17,18)

TEMPERAMENT

Temperament is the manner or internal constitution with respect to how an individual behaves, reacts, or thinks; an individual's peculiar physical or mental character; a disposition.

Psychology tells us that temperament is the inborn, genetically based, natural aspect of an individual's personality. One can be an introvert or an extrovert. When temperament is molded with character along with the learning process, the two together then form personality.

Our attitudes are based on likes and dislikes.

Temperament then, unlike character, is somewhat inherited. There are different ways of evaluating temperaments. The following are some distinguishing types:

> ***Temperament Characteristics***
> Activity
> Adaptability
> Distraction
> Initial Reaction
> Intensity
> Mood

        Persistency (Attention Span)
        Regularity (Rhythmicity)
        Sensitivity (Sensory Threshold or Responsiveness)
Classical Temperaments
        Choleric
        Melancholic
        Phlegmatic
        Sanguine
        Supine

Throughout the ages, surveys have found that temperance can be enhanced by the building of character, which is better accelerated at a very young age. Family life plays an intricate part in the development of character and personalities.

> "The lack of emotional security of our American young people is due, I believe, to their isolation from the larger family unit. No two people – no mere father and mother – as I have often said, are enough to provide emotional security for a child. He needs to feel himself one in a world of kinfolk, persons of variety in age and temperament, and yet allied to himself by an indissoluble bond which he cannot break if he could, for nature has welded him into it before he was born."   – Pearl S. Buck –

If you like to cook as much as I do, you probably have gathered many recipes. Some of which have become your favorites. The reason for the recipe is not only to give a guideline as to how to prepare the food, but most importantly, it gives a list of ingredients.

In order to arrive at the intended end result, you must include all of the listed ingredients. Omitting an ingredient can make a disastrous change in the outcome of whatever it is that is being prepared. What if there was one of the ingredients that had been left out? What if that particular ingredient was the most essential one in the recipe? Let's take a look at the ingredients needed for *good health*, and for most people, a regimen has to begin with A NEW START.

A – Acceptance

N – Nutrition
E – Exercise
W – Water

S – Sun
T – Temperance
A – Air
R – Rest
T – *Temperament*

Acceptance – In order to activate any new regimen, we have to accept the fact that we *need* change, and must allow ourselves to start. The lack of acceptance is the reason that so many fall into, and stay in many different types of addictions – be it alcohol, drugs, nicotine, sex, etc. The *acceptance* of change, the *attitude* – is the primary step toward the accomplishment of anything. It is always advisable to consult your doctor prior to any change to your regimen, especially your exercising or eating habits.

Nutrition – is basically what fuels our bodies. People are concerned about the type and quality of fuel that they use in their vehicles or furnaces. The body is much more delicate and fragile than a mechanical unit. We wouldn't want to put too many additives in our vehicle's engine, as it would start to take away from the engine's performance. The same applies to our digestion. The type of nutrition we ingest makes us who we are, how we feel, how susceptible we are to sickness and disease. There's an old saying that says that, "We are what we eat!" What should be added to that also is – "and what we can digest", because a lot of our foods are not digested properly, or not digested fast enough.

The human body, if we look at it as a chemical processor, was created in a certain way for a particular purpose. Most people try to have the body do things it wasn't meant to do. The body was intended to process mostly grains, legumes, vegetables, and fruits, preferably raw. The storage and cooking of the foods diminishes its quality and nutrients, decreasing in value from each and every process the food has to go through before it reaches the table. In order to give food a longer shelf life, and to enhance its appearance and flavor, many chemicals are added.

There are a few simple guidelines to remember about food consumption. The more different foods that are ingested at a given meal, the longer it will take for that meal to digest. One food might cause a chemical reaction to the other. For instance if we were to take the proper amount of Hydrogen, and the proper amount of Oxygen, and mix them together, we would end up with *water*. A Chemical reaction. The idea then is to avoid the clashing of certain foods that will alter the *chemical* digestion process.

The ideal way of eating is to have a meal digest in three hours or less, while the food is still fresh. This way the body gets the full benefit of the *fresh* nutrients reaching the intestines. Anything left in your stomach by the time another meal is ingested, it will make digestion even more difficult, and slow down the digestive process. If the body doesn't have time to process all it needs to before the next ingestion, it will store some of it as fat. By being able to digest a meal in three or less hours, the stomach now has a chance to start to break-down that stored fat and process it. So the more we can give the stomach some *empty time* the more it can process the unwanted fat. A natural method of stabilizing weight. By adhering to this process the body will automatically work at maintaining its proper weight.

Fruits for instance should be eaten at lest a half-hour before a meal, or a least three hours after a meal, but not included in a meal, as they will cause the whole meal to ferment, so by the time that meal reaches the intestines, it has lost most of its nutritional value.

In order to get a meal to digest in the proper amount of time, the selection and the compatibility of the foods is the most important. An easy rule to follow is to have only fruits or fresh fruit juices for breakfast. This allows for fast digestion and allows your stomach to empty. The other meals can consist of as many vegetable as you care to have, along with a generous portion of the choice of only *one* of the following: meat, poultry, fish, egg, pasta, rice, or potatoes. This combination should allow for fast digestion. Some meals, including a variety of many types of food, especially like the ones being consumed at Holiday times, could literally stay in your stomach for over thirty hours.

Exercise – Special consideration should be given to the implementation of any physical activity. Again consulting a doctor prior to any new activity is always advisable.

The human body was intended also, to be active. By being inactive too long the body loses strength and stamina. An exercise program should be one that starts so gradually that the body can easily adjust and get accustomed to it. Progression should be *slow* but *challenging*. Most people try to do too much too quickly, with results of either pain, frustration, or both. The media talked about a lady that was able to walk through several states. She said that when she first started her walking exercise, she would walk alongside her road, and every day she would walk up to one more telephone pole than she had walked the previous day. Eventually she was able to walk for miles. The same goes with any exercise program. Progress must be seen, but the effort has to be limited.

Water – Our body consists largely of water. The proper intake of water is needed to allow the body to function properly. The water we drink is helpful in helping to cleanse our system, and to help with detoxification. Not only is the quality of the water we consume important, but the quantity is as well. Quantity varies with different people and different circumstances. Other beverages, such as coffee tea, alcoholic beverages, sodas, etc., should be ingested with moderation. Milk clings to the inside of the intestines and can slow the absorption of nutrients.

Sun – The exposure to the sun, not only gives us special vitamins, but the psychological benefits are also very essential. Daylight, and especially sunlight, has a way of perking up a day. Not only does sunlight make it easier to see, but it also seems to light up a more joyful nature. For this reason, many hospitals try to expose certain patients to sunlight as often as they can.

Temperance – We have to live our lives in a well balanced manner. Not having enough of something could be bad for us, but having too much could be even worse. We need a certain amount of water to survive, but if we ingest too much, it will poison our system. Researchers say that a glass of red wine is good for the heart, but if you have four bottles it might kill you. Moderation is the key. Enough – but not too much!

Air – We can go without water for quite a while, but time is limited when it comes to air. Our lungs are very fragile, we should treat them with special care – by being careful of our surroundings, and what we allow ourselves to breathe. We should take precautions in filtering out anything that might be harmful.

Rest – In order to recharge our battery we must devote ourselves to the proper rest. One cannot continue forever without the required amount of sleep or rest. The body will not function properly, and soon the brain will lose its efficiency and tenacity. Even God took a day off and rested on the Seventh Day. We should imitate Him!

Temperament – *Temperament* is indeed one of the *most* important part of attaining and maintaining good health. It is sadly overlooked. When most people talk about wanting to enjoy good health, the emphasis seems to be towards diet and exercise. Very few would consider temperament as something considered as necessary for the enjoyment of good health. A person can include all of the above mentioned requirements for good health, but if there is something inside of you that is eating up your insides, it can do more damage than deleting any of the other requirements. We have to deal with what makes us psychologically and emotionally tick inside, with the same care we give to the food we eat, the exercise we get, and the air we breathe. If we don't give our temperament the proper attention that it should be given, bad feelings could start a degenerating process. Whether it is something that has been annoying us for some time or for some reason. Whether is was a hurt that we have suffered – the loss of a loved one, a pet or a friend, whatever the hurt, if we don't allow ourselves to heal whatever it is that is causing us unrest, we can rest assured that eventually it will get the best of us. It will intensify and cause even greater pain and can even result in physical pain. We have to treat our temperament well because it gives us the needed motivation that leads us to the application of all the other ingredients of good health. We have to guard our temperance very well, for it affects everything we do.

Studies have found that the way we feel affects our health, and that our health affects the way we feel. Physical health is related to psychological health – and one can affect the other. Because health has a direct impact about the way we feel emotionally or psychologically, health can have relevance to our spiritual well-being and vice-versa. The way we feel can affect us spiritually, and our spiritual well-being can affect our health. Temperament is indeed one the most important ingredients of good health – and a little bit of laughter can add several years to your life.

"Please Lord teach us to laugh again,
but God, don't ever let us forget that we cried."
– Author Unknown –

Doctors are now treating
the effects
of mal-nutrition.

Ulcers are caused not so much by what we eat,
as to what's eating us.

COMMUNICATING WITH ONE – ANOTHER

The act or process of communicating, transmitting, or interchanging; to impart, make known, convey, or transmit some information; to have an interchange of thoughts, opinions, or ideas; to converse; to be connected; join.

Communicating can be accomplished in many different ways, as a means of sending messages, orders, or information. Speech, telephone, telegraph, radio and television are the more common methods. There are yet many other manners that relate to communication, such as: books, dreams, facial expressions, frowns, gestures, nods, sign language, signs, smiles, visions, writing.

The way that we communicate seems to change according to whoever it is that we are communicating with. The way we deliver our message, the method being used to convey it, even the tone or choice of words is dictated by who it is that will be receiving it. The method could vary in accordance to the many different recipients: a spouse, children, parents, relatives, friends, teachers, students, work or business associates, etc.

Special ways of communicating apply when interchanging ideas and information with the deaf, the mute, or other impaired, as Alzheimer's patients. Much helpful training and information is available for such communicating.

Have you ever played the game where you have a few people form a line, and give a message to the person at one end of the line, then having that person repeat it to the next person, then each passing it down to the next, until it reaches the last person in line. It is amazing how the message gets distorted by the time it reaches the last person. This shows the importance of making sure that message doesn't lose its intended meaning as it is passed along.

A message should be given clearly, distinctly, and in an understandable manner and language, being careful to not leave anything to assumption. It is also a good idea to keep in mind the importance of choosing the appropriate time and place, as this could have an impact on how the message is received.

The power, usefulness and purpose of communication is in regards to: answers, apathy, emotions, feelings, ideas, information, like or dislikes, opinions, questions, sympathy, thoughts, etc.

In conversations, what we say, how we say it, our choice of timing, our choice of words, our choice of tone, all of these could be revealing of who we are – because it comes from the heart. It denotes our character, our personality, our understanding, our compassion, our feelings, our patience, our tolerance, our attitude, and the very *weigh and essence* of our being. If we could listen to, and in fact analyze the method we choose to communicate, we would learn a great deal from it.

The lack of communication is the primary reason for failed relationships. It is so important to be open and honest with each other. It allows us to learn, to know, and to understand one-another. For this reason it is so important to visit one-another, loved ones, friends, relatives, acquaintances, as often as possible – by keeping in touch, phoning, or writing letters. Whatever happened to the joy of receiving a letter through the mail?

> "Worry weighs a person down; an encouraging word cheers a person up." (Pr 12:25)

The real art of conversation consists not only of saying the right thing at the right time, but also leaving unsaid the wrong thing at the tempting moment.

Family life is where good communication examples should start. There should be a saying that implies that families that talk together – stay together. The spouses being able to converse with each other and with the children, and children being able to talk with each other, and with the parents.

> A man came up to his wife and told her that he had heard through a survey that women talked more than men did. He said that the amount of words that women used, averaged 30,000 a day, and that men only used 15,000. The wife then

said that the women *needed* to use *twice* as much as men, because the have to *repeat* everything to them. The husband replied, "*What?*"

In conversation, if a question is being asked, it should be precise, then too the answer should be precise. When a definite answer is anticipated, a definite answer should be given, and not a probable one, or one that would leave one up in the air. A definite answer would show consideration to the person requesting the information. In this way we show care for the person awaiting the response.

We must not be misleading in our communicating. Lies and deceitfulness are fabrications and unworthy conveyance of information, so is gossip. We were warned through and old saying that, "Loose lips, sinks ships." There is so much harm that can come from improper communication.

> "A gossip is one who talks to you about others, a bore is one who talks to you about himself; and a brilliant conversationalist is one who talks to you about yourself."
> – Author Unknown –

The power of the tongue is limitless, and so are the consequences. Words can bring forth life, or can bring forth death. It can bring joy, or sadness.

> "....but no one can tame the tongue. It is an uncontrollable evil, full of deadly poison. Sometimes it praises our Lord and Father, and sometimes it breaks out into curses against those who have been made in the image of God."
> (Jas 3:8,9)

Quite a few years ago I was very fortunate to learn a true meaning and importance of communicating. I was invited to a family gathering, and of the many people who were invited and attended, I was the only one who wasn't a relative. I was though, a close friend to the couple who were hosting this assemblage. I was kind-of reluctant about going. One of the reasons that I was hesitant, was that I was planning to attend this event unaccompanied. I didn't want however, to disappoint my friends, as they really wanted me to be there – we hadn't seen each other for a while, and maybe we'd probably have a chance to visit a little. The other reason that weighed on my decision making, was that I wondered how the evening would turn out, because, the only people that I would actually know there would be the ones in charge of entertaining their guests, and that would undoubtedly keep them very busy.

I had been asked to arrive earlier than the others, because my friends wanted to allow some time for us to talk, and try to catch-up on the many different things that people like to get current about. I really anticipated this special time with them. It was so nice of them to be so thoughtful and considerate – to allot some extra time, just for me. They were busy people. That's what good friends are made of, loving, caring, and giving a feeling of inclusiveness.

Some of the guests started arriving. The first two couples were my friends parents. I had never had an opportunity to meet them, as they lived out of state. It was so nice to be able to talk with the parents before the others would arrive.

It didn't take long for the rest of the guests to join in. All seeming like very nice and likable people. The more people I got to meet and talk to, the more I started to relax and be comfortable with them, and I hoped, them with me.

As the evening progressed, I had found myself having talked to many different people, all whom I found to be quite interesting. There was one person that seemed to stand out from the rest, and I hadn't had an opportunity to speak with her. She was a lady, probably in her fifties, neatly dressed, and very conservative in her appearance. From what I could gather, she had come with one of her nieces. I walked over and introduced myself, and she to me, on a first-name basis. Our conversation was enjoyable. I found out how she was related to some of the people that were there. Our talk was pretty much limited to, lets say, soft talk, not getting into anything in particular.

After having spent some time with other guests and finding out more about this wonderful family, something told me that I should go talk to that woman again. When she was free to talk to, I went to see her and asked if I could sit and chat with her for a while. She seemed so interesting. I just wanted to spend more time with her. This time it didn't take long for our conversation to get going.

I found out that she was a nun, that she was on a sabbatical, and that she had come to stay with her niece for a while because of health reasons. After talking about her health, I decided to ask her where she had served as a nun. The countries mentioned were numerous. But of all the places she had been, the one that would stand out the most, was Calcutta. She had served for some time with Mother Teresa. I felt so privileged to have her spend time with me, sharing with me some her experiences.

I had decided to talk with other guests, as somebody else wanted to take my place to talk to the lovely nun.

The evening had really materialized for me as some time enjoyably well spent, and not at all what I had imagined it to be.

I found myself and friends having an opportunity to get together again for a few minutes, and the minutes were few, as they were so into their chores.

The person who had taken my place, and had been talking to the nun, had now left. I imagined he had gone to see her to say goodnight before he had to leave.

Something again was telling me to go talk to this woman. I didn't know why I was being drawn to her direction. So once again, I decided to go chat with her. This time, we started talking about her early family life. She had been born in Canada, and had come to this country when she was a teenager. I told her that my parents had also come from Canada with their families when they were also in their teens. She asked me my parents' names, and it almost shocked me when she said that not only did she remember my mother, but that her family and my mother's family, not only lived on the same street, but actually lived as neighbors. She told about how the families would talk together at the picket fence separating their homes.

Her sister and my mother's sister were the best of friends, and so was her brother and mother's brother the best of friends. It seems that my aunt would accompany her sister when she went for piano lessons. All this information – I was overwhelmed.

There was so much more information revealed through the joint contribution of our thoughts, and open sharing.

The next day I rushed over to my mother's home with all this information concerning the early acquaintances of her first few years in this country. Needless to say, she was very excited. It brought back for her, so many good memories. It was like it allowed her to relive a little bit of her past, a part of her life that she had enjoyed so much.

The reason why this is being related at this time, is not because it was intended to be descriptive about a night out with my friends, but mainly for the purpose, and reason, of being aware of what can be gained through, or can be missed by the lack of, conversations. I had no idea what information this person had stored in her mind, nor would she have known about relating me with some of the things that went back to her past.

Since that occurrence, that event not only caused me to be less reluctant about talking openly with people, but it encouraged me to pry a little more if my intuition seemed to be demanding it. What I find incredible, is that I could be walking right by a person, that could appear at the time to be a complete stranger, but I could, or this person could, be carrying a valued amount of information that could, and sometimes *should* be shared by each other. Only through the mutual expressing of information, can we unlock and open up the treasures that are there to be shared, otherwise they would stay dormant forever.

> "Don't forget to show hospitality to strangers,
> For some who have done this
> have entertained angels
> without realizing it!"
> (Heb 13:2)

Another notable and similar incident took place just recently, and it happened again quite unexpectedly. My wife and I had gone to a local small business which was operated at this person's home, to have something serviced. The service actually didn't take more than fifteen minutes, but the conversation was quite lengthy, and very enjoyable. As my wife and I were getting ready to leave, I told the serviceman how I admired his new vehicle sitting there in his driveway. After talking about cars for a while, he asked if I would like to see a car from the 60's that he had restored, which he had in his garage. As I walked into his garage and stared at the vehicle, I couldn't believe what I was seeing.

Years ago, after my father died, we thought our Mom should learn to drive and be able to be self-dependent. She was a short woman. Whenever we went looking for a vehicle, a problem we had to overcome was that, with her being short, it was difficult for her to have good visibility while sitting a the drivers seat, as the steering wheel would obstruct her vision. After trying dozens of cars, I happened to spot this one vehicle sitting at the dealership's showroom. Among all of the other vehicles, this particular one was very unique. It was a bright red Camero, with white racing stripes and black and white checkered seats. I said, "Mom, this is your car!" She sat at the wheel, and not only did she feel comfortable and have good visibility, but she actually bought the car. It changed her life! It didn't take long for her to travel up and down the turnpike to go visit her sister. This Camero, and the Camero that we saw in that serviceman's garage were identical. Same year, same model, same color, same stripes, same checkered seats and interior. If I would have left this man's driveway two minutes earlier I would have missed this experience.

Even in our own everyday relationships, with our own families, or friends, things are sometimes left unsaid. It might be because of the fear of hurting someone's feelings.. It might be because the time doesn't seem to be right. It could be for the searching of the right words, or maybe the feeling that it was not noteworthy. But that extra push can sometimes get something going. It is these incidences that make you appreciate conversing and communicating, and especially unearths such wonderful buried treasurers.

While conversing it is always more interesting to find information about the other person or persons. We already know about our stored-up information. It arouses the interest more to share the information that others have stored-up. We have learned practically everything we know through others. So, by being a good listener, we can learn even more.

When we are the ones doing the talking, the main thing to keep in mind, is not to dwell about ourselves, or take center stage, and especially to not brag about ourselves, or about what we've done or what we've accomplished. This doesn't make for good conversation – in fact it usually turns most people away.

> "Kind words are like honey – sweet to the soul and healthy for the body." (Pr 16:24)

> "Heaven and earth will disappear, but my words will remain forever." (Lk 21:33)

Communicating takes on a very special meaning for Christians as it relates to the partaking in the Lord's Supper, by receiving Holy Communion, the Blood and Body of Christ. The highest form of Communicating.

COMMUNICATING WITH GOD

Communicating with God is not any different than communicating with one another. The only important difference is that we have to realize *Who* we are in touch with. We have to approach Him with Reverence and Humility. Our conversations with Him don't always have to be in the form of prayer. We can just talk to Him as we would while walking with a favorite friend.

God being our Father is also the very *best* friend that we could ever have. He can be referred to as God, Father, Daddy, Abba, or any other intimate name we choose. He is always ready to have a very intrinsic, personal, or private conversation with us, at any time. He is always available, always anxious, and never too busy. He is also the best listener we'll ever find. We can talk to Him as we would any other friend.

How many times do we get in touch with a real close friend, via either mail, phone, online, or cell phone? How long do the messages last? What kind of anticipation do we have for the upcoming sports game, theater performance, newscast, dinner engagement, meeting with friends or a long awaited telephone call? The closeness to our best friend, God, should be just as anticipated, even more. He is by far more important than any other relationship that we could ever dream of having. The conversations that we have with our friends are very important to us, as they are also important to our friends. So also should be, the shared conversations with God. We must consider the importance of talking with the *One* that loves us *the most*.

Communicating with God is as easy, as simply talking to Him any time or any place, as we would any other person. When we're in our car driving somewhere, or standing in line at a checkout counter, anyplace. We should always remember that His intimacy with us is so intense that He actually knows everything about us, even our most inner thoughts or feelings.

We shouldn't let God become out of sight – out of mind. If we want to have a *Close Relationship* with God, we have to become *close* to Him. He is already close to us. He is patiently waiting for us to make the move to get closer to Him. We can not find anyone that is more important or more interesting to spend our time with.

As we start to get closer to God, we find so many things to talk to Him about. At times when we need to open up to someone – He's always there to listen to anything we want to say or share with Him. He *cares*, and is *interested* in anything and everything we want to talk to Him about. Not only will we feel good about having shared things, but we shouldn't be surprised if we get a response.

Church is also another means of getting closer to God. Going to church isn't because we find ourselves better than others; it is because of our need for direction, to become closer to Our Creator, to take the time to show Him our appreciation for all He does for us, to give Him reverence, by taking time to give Him His well deserved praise.

> "No, O people,
> the LORD has already told you what is good,
> and this is what he requires:
> to do what is right,
> to love mercy,
> and to walk humbly with your God."
> (Mic 6:8)

Chapter 7

REDEMPTION

CALVARY
(Golgatha)

"God showed us how much he loved us by sending his only Son into the world so that we might have eternal life through him. This is real love. It is not that we loved God, but that he loved us and sent his Son as a sacrifice to take away our sins." (1 John 4:9,10)

REDEMPTION

R esolved was God's love, to rescue us from our sins;

E ver inclusive, from our parents' origin.

D ecided to send us, His only Begotten Son;

E ternal relief from all our burdens, Christ would don.

M indful of our consequences, rescued us from strife;

P romising us through belief, an everlasting life.

T ormented, spat upon, flogged, and unjustly crucified;

I mpassioned to save us, and set us free, He died.

O ur own achievements, were not enough to pay the price;

N eeded to recover, was Jesus's Holy sacrifice.

REDEMPTION

Our Redemption was in God's plan even before man was created, for God knew that we would have to be saved because of our sinful nature. Being saved not by our own capacity, but through Divine Grace. Our only means of Redemption and Salvation would have to come from God Himself through His Son the Christ.

It was foretold in the Scriptures, that a Savior, our Messiah, would be conceived by a virgin from the Royal Family of David, and his name would be Immanuel, meaning 'God is with us'.

"The mother bore Him in her womb, let us bear Him in our hearts."
– St Augustine –

The setting for the birth of our Savior was not that of Royalty. Not at all what we would expect for a Divine birth. The little town of Bethlehem, was actually that, a little village. Mary and Joseph were refused a room at the Inn, and had to conform to a stable for shelter.

A group of Shepherds were startled when an angel came to them, and the radiance of the Lord's glory surrounded them. The angel gave them the good news that the Savior, the Messiah had been born that night in Bethlehem, in the city of David, and they would recognize Him, as He was wrapped in strips of cloth, and they would find Him in a manger.

Whenever a star is mentioned in the Old Testament, it seems to refer to an angel. It is then properly fitting that the star the three wise men followed, was an angel directing them to the birthplace of Jesus. The wise men had brought with them gifts of gold, frankincense, and myrrh. The gifts represented Royalty, Humility, and Divinity. The gifts were quite suitable for the occasion, because *Divine Love* had come down from Heaven.

> "For God so loved the world that he gave his only Son, so that everyone who believes in him will not perish but have eternal life." (Jn 3:16)

God sent His Son, the promised One, because we were utterly helpless, and in order to buy us freedom – for us who were sinners and slaves to the law. God was pleased to live in Christ, and through Him He could reconcile everything to Himself. The Lord could then adopt us as His very own children. This peace and freedom between Heaven and Earth would only come by the means of Christ's blood shed on the cross, which opened the door to the world, and revealed our long awaited *hope*. Christ through His cross, purchased our happiness. Where can we find true meaningful happiness, in other than Him?

$$1 \text{ Cross} + 3 \text{ Nails} = 4\text{-Given.}$$

"For since we were restored to friendship with God by the death of his Son while we were enemies, we will certainly be delivered from eternal punishment by his life."
(Ro 5:10,11a)

Prior to His crucifixion, He was treated harshly and was oppressed, but never said a word. A lamb, the lamb of God, being led to slaughter. He never opened His mouth, as a sheep is silent before the shearers. From the trial at prison He was led away to His death. No one among the people realized that He was dying for their sins, and was actually suffering their punishment, for He had done no wrong. Although buried as a criminal, He was put in a grave of a rich man.

He died for us, every single one of us, so that we no longer would live to please ourselves, but live to please Christ. As we live to please Him, we become new persons. As He came to bring peace to the world, His coming would also bring strife and division. A division even in families, as not everyone would accept Him and follow His teachings.

Just as Moses lifted up a bronze snake on a pole in the wilderness so that the people that had been bitten by the snakes would recover, so too was Jesus lifted upon a pole so that sinners would recover. Through His blood He brought us into the very presence of God, that we would be blameless as we stand before Him without a single fault. But we must continue to stand firmly, not drift away, and believe in this truth, for it is in believing in Him that we gain eternal life.

"The Scriptures tell us, 'The first man Adam, became a living person,' But the last Adam – that is Christ is a life-giving Spirit. What came first was the natural body, then the spiritual body comes later. Adam, the first man, was made from the dust of the earth, while Christ, the second man, came from heaven. Every human being has an earthly body just like Adam's, but our heavenly bodies will be just like Christ's. Just as we are now like Adam, the man of the earth, so we will someday be like Christ, the man from heaven." (1 Co 15:45-49)

"When Adam sinned, sin entered the entire human race. Adam's sin brought death, so death spread to everyone, for everyone sinned. Yes, people sinned even before the law was given. And though there was no law to break, since it had not yet been given, they all died anyway – even though they did not disobey an explicit commandment of God, as Adam did. What a contrast between Adam and Christ, who was yet to come! And what a difference between our sin and God's generous gift of forgiveness to many through God's bountiful gift. And the result of God's gracious gift is very different from the result of that one man's sin. For Adam's sin led to condemnation, but we have the free gift of being accepted by God, even though we are guilty of many sins. The sin of this one man, Adam, caused death to rule over us, but all who receive God's wonderful, gracious gift of righteousness will live in triumph over sin and death through this one man, Jesus Christ.

Yes, Adam's one sin brought condemnation upon everyone, but Christ's one act of righteousness makes all people right in God's sight and gives them life. Because one person disobeyed God, many people became sinners. But because one other person obeyed God, many people will be made right in God's sight.

God's law was given so that all people could see how sinful they were. But as people sinned more and more, God's wonderful kindness became more abundant. So just as sin ruled over all people and brought them to death, now God's wonderful kindness rules instead, giving us right standing with God and resulting in eternal life through Jesus Christ our Lord." (Ro 5:12-21)

After Christ died to cleanse us from the mortal stain of sin, He then went to Heaven to sit in the place of honor at the right hand of the Majestic God of Heaven.

"For every time you eat this bread and drink this cup,
you are announcing the Lord's death until He comes again."
(1 Co 11:26)

DELIVERANCE – SALVATION

God's design and purpose for His plan of Salvation was intended to be very simple and easy to understand. Up until a few generations ago, His message remained fairly constant. We are now living in a very changed environment. Everything has changed, and is changing drastically. People have become opinionated and diversified. Their words to some, seem to mean more than God's Word. So much diversity and liberalism has entered our homes , our schools, our places of work, our politics, and even our churches. Where there is diversity and opinions, confusion reigns. Where there is confusion, the Devil reigns. He loves confusion. God's simple message however has not changed, the one and *only* way that we can be rescued from our sinfulness is through Jesus, His Son. He told us that He was *The Way,* that He was the *Truth* and that He was the *Life.*

> "We are all infected and impure with sin. When we proudly display our righteous deeds, we find they are but filthy rags. Like autumn leaves, we wither and fall. And our sins, like the wind, sweep us away." (Isa 64:6)

Unlike what many believe, we cannot gain Heaven on our own, through our own achievements, or something we can boast about, or take credit for. Only through *grace*, an undeserved supernatural gift from the benevolent nature, and the extreme love of God, can we be assisted in achieving salvation, the salvation of our souls.

> "God saved you by his special favor when you believed. And you can't take credit for this; it is a gift from God. Salvation is not a reward for the good things we have done, so none of us can boast about it." (Eph 2:8,9)

The Bible tells us that there is no salvation in anyone else, that there is no other name that we can call on to save us. It was only due to God's kindness, mercy and love that we were saved, otherwise we would not have had any *hope* – our hope came through His Son that paid the price for our sinfulness, not in any way to condemn us, but to save us, and cleanse us. This hope and joy became a reality by our trusting, having faith in, and believing that it was Christ that became our Savior, the propitiation, the means of appeasing our sins, and that He opened the door for us to share a life with Him and His Father for all eternity.

> "I assure you, those who listen to my message and believe in God who sent me have eternal life. They will never be condemned for their sins, but they have already passed from death into life." (Jn 5:24)

Our hope of Salvation was made possible only through His Resurrection. As Jesus died for our Deliverance and Salvation, we also must die of our old ways and rise up in a new life in Christ, a life that will also resurrect us to the joy of an everlasting life to be shared with Him that loves us so much – that He died for us.

"In love the Saviour died for me. He shed His blood upon the tree. That I a ransomed soul might be, With Him in Heaven, eternally!"
– Author Unknown –

"And endurance develops strength of character in us, and character strengthens our confident expectation of salvation." (Ro 5:4)

ACCEPTANCE

Acceptance is the act or the process of taking something being offered; the condition of something being accepted or acceptable; a favorable reception; approval; mindfulness.

When something is being offered, we have a choice of acceptance or resistance. Acceptance shows willingness to receive. While resistance shows non-approval of what is being offered.

Many people literally *die* to belong to fraternities, sororities, or many other organizations. Some for notoriety, some for friendship, and some for power. They will do *whatever* it takes to be accepted by these groups. They want to be part of a society of their own. One that is different from the norm, and they will go along with any of the rules and regulations that govern them, no matter what the cost.

"There are two principles of established acceptance in morals; first, that self-interest is the mainspring of all our actions, and secondly, that utility is the test of their value."
– Charles Caleb Colton –

When it comes time to accept the gift that God is offering us, do we have that same kind of elation and excitement? Do we show a longing, an anticipation or excitement to receive that offer; and to do whatever it takes to follow the path awaiting us if we accept this Gift? Accepting or resisting is a decision, one that can have a dramatic influence on our eternal life.

> "If you bring a peace offering to the LORD from the herd or flock, whether to fulfill a vow or as a freewill offering, you must offer an animal that has no physical defects of any kind." (Lev 22:21)

What the Bible is probably trying to tell us in the preceding verse, is that by accepting God's ways we must willingly cleanse ourselves of our spiritual defects, as our offering to Him. Scriptures tell us that it is easier for a camel to go through the eye of a needle than it is for a rich man to enter God's Kingdom. If we really desire, and want to acquire something, we must be willing to do whatever it takes to achieve or receive it.

The Bible also tells us that if we believe in our heart and confess with our mouth that Jesus is Lord, and that God raised Him from the dead, that we will be saved. The following is a testimony that can be said, alone, or with others, to choose Christ as the Lord and Saviour:

> Dear God, I admit that I am a sinner and can not go to Heaven based on my own works. Thank you for sending Jesus to pay the punishment for my sins by dying on the cross, then raising Him to life again. I turn now from my sins and receive Christ as my Lord and Saviour. Amen.

REPENTANCE

Repentance is the remorse or contrition we have for our past conduct or sin; the act or process of repenting; a state of being penitent with amendment to life; penitence.

"Our repentance is not so much regret for the ill we have done,

as fear of the ill that may happen to us in consequence."
— Francois de La Rochefoucauld —

Repentance is a cleansing process, as it cleanses our conscience. In the New Testament, the word repentance is applied from the Greek word *metanoia*, which has a compound meaning of *to think differently after*. Repentance, or metanoia, would bring about a change of mind and heart, or a change of consciousness.

"Repentance may begin instantly
but reformation often requires a sphere of years."
— Henry Ward Beecher —

We are all sinners, and have rebelled against God, and against His commands and regulations, but the Lord always fulfills His promise of unfailing love to those who keep His commands. This is why we must not allow ourselves to follow a self-destructive path. Once we have found God, and then turn away from Him, is like nailing the Son of God to the Cross again by rejecting Him.

"Mere sorrow, which sweeps and sits still, is not repentance,
Repentance is sorrow converted into action;
into a movement toward a new and better life."
— M. R. Vincent —

Jesus said that in order for us to get into the Kingdom of Heaven, that we should become like little children. Little children are innocent. God has been very kind, tolerant an patient with us – he has given us much time to turn away from our sinfulness. Our time is limited, another reason why we should take advantage of the time we have left is for self-restoration, gaining for ourselves a new heart and a new spirit. It is from the turning from our wicked ways and doing what is just and right that we will live, and live in a peacefulness with others and with God. A peacefulness, a calmness, a serenity, that has a ripple effect.

> "True repentance means making amends with the person
> when at all possible."
> – Lawana Blackwell –

True repentance should not include show or pretense, but what comes from confessing our wrong doings and sins to God and asking Him forgiveness. It should start by testing and examining our ways. We should have tears, sorrow and grief for the wrongs we have done. Confession is also called: conversion, forgiveness, penance or reconciliation. The confession of our sins must include repentance and the intention to make reparation. God will refresh the humble and contrite, and give new courage to those with repentant hearts.

"Instead, let us test and examine our ways. Let us turn again in repentance to the Lord." (Lam 3:40)

"For God can use sorrow in our lives to help us turn away from sin and seek salvation. We will never regret that kind of sorrow. But sorrow without repentance is the kind that results in death." (2 Co 7:10)

"In the same way, there is joy in the presence of God's angels when even one sinner repents." (Lk 15:10)

ATONEMENT

Atonement is amends or reparation made for an injury or a wrong; satisfactory reparation for an offense; appeasement; reconciliation; concord.

The word atonement was a word invented from Hebrew and Greek manuscripts to more thoroughly explain the doctrine of the sacrifice of Christ, which accomplished the remission of sin and also the reconciliation of man to God. The word came to be by the joining of the two words *at* and *onement* – combined together giving a singular meaning to the three words reconciliation, propitiation, and forgiveness.

Other words that are used to denote atonement, would be:

>Expiation – to atone for.
>Reconciliation – to sit again with.

Found in the Hebrew Scriptures, is man's reconciliation with God because of the transgression of the covenant. In the New Testament it refers to Christ's Redemptive incarnation, life, sufferings and death, which brought the reconciliation of God and man.

There are three Christian metaphors in understanding atonement, which may vary according to denominational or theological perspective:

>*Chistus Victor* – the theory that the Son of Man came for the purpose of giving His life for many, liberating mankind from the slavery to Satan, and thus giving His own life as the ransom.
>
>*Satisfaction Theory* – Because of a debt to our Sovereign God Himself, only a perfect sacrifice could satisfy our sinful insults given to God – affronts to His honor. Jesus who became God and man, was the perfect sacrifice.
>
>*Moral Influence* – Through God's great love for us, shown to us by the demonstration of Jesus' death on the Cross, makes us respond, and transforms us by the power of the Holy Spirit.

The wonderful reason for atonement, is that it brings about restitution, it sanctifies, and it purifies.

Christ died as atonement for our sins. He actually carried all of our sins in His body and to the Cross to satisfy God's anger against us, and also that we could live for what is right and be free from sin. But those sins were ours, not His. We should also do *our* part in the atonement of those sins, by *our* reparation, and *our* own self-sacrifice. In this way we can show God, that not only do we appreciate what He has done for us through Christ, but we can do our part in showing Him atonement for our own sinfulness.

"For even I, the Son of Man,
came here not to be served but to serve others,
and to give my life as a ransom for many."
(Mk 10:45)

"But Christ has rescued us
from the curse pronounced by the law.
When he was hung on the cross,
he took upon himself the curse for our wrongdoing."
(Gal 3:13a,b)

Chapter 8

CHOICE

SCALE OF JUSTICE

"I know all the things you do, that you are neither hot or cold. I wish you were one or the other! But since you are like lukewarm water, I will spit you out of my mouth!" (Rev 3:15-16)

CHOICE

C arefully selecting, from the things at hand;

H aving so much to sort, and to comprehend.

O pting for maybe this, that, or the other;

I t's difficult, to elect, or smother.

C alculating, through all the alternatives;

E merging at last, as to be decisive.

DISCERNMENT

Discernment is the keenness in detecting, distinguishing, or selecting; quickness or accuracy in discriminating; acumen; perception; penetration; insight.

> *Acumen* – characteristic penetration combined with keen judgment.
> *Discrimination* – the ability to find or select the excellent, or what is true.
> *Insight* – depth of discernment, and understanding sympathy.
> *Penetration* – a searching mind that goes beyond the reach of the senses.
> *Perception* – a quick discernment of delicate feelings.

Discernment, in Christian application, describes the process of being able to discern God's will for one's life. It is a search of our interior, or conscience, to find answers to the questions of right or wrong, as it applies to our way of living. Our conscience is our *inner core* that identifies our *choices*, either good or evil, through right reasoning and proper teachings. It is a spiritual influence that guides our will toward what is good, or what is evil. It is also applied towards finding a proper path, or deciding about one's vocation.

Charism comes from the Greek word *charismata*, which implies a *free gift*, as well as other spiritual gifts, and also answers to prayers, or eternal life. Charismata are then special gifts that make obvious to us the work of God, which He does through the Holy Spirit, for our common good. The gifts always show direction to the giver.

Since Our Creator had willed that we would have communication with the angels, and the angels being of two kinds, we then have the influence of both the good and the evil angels, all trying to get our attention, and desperately trying to sway us in their direction.

In order to use discernment we must acquire the proper knowledge to be able to evaluate our decisions. We can learn what is right by looking at the Ten Commandments, and learn as well, what is wrong, by looking at the Seven Deadly Sins. The decision is then made according to our *free will* given to us from God.

When God created us, one of the most generous and important gifts that was given us, was the gift of free will. A free will , so that we could be our own person, letting *us* decide and determine for ourselves, what we as humans want to select as our preferences to mold our own way of living. A capability or faculty of making a choice according to reason among several alternatives. It underlies the fact of moral responsibility. This means that our choices, ultimately are voluntary, free of pressures, and not determined by external causes. Through this free will we can reject God's grace and His gift of eternal life. Through this gift of free will we can recognize the place of God in our lives, and respond to His invitation to live in His light, free from sin, or enter into darkness. What we choose – is what we get!

Having been given this wonderful freedom, we were also made to be responsible for each of these decisions, or choices. Some of these choices can be either good for us, or maybe not quite so beneficial, and sometimes very harmful to our well-being, or even be very detrimental to our eternal destiny. We not only have to choose *wisely,* but we have to choose *seriously*!

> "Life consists not in holding good cards but in playing those you hold well."   – Josh Billings –

As we go through our mortal journey we are faced with innumerable choices, some not as easy as others to decide. Before making a choice, or choices, we must *learn* to be knowledgeable, and we must *learn* how to use discernment. While learning to be knowledgeable we acquire and accumulate proper information, and look intently at the facts, and weigh them with significance, before we can justifiably, intelligently, and more importantly, *morally* make a proper and right decision. Most choices and decisions are generally more effective, if given the proper amount of time for reflection.

> "There are two ways to look at life and the world. We can see the good or the bad, the beautiful or the ugly. Both are there, and what we focus and choose to see is what brings us feelings of joy or feelings of despair." – Lloyd Newell –

We are living in a time, where so many people are purposely trying their best, and with all their resources, to influence us to buy, try something, or accept their way of thinking or belief.

The ever so powerful, manipulative media, which seeks its self-interest, will do anything it possibly can to capture the public's attention. For their own gain, purpose, and self-gratification, some, are for the most part, outstandingly bias or completely opposed to the facts. This diversion can affect, and lead to so many changes in people's lives. Changes that wouldn't have been realized if the truth had not been intentionally distorted, or if the actual facts had been properly told. Will the media ever realize, and admit that they purposely misled so many people and situations, by not being entirely truthful or accurate? All for the sake of drawing attention to themselves, for the purpose of trying to get better ratings, and selling more *ads, magazines,* or *newspapers – looking out more for the bottom line, than the truthfulness of what they are conveying.* Whatever happened to decency and dignity? Some are honest in their message. Bless them! It is because of all these diversions and alterations to the facts, that we must be selective of what it is that we read, watch or listen to. We can't allow ourselves to be that easily swayed. When we leave the window open – bugs come in! We must be cautious of what gets in!

The devil is not without his charms.

Throughout the thousands of years that man has existed, the meaning of morality has not changed – people's idea, or interpretation of morality has changed.. What we are told as being *O. K.,* or *Cool,* and of some things that are being taught at some of our schools by some of the teachers, may be acceptable to some, but it certainly doesn't mean that these things are morally right. Just because the majority wants something – doesn't make it moral, nor right. It was for that reason that it was so difficult to find a handful of people so that God would not destroy a City.

> *There are reasons for doing good.*
> *There are many excuses for doing bad.*

"True understanding is possible only when we are fully conscious of our thought, not as an operative observer on this thought, but completely and without the intervention of a choice." – Jiddu Krishnamurti –

Some of the advertisements of today are quite dreadful! They leave almost nothing to the imagination, and shown so that children can see them. Violence is glorified. Promiscuity, sex, and genders are mixed, not only at a rampage, but have become common-day occurrences, and enjoyably acceptable in our society. The pop-culture media are pandering to, and targeting the young people to get their attention towards food, clothing, music, consumer goods, electronics, idols, sex, homosexuality, and even religious belief. The pandering newspaper tabloids are pandering to a public craving for scandals. This is why discernment is such a beneficial and necessary tool. We must avail ourselves of it so we can learn and apply its principles. We must exercise wisdom and good judgment in all of our daily decisions.

Not too many people today talk about the subject of discernment. Why? Because most people are living a *liberal* life in the fast lane. They like to make fast decisions. Many have been used to accepting what the majority wants, or seem to want, or are being told they want, especially when it comes to politics. Every one of us is special, and in being special, we need not conform to the norm, just for the sake of being *accepted.* We should choose what's *right* for us – and live our own life according to the proper principles.

> "The fundamental qualities for good execution of a plan is first: intelligence; then discernment and judgment, which enable one to recognize the best method as to attain it; the singleness of purpose; and, lastly, what is most essential of all, will-stubborn will."   – Ferdinand Foch –

Horses are sometimes seen with *blinders* attached to their bridle, so as to curtail side vision. When applied, these blinders restrict the horse's vision to only what is in front of it, and keeps it from any distraction from whatever could be seen on either side. Blinders play a very essential part in focusing on our values. By utilizing them they help us to see, and stay on, a proper direction needed to keep us from all the worldly things that are placed there to distract and tempt us.

Whatever we choose in life becomes our master. We can become slaves to impurity and lawlessness, or choose to be slaves of righteousness and live a holier life that results in eternal life. We must find the truth and remain faithful to the things that we learn, and find trust and honesty in what we are being taught. Christ, God Himself, was our best teacher. His Word in Scripture is a Holy inspiration, and is our useful tool to teach us what is true, what is wrong in our lives, how it can straighten us out, and show us what to do, and do what is right. God gave us these tools in order to prepare us in every way so that we would be fully equipped for every good thing that God is expecting from us, what *we* should want for ourselves, and what *we* should want to give Him. We have that choice to either serve ourselves in giving in to our worldly desires, or we can serve God.

Life has rules –we must learn to live by them.

We can sin against Gods's love in many different ways:

> *Aceda* – better known as spiritual sloth, is when we go as far as refusing the joy that comes from God, and be driven back by divine goodness.

Hatred of God – derives from pride. It contrasts the love of God, denies its goodness, and presumes to curse it as the one who prohibits sins and imposes consequences and punishments.

Indifference – when we neglect or refuse to manifest the divine good will; when we fail to examine or study its prevenient merit and deny its power.

Ingratitude – when we don't, or refuse to admit divine goodness or charity, and don't reciprocate the Divine love given to us.

Lukewarmness – When we hesitate or neglect in replying to God's divine love; it can express a refusal of giving oneself over to the prompting of charity.

Each of us have set a path before us that *seems* right, but although it *might* seem right, it doesn't always lead us in the proper direction. What is required is an informed conscience in order to find ourselves on the right and proper path. Morality gives us a healthy conscience. A healthy conscience will produce good fruit, and an unhealthy conscience will produce bad fruit. We all have the responsibility of becoming more familiar with the teachings of Scripture or of the church on moral and religious issues in order to properly form our conscience according to what is true and good for us, and also good for those around us.

People are in hell because of what they have *loved* too much avarice, envy, pride, gluttony, lust, sloth, or wrath.

Is anything worth more than concentrating on the goodness of our soul? What would we trade Heaven for? What benefit would we obtain by gaining the whole world and losing our soul? If we refuse to serve or obey God, who then will we serve and obey? We have to chart our own course. We were created with a will and ability to make these choices by applying wisdom. We should fill our thoughts about heaven, and not about things of this world.

We can all have a change of heart. St Paul used to scoff at the name of Christ, and hunted down his people, and harmed them in every way he could. But God had mercy on him because he had done those things in ignorance and unbelief. God is so gracious! If we just believe in Him, He can fill us all with faith, grace us with His love, and our lives can also turn around, like Paul's was. God tells us that if we hear Him calling, and open the door, that He will come in and share a meal with us as friends.

"Watch out for attacks from the Devil, your great enemy. He prowls around like a roaring lion, looking for some victim to devour. Take a firm stand against him, and be strong in your faith." (1 Pe 5:8,9a)

PRIORITY

Priority is the preferred order of, or the right to be considered before others because of, importance, merit, privilege, or urgency; one of many items ranked to urgency or importance; the quality or state of being prior; a superiority in position, privilege, or rank; something meriting or given attention ahead of competing alternatives; precedence.

"Priority is a function of context." – Steven R. Covey –

Choices, choices, choices, we have so many choices. *We live our lives according to our priorities.* Every decision we make is based and governed by what our priority happens to be at that moment.

Priority then brings us to a decision in making a choice or choices. What we favor most captures our attention and our priority, which leads us to ultimately make a choice.

Our priorities are sometimes based on urgencies or importance, but most of the time they are categorized according to our preferences, or our *likes* and *dislikes*, because we are more prone to prioritize something we like over something we do not like. Our priority then brings us to a decision in choice making. What we favor the most is what captures our attention and our priority, and leads us to a particular choice being made.

> "Make service your first priority, not success
> and success will follow."
> – Author Unknown –

In order to have the proper precedence of priorities and choices, we can only achieve that by virtue of true wisdom, in which we will find a joyful life.

> "It's fantastic knowing you're going to die;
> it really makes having priorities
> and trying to follow them very real to you."
> – Susan Sontaq –

Through our journey of many choices, if we chose to do right, it was because *that* was a priority at the time. If we chose to do wrong, whatever it was, *was* a priority at that particular moment.

In order to show God priority in our lives, we must show Him that He merits our time, our love, and especially our attention, above all other worldly competing alternatives.

> "God makes Man, His first priority.
> But Man makes God his last resort."
> – Ceasar Rodriguez –

The all inclusive and accumulated choices gathered to form the book we will have written for ourselves, however good or bad will determine our destiny.

HOW TO FIND OUR FAITH AND DESTINY

When we plan to take a trip, we first find a place of interest and the location we want to go to. We decide what we want to do or see there. We determine how long we are intending to stay, and who and what we should bring with us. Then decide how we're going to get there.

A person has to prepare for a working career, for the fulfillment of being able to enjoy his type of work according to his talents and capabilities. He wants to arrive at that certain stage in life, where he has now acquired that applicable knowledge necessary to reap the results intended. All this preparation involved much time, studies, much effort, and much work. It is not unusual to study for a specialized career for two to eight, or even more years. Whatever is needed to accomplish a specific goal. All this special training for a profession that may only last a mere forty to sixty years, if that long.

Let's take a look now, as to why we are in existence. It isn't only for the reason of taking trips or enjoying a career; it is to get ready for the *inevitable* trip, and that long lasting *career* that awaits us. A trip and career that will last forever, for eternity. Yet, in comparing the eternal destination to the vacation trip, or to the extensive earthly career, most people are still more concerned with their present itinerary.

Where is our logic? Where is our priorities? What are we focusing on? Surely the career and the trips and vacations are important, and sometimes very necessary. But which is obviously, ultimately more important, and will last the longest? The eternal destination requires only a *one-way* ticket, it has to be used at a very *specific* time, and it is *not refundable*.

How do we find our Faith and Destiny? We find those answers in the same manner that we obtain the information about taking a trip or traveling, or how we go about studying for a career. First, and most importantly, we must accept the importance and necessity of this endeavor, as being above anything else that could be attempted or achieved. We must devote the time to study and accumulate knowledge in regards to where it is that we are going, and what is needed to get there. Happiness comes from a decision – so do our choices and destiny.

In trying to find our faith and our destiny, we shouldn't trust, or rely on our own judgement, but instead seek whatever is needed to justify the proper outcome of having decided wisely.

By having faith and believing in God's message about His Son, we have His word to assure us that heaven is our destiny. The alternate is also very clear in the Bible to those who don't respond.

> A saint is a sinner who discovers God's love.
> – Author Unknown –

At any moment our departure can be realized. It is *vital* that we must be forever mindful of our faith and destiny.

> Finding happiness – is from the inside out.

We should prepare for our spiritual growth, in the same manner as we do horticulturally. Cultivating, planting seeds, pulling weeds, nourishing and enriching the soil. After the preparation and planting has been accomplished, we can be patient for the harvest.

> "Turn my eyes from worthlessness, and give me life through your word." (Ps 119:37)

The Bible, like a lighthouse, is what directs each of us to our Saviour and a heavenly harbor. In order to erase the sins of mankind, God required a sacrifice acceptable to Himself. We could not have been saved in any other way. This is where we find our faith. It is by *accepting* and *believing* this very simple message. Reading the Bible will keep us from sin, and sin will keep us away from the Bible. Again it is a decision.

> "Die to earthly things. The Saints in Heaven, comprehending

by the same divine light these mysteries, are astonished at themselves for not having paid more attention to them during their life." (Gal 2:20)

We have to soften our hearts, and come to God, surrendering ourselves to Him, as little children.

> "I listen to his little prayers at night with quiet joy –
> And when I hear the pure in heart I hear a little boy.
> He hasn't reached the age as yet to question and to doubt;
> He gravely takes his mother's words and that's what life's about.
> Each day is gold, a shining thing without a wrong allow –
> And when I hold the pure in heart I hold a little boy."
> – Gwen Belson Taylor –

We have been called to start enjoying this heavenly freedom now. We will find this freedom, not in trying to satisfy our sinful nature, but in the freedom to serve one another with love.

> "Is anyone thirsty? Come and drink – even if you have no money! Come, take your choice of wine or milk – it's all free! Why spend your money on food that does not give you strength? Why pay for food that does you no good? Listen, and I will tell you where to get food that is good for the soul!" (Isa 55:1,2)

In learning the truth from Scriptures, we have to throw away our old evil nature, and our former way of life, which is full of lust and deception, and replace it with a spiritual renewal of our thoughts and attitudes. We will be blessed by hearing, listening, and reading the Word of God, but more importantly by putting it into practice. We do this because we want to become a creature of God's likeness, righteous, holy and true, so that we may, and be ready, to live new lives. We also want to help our loved ones, and as many others as we can, by sharing with them spiritually.

"I, wisdom, live together with good judgment. I know where to discover knowledge and discernment. All who fear the LORD will hate evil. That is why I hate pride, arrogance, corruption, and perverted speech. Good advice and success belong to me. Insight and strength are mine."
(Pr 8:12-14)

Whatever we accumulate here on earth will be but worthless matter. What will matter most, will be the treasures that we will have stored in heaven. Our treasures will be safe there, not to be stolen or destroyed. Our hearts and thoughts will be wherever our treasures will be.

"Then Jesus said, 'Come to me, all of you who are weary and carry heavy burdens, and I will give you rest. Take my yoke upon you. Let me teach you, because I am humble and gentle, and you will find rest for your souls. For my yoke fits perfectly, and the burden I give you is light.'"
(Mt 11:28-30)

"Man is asked to make of himself what he is supposed to become to fulfill his destiny."   – Paul Tillick –

OBEDIENCE

The act, condition, example, fact, or quality, of being obedient to a wish, request, demand, or command. To have acquiescence; to consent or comply without protest; to assent; to express agreement; to consent. In some instances obedience might be described as submission, compliance, or submissive compliance. *Conformity* would be different as it is a behavior to go along with the majority. *Obedience* is usually related to social influence or control and submission. It is the willingness, the ability, or the caring to comply with the request of another.

Obedience is one of the greatest virtues.
All other virtues are through the obedience of God, who is Love.

It is surprising that people have been so obedient in the presence of figures of authority. Most of the time the compliance to authority is the norm and not the exception.

> "Through Christ, God has given us the privilege and authority to tell Gentiles everywhere what God has done for them, so that they will believe and obey him, bringing glory to his name." (Ro 1:57)

Obedience is regarded as a moral virtue in most cultures. Children throughout the ages have been taught and expected to be obedient to their elders. Obedience and honoring of parents and authority has declined since the Second World War, due to the exposure to a degrading, liberal and permissive society. Obedience is now regarded by many as less favorable than individual judgment, for moral decisions.

Obedience starts with the modification of behavior in children. Parents try many types of techniques to achieve a satisfactory goal.

The gradual training given to soldiers and servicemen to instill order and obedience, through persistent effort, grows in effect to such a point that an untrained person could not follow those given orders. The training that prompts, a simple order, that can place a soldier into the midst of gunfire. All due to the *obedience* of a superior. That same *obedience* that Abraham was willing to abide by, in sacrificing his son Isaac.

> "If they listen and obey God, then they will be blessed with prosperity throughout their lives." (Job 36:11)

To be obedient we must become humble, gentle, docile, manageable, and easily taught, and able to teach ourselves and our children the principles of obedience to all authority.

After Jesus was found in the Temple at Jerusalem, he returned home with His parents, and was obedient to them. It was also through the obedience to God His Father, that Christ suffered and died to redeem us.

"So even though Jesus was God's Son, he learned obedience from the things he suffered." (Heb 5:8)

The Scriptures remind us of the good that comes from obedience. Through Noah, Moses, Mary, Paul, and so many more that listened and obeyed, God's purpose was fulfilled. Will we listen to, and obey God, so that He will fulfill whatever is intended through us?

Obedience is better than sacrifice.

God made it very clear about obeying His Commandments. The Bible tells us that if we obey His laws and teach them, we will be regarded great in His Kingdom. If we however break the smallest of His Commandments and teach others to do the same, then we will be considered as the least in His sight.

"And this world is fading away along with everything it craves. But if you do the will of God, you will live forever."
(1 Jn 2:17)

PERSEVERANCE – PERSISTENCY

Perseverance is holding to course of action, purpose or belief without giving way; the persistence in any enterprise that one undertakes, in spite of influences of opposition; being steady in a course of action even among difficulties; to go beyond obstacles or discouragement; doggedness; persistency; steadfastness; tenacity.

Persistency is quite similar in meaning – while perseverance would imply a follow-through, persistency would imply repetitiousness.

In theology, it would imply continuing to the end in the state of grace, which would lead to eternal salvation.

A rock or an object in the middle of a stream will cause the flow of water to take a different course. The same is true with daily living. There are many things that come up during the course of the day or throughout our lives, that tend to divert whatever was expected, and force it to flow towards a new direction.

> "The drops of rain make a hole in the stone not by violence but by oft falling."   – Lucretius –

We must be able and ready to utilize perseverance in our lives. Life today is getting more and more complicated – filled with obstacles. We must have determination, patience, and stick-to-it-tiveness in order to work through, deal with, or overcome some of the difficulties that face us.

> "When the going gets tough, the tough get going."
> – Joseph Patrick Kennedy –

> "It's not that I am so smart, it's just that I stay with the problems longer."
> – Albert Einstein –

We are not alone going through hardships. God is always there for us to turn to. His help and guidance makes it easier for us to persevere. Not too long ago I saw a teenager that had a T-Shirt with an imprinted saying that read, "Don't worry about tomorrow – God will be there." We mustn't forget to ask for His help. But God wants us to work hard to prove ourselves to Him. We should labor until all love of self within us has died.

> "Perseverance is the hard work you do after you get tired of doing the hard work you already did."
> – Newt Gingrich –

> "The greatest oak was once a little nut who held its ground."
> – Author Unknown –

> "....so run from all these evil things, and follow what is right and good. Pursue a godly life, along with faith, love, perseverance, and gentleness." (1Ti 6:11)

Abraham was persistent when pleading to save the people of Sodom and Gomorrah, because God saw them to be extremely evil. Abraham asked God if He would spare them if fifty innocent people were found, then forty-five, then forty, then thirty, then twenty, then because of Abraham's perseverance and persistency, God saved the people because of *ten*.

> "The toughest thing about success is that you've got to keep on being a success." – Irving Berlin –

We must exercise this same persistency when praying. If we are not alert and pray with tenacity, temptation will overpower us, because even though our spirit might be willing, our body is weak.

Answers to prayers don't always come instantly, although sometimes they might. Some require persistency, as Jesus explained in a parable, that we shouldn't give up with prayer. If we keep on knocking, or asking long enough we will receive an answer.

> "And so I tell you, keep on asking, and you will be given what you ask for. Keep on looking, and you will find. Keep on knocking, and the door will be opened. For everyone who asks, receives. Everyone who seeks, finds. And the door is opened to everyone who knocks." (Lk 11:9,10)

DEVOTION

Devotion is an ardent attachment of affection; an act or state of religious observance as a group, and especially in private; paying homage or showing honor; ardent affection; dedication; fidelity; piety; prayers; religious ardor, fervor or praise; supplications; worship; zealous attachment.

Through devotion, a reverent manner of praying, we show our desire to dedicate ourselves to God's service. Prayer humbles us, and leads us to animate ourselves fully to God's will – to Him Who is the core of sanctity. Prayer brings us to experience consolation.

> The desire of the moth for the star.
> Of the night for the morrow.
> The devotion to something afar
> from the sphere of our sorrow."
> – Percy Bysshe Shelley –

"So our daily worship of God is not really the process of gradual acquisition of him, but the daily process of surrendering ourselves, removing all obstacles to union and extending our consciousness of him in devotion and service."   – Rabindranath Tagore –

> "True strength lies in submission
> which permits one to dedicate his life,
> through devotion, to something beyond himself."
> – Henry Miller –

"This, and this alone, is Christianity, a universal holiness in every part of life, a heavenly wisdom in all our actions, not conforming to the spirit and temper of the world but turning all worldly enjoyments into means of piety and devotion to God."   – William Law –

"We should live in this evil world with self-control, right conduct, and devotion to God, while we look forward to that wonderful event when the glory of our great God and Savior, Jesus Christ, will be revealed. (Tit 2:12,13)

PRAYER – FASTING

Prayer is an act, instance, or practice of praying; expression of human hopes, needs, or thoughts as directed to God; an arrangement, or formulation of words used in speaking or making an appeal to God; an earnest appeal; the offering of adoration, thanksgiving, confession, or supplication to God; a plea; a request; entreaty.

>We must pray like it depends on God,
>and work like it depends on us.

>The dependence of prayer is essential
>to safeguard against temptation.

There are different methodologies and a variety of distinctive ways of understanding and applying prayer. They range in the belief that:

- God can actually have communication with Man;
- God has an interest in communicating with Man;
- prayer is intended to implant certain attitudes on the one praying rather than being influenced;
- prayer is intended to affect and bring forth, reality as we see it;
- prayer is a substance creating in us a change, or in our circumstances, or those of others;
- the one praying appreciates and desires the act of praying.

According to some anthropologists, through some attested written sources, the belief is that some of the earliest modern humans, going back some 5000 years, practiced a recognizable form of prayer.

We shouldn't have a relationship with God because of dutiful obedience to His law. It should rather be because we are excited in coming to Him in order to show Him praise and appreciation for the Being that He is. Anxiously wanting to show Him His deserved love and reverence.

Prayer is more than asking God for a favor. It's an investment of our time. It is communicating with the Creator of the Universe, a Supreme Being, our Lord, and our God. We must humbly and respectfully be aware of *Whom* it is that we are interchanging with, and who *we* are in comparison. The most effective prayers, are those that come from the heart.

In order to follow a sequence that would show proper reverence, priority and importance should be aligned in a proper order:

> – the primary and opening reason for prayer is to fervently pay homage to God by praising, adoring, and showing Him reverence. We need to take some time to praise and show Him our love and dependence.
> – showing gratitude and thankfulness for the many graces and things received through God's mercy and generosity. It would be shameful for us to ask Him for anything more, if we had not showed Him gratitude for what we have already received.
> – expressing our sorrow, and imploring His forgiveness for sins committed.
> – being attentive, in listening to God's message that He might have for us.
> – a plea can then be made in the form of an earnest request, in faith, trust, and with the belief that He can answer. Many do not make any pleas, but instead ask that His will be done. A true petition is one that will be according to, and in line with His will.

A prayer, or prayers, can take the form of: adoration, a morning or evening prayer, graces or blessings before a meal, thanksgiving, or a constant communication with God during daily activities.

Some adopt a form of prayer that is made through an intercessor. Relying and having faith in the intercessor to plead in one's behalf.

Prayers can be said privately, individually, or corporately in the presence of fellow believers. Answers to prayers can be either audible, physical, or mental epiphanies.

Some of the reverent acts that can accompany prayer would be: lighting candles, anointing with oil, the ringing of a bell or bells, the sign of the cross, or the burning of incense.

Body posture can also be applied signs, or an enhancement of reverence: standing, sitting, kneeling, bowing of the head, prostrated on the floor, eyes opened, eyes closed, hands folded, hands clasped, hands upraised, holding hands with others, the laying of hands on others.

Prayers may be read from a book, listened to, recited from memory, or spontaneously composed as they are prayed.

There are prayers for different reasons and occasions. Some of which include: the birth of a loved one, the death of a loved one, a wedding, a healing, for guidance or direction, a significant event, Holy Days, or certain significant holidays throughout the year.

Prayers could be: silent, spoken, chanted, sung, with or without musical accompaniment, or in the form of outward silence while prayers are offered mentally.

Besides praying for our own needs, we must keep in mind that everyone, and every situation, needs our prayers. We must also pray for those who fail to do so. It is important to also pray for, and especially for, our enemies.

When do we pray? Where do we find the time to pray? How much time are we spending on our cell phones, or on our computers? How much time do we spend driving or traveling, or waiting for a red light? How much time do we spend in line at a check-out counter? How often do you lay in bed – sleepless? All missed opportunities for beneficial prayer time.

Life is fragile – handle with prayer.

We have a biological clock that tells us when we're hungry, tells us when it's time to go to sleep, and when its time to wake up. We should set, and utilize this biological clock to let us know when it is time to pray. We should utilize this clock in reminding us of the importance of being prayerful *always*.

> "For prayer is nothing else
> than being on terms of friendship with God."
> – Saint Teresa of Avila –

Families today are faced with a *battle* with time. More families have both the mother and father involved in careers, demanding most of their time. When their workday is done, they seem to disappear to board meetings or business dinners, workouts at the gym, PTA meetings, or an evening out with some friends. The children are rushed to and from, sports practices, games, or music lessons. So that some of the parents won't feel guilty about having left the children alone for long periods, they will shower them with high-end gifts of clothes, electronics or sporting goods. Their meals are hurried and frenzied. Eating as a family is needless to say, very uncommon. When holidays or vacation time comes, it is a get-away. All of these concentrated efforts, take away from the concentration of the real purpose and enjoyment of family life. Not having enough time for family bonding, or to get to know each other intimately, and more importantly, denying each other of an opportunity to participate in a rewarding, and bonding spiritual life – being even too busy to attend church. It is by praying together, communicating with one another, and playing together, that we stay together.

> "There are more tears shed over answered prayers
> than over unanswered prayers."
> – Saint Theresa of Jesus –

Meditation is the concentrated attention on an object of awareness or thought. It involves focusing the attention inward to a particular reference. It is the entertainment of deep thoughts, reflection and contemplation. A higher state of consciousness can be benefitted from its practice.

Meditation gives us a feeling of closeness to God – like being in His presence. A silent, quiet, serene surrounding can enhance effectiveness and performance. If we spend time with Him during our life, He will be with us at the time of our death.

We are told through Scripture that we should pray to God, joyfully, thankfully, to show Him our love, and that this should be done with all our heart, all our soul, all our mind, and with all our spirit and strength.

> "Don't worry about anything; instead, pray about everything. Tell God what you need, and thank him for all he has done. If you do this, you will experience God's peace, which is far more wonderful than the human mind can understand. His peace will guard your hearts and minds as you live in Christ Jesus." (Php 4:6,7)

In the year 1534, a religious Order was formed, called the Jesuits. An Order founded by Ignatius Loyola (Saint Ignatius). The members of the Order took vows of poverty, chastity, and obedience. Part of their Creed included, and does to this day, that they would see God more clearly, love God more dearly, and follow Him more nearly. The essence of this Creed was utilized in a Broadway Musical. But we should remember daily, day by day, to pray in these three ways: to see God more clearly, love Him more dearly, and follow Him more closely.

There is no better way to start the day than with prayer, especially being thankful that we made it through the night. Some prayers need not be long to be effective, such as:

> Thank you Lord for the sleep and rest,
> today I offer you my very best.

> Thank You, Lord, for receiving me joyfully
> no matter how far afield I've run.

Jesus Himself prayed fervently, and gave us a wonderful way of expressing ourselves to the Father, by teaching us the "Lord's Prayer".

Fasting is to avoid, or consume very little of, or to go without certain food or drink; the act, time or period of fasting; to abstain willfully; to abstain as a religious exercise or as a token of grief; to eat sparingly.

It is primarily a willful act of abstaining from all food, drink, or both for a certain period of time. It could be a partial, or total abstinence. It usually involves certain types of food – such as the deprivation of meat was a form of abstinence on Fridays, and still is for many during the season of Lent.

Medical fasting is usually a way to promote detoxification. It also helps the stomach, by giving it a rest from digestion.

The exercise or act of fasting, along with time, and rest, as part of human custom for spiritual or religious reasons, is mentioned in the Bible, going as far back as Leviticus. Scripture also tells us that there is a time for rest, fasting, prayer, mourning, and weeping.

> "When the stomach is full, it is easy to talk of fasting."
> – Saint Jerome –

> "And when you fast, don't make it obvious, as the hypocrites do, who try to look pale and disheveled so people will admire them for their fasting. I assure you, that is the only reward they will ever get. But when you fast, comb your hair and wash your face. Then no one will suspect you are fasting, except your Father, who knows what you do in secret. And your Father, who knows all secrets, will reward you." (Mt 6:16-18)

FOLLOWING FOOTSTEPS

Whenever we want to arrive at a new given destination, we have a choice of attempting to find our way in getting there on our own, or we can seek information as to how to get there.

Having spent many years on the road, there were many times that it became a necessity to stop and ask for information or direction. Some could give very precise and clear directions even drawing a map with approximate mileage, and noting certain things to look for along the way. Others left the charting of the course very vague, to say the least – leaving a lot to assumption. There were a few people that were not only helpful, but quite accommodating, in saying, 'I happen to be going in that direction, just follow me!" Following someone who knew where they were going, was much easier than to attempt some questionable route. In becoming a follower, we can then rely on, and have confidence in the person we are following, because the one we are following knows where we want to go, and he knows how to get us there.

I have also found that there is safety in numbers, especially when traveling. Two heads are better than one, and it allows us to not only enjoy having the company, but we can share our experiences and any burdens along the way.

Our spiritual walk and journey shouldn't be in any way dull or boring, or appear to be a duty. It should be instead, anticipated, exciting, joyful, exhilarating, and stimulating. We should regard our being able to follow in Christ's footsteps as a blessing. A chance to follow in the values of the One who, by His Words, taught us, and left us with such Holy examples, and described directions. Because He told us that He was the Way, we are certain of being on the right path leading us to His promised destination.

When Jesus asked His disciples to follow Him, they left everything behind and were, at that very moment, ready to start their new journey. They didn't know what to expect, what they would do, or even how they would do it. The only answers they had to those many questions, were found in the trusting, the faith, and the belief that they had in the One they were following.

We were not only asked to imitate Christ in everything He did, but we were also asked to *follow,* as He asked His disciples to follow.

He wants us to not only *walk the walk* but to *talk the talk*. He came to serve – not to be served. He wants us to imitate Him in every way, even through our service and sufferings. This is our way of showing Him appreciation for all that He has given us, the good as well as the trials we are challenged with. It is easy to give thanks for graces and blessings, but through the difficult things that He allows us to experience, we are tested, by how we react to them. If we react favorably, we will receive even more blessings. It is a test of our endurance, our faith, our trust, how much we believe in Him, and how much we love Him. We must remember that Christ was also tested, and that He also suffered. All of these tribulations and testings will come to pass – so will our lives. We can then only look back to see how we had handled these given situations. Following Christ is not only rewarding, but needless to say, very challenging. The results can't help but be gratifying because of all the changes that would take place in our lives, especially in making a committed decision to follow.

Jesus told us that if we are to follow Him that we must leave *all* our baggage behind. He said that *nothing* or *nobody* should stand in the way in our deciding to follow Him. Whatever it is that keeps us from being His follower, is what we prefer to love over Him.

In our desiring and accepting the choice to humbly follow Him, we not only accept the invitation to follow, but we are reminded that we are following the greatest leader and teacher the world has ever known, or will ever know. He not only gave us direction, but He will lead us there to our eternal destination. He not only gave us a blessed direction, He wants to lead us there. He also gives us hope and assurance through His guarantied and promised reward, that we will be saved because of Redemption and Salvation. The path that He gives us to follow is a *safe* path, it is an upright path that leads us to goodness, and away from evil.

> "I am the way, the truth, and the life.
> No one can come to the Father except through me."
> (Jn 14:6)

Christ was here with us for a very short time. Great crowds *followed* Him. He devoted and utilized His time to teach us, give us direction, and most importantly, to expend His entire life with us as to become an example. An example, a method, a way of living, that if we are to be His followers, must also imitate. Christ had many difficulties, hardships, and sufferings to overcome, but faith and trust in His Father's desire, made Him accomplish His intended mission. Salvation is *free,* but not *cheap.*

"So be careful how you live, not as fools but as those who are wise. Make the most of every opportunity for doing good in these evil days. Don't act thoughtlessly, but try to understand what the Lord wants you to do." (Eph 5;15-17)

When the shepherd calls his sheep, they know that he is the one they should follow. We are the sheep and Christ is our Shepherd – we must follow Him.

God has a plan for us. It is a plan that will bring us good and not disaster, a plan with a future and hope.

Our decision to follow Christ sometimes brings about mockery, being lied about, and sometimes even persecuted. But if these happen, we should be happy, and be very glad because a great reward awaits us in heaven.

It might also bring division, as some will decide to follow, and others wont.

"But those who endure to the end will be saved."
(Mt 10:22b)

"The truth is, when you were young, you were able to do as you liked and go wherever you wanted to. But when you are old, you will stretch out your hands, and others will direct you and take you where you don't want to go. Jesus said this to let him know what kind of death he would die to glorify God. Then Jesus told him, 'Follow me.'" (Jn 21:18,19)

HEEDING

Heeding is paying particular, close, and careful attention; regarding with care; concentrating on some particular features of the environment that others don't; noticing; caring; being obedient.

> "Take heed, you do not find what you do not seek."
> – English Proverb –

There are so many influences around us – attractions, distractions. Any of these can cause us, and lead us to follow a certain way of life.

> "If the world despises you because you do not follow its ways,
> pay not heed to it. But be sure your way is right."
> – Author Unknown –

As God punished Adam and Eve for following the advice of the serpent, we also must be careful of the influence or advice of others that might cause us to go astray.

> "It is vanity to desire a long life
> and to take heed of a good life."
> – Thomas a Kempis –

We cannot go through life being on the fence, being lukewarm, negligent, uncaring, or oblivious, to what is going on around us. A fine example of being oblivious, is how the world, in the 30's, did not heed or react fast enough to the building up of the Third Reich. Millions of lives could have been saved. We should shed light upon, and heed the efforts of any terrorists who would be planning attacks, and would want to take control of the world.

We have to cure our blindness, we must become observant! We cannot risk falling into a trap because we decided to make decisions based on appearance instead of good judgement. How much is God's work being destroyed – by so many people, the media, schools, and those that some regard as idols? How much of our lives, our society, our culture is being liberalized?

> "Then Jesus said to his disciples. 'I tell you the truth, it is very hard for a rich person to get into the Kingdom of Heaven. I say it again – it is easier for a camel to go through the eye of a needle than for a rich person to enter the Kingdom of God!'" (Mt 19:23,24)

We have a God that wants an endearing relationship with us. Is our relationship with Him just enough to get by? Are we careful of who we associate with, and what kind of direction could be realized through our behavior? The easiest way, and the fastest way to *grow up,* is to surround ourselves with people who are smarter than we are. If these people are spiritual, then we will have heeded well in our selection.

> "Turn on the prudent ant thy heedful eyes,
> Observe her labors, sluggard, and be wise."
> – Samuel Johnson –

Who doesn't like to receive and read a letter, especially a *love letter.* The Bible is exactly that, a love letter, telling us how much our God loves us, what He can and wants to do for us, what kind of life He wants to share with us, and of the many gifts He has waiting for us. By reading the love letter, we discover how much He cares about us. It makes us aware of how much we should be devoted to *Him.* We should take more time to be with the One that loves us the most.

> "The will is deaf and hears no heedful friends."
> – William Shakespeare –

The gate to God's Kingdom is very narrow. Many are being called, but few will answer the call. The gate to hell is wide for those that choose the easier way, and its highway is broad.

Chapter 9

ETERNITY

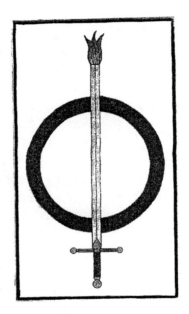

**The CIRCLE is a symbol of eternity,
not having a beginning or end.**

The FLAMING SWORD is a symbol of judgment.

"After banishing them from the garden, Lord God stationed angelic beings to the east of Eden. And a flaming sword flashed back and forth, guarding the way to the tree of life." (Gen 3:24)

TRINITY

ETERNITY

ETERNITY

E verything thus was made beautiful for its own time;

T he Lord's great creation, is majestic and sublime.

E ndeavoring to show, and share with us His wisdom;

R eassuring us of His awaiting, loving Kingdom;

N ecessity, being the price of our Redeemer,

I nsures us now, His gift, of blissful joy forever.

T hanks to Him, having made us in His image;

Y es, the glory belongs to God, through all the Ages.

WHAT IS ETERNITY ?

As it applies to God and His divinity, eternity is: the totality of existence without beginning or end; the condition or quality of being eternal; a very long or seemingly very long time; existing for an everlasting, limitless amount of time; an endless or immeasurable time; eternal existence; infinite duration; infinite time; timelessness.

As it applies to the mortal state of being, it is: the endless period of existence following death; the state after death; the afterlife; immortality.

In the writings of St Augustine, he cites that time exists only within the created universe – God existing outside of time. There is no past, present, or future for God, only eternal presence.

TIME

Moment before death.
Moment during death.
Endless existence after death.

God being the Creator of everything, is completely independent of anything or everything else that exists, because He created everything. Yet, everything that He created is part of Him, as He created it.

Time is irrelevant to God, He existed before time began, exists during our mortal periods of time, and He would continue existing even if somehow the universe and time itself, as we know it, would cease to exist.

The Brothers Grimm told a story about a Shepherd Boy who was brought to a King to answer three questions. The third question the King asked him was "How many seconds of time are there in eternity?" The Shepherd Boy replies, "In Lower Pomerania is the Diamond Mountain, which is two miles and a half high, two miles and a half wide, and two miles and a half in dept; every hundred years a little bird comes and sharpens its beak on it, and when the whole mountain is worn away from this, then the first second of eternity will be over.

When we talk about Heaven, we try to describe and understand beyond our comprehension a visual picture of a celestial and Divine dwelling place – be it spiritually or physically.

When we think about eternity, our foreseen eternal existence, the first thing that comes to mind, is the ageless period following death, or maybe of ever-lasting life, infinite time; or joining the totality of existence that has had no beginning, nor will it have an ending.

Being mortals, we experience life as something that is around for a certain duration. Our pets are with us for a certain number of years, then they are taken away. Our vegetation, trees, and seasons, are but temporary. Our forests are governed by a certain life-span, that keeps them in renewal. Even the parts of our bodies are constantly renewing themselves – our skin, our organs, even our bones. Members of our families are only with us for so long, then God decides when He wants to take them. We are used to looking at life as something that has an ending.

> "Lord remind me how brief my time on earth will be. Remind me that my days are numbered, and that my life is fleeing away. My life is no longer than the width of my hand. An entire lifetime is just a moment to you; human existence is but a breath." (Ps 39:4,5)

It is *awesome* to think about God.
He is someone who always was, is now, and always will be.

"I am the Alpha and the Omega – The Beginning and the end."
(Rev 21:6)

"The best use of life is to spend it for something that outlasts it."
– William James –

So is it with eternity, it always was, is now, and it always will be. But the present, being a temporary condition for us, is also part of eternity, and must be included in its entirety.

Everything that God has made is beautiful, full of wonder, for a purpose, and for its own time. Even though He has implanted eternity in our hearts, we cannot see the whole scope of God's work from beginning to end. It is too majestic! Never to be comprehended because of our mortal minds. God wanted to share His love, architectural brilliance, and His awesome, intricately combined, creativity.

The gift of eternity is *more precious* than human life.

This *eternal* city which we call heaven,
is usually referred to in the Bible as the *New Jerusalem.*

"Look, the home of God is now among his people! He will live with them, and they will be his people. God himself will be with them. He will remove all of their sorrow, and there will be no more death or sorrow or crying or pain. For the old world and its evils are gone forever."
(Rev 21:3,4)

God had a plan for each and every one of us as individuals to fulfill His intended plan of creation. Every individual being gifted, and having special talents and purposes, with specific reasons for the utilization of those abilities, unite these efforts to accomplish the realization of God's plan. In putting these talents to good use we are helping God do His work here on earth, by helping and showing love to one another; to share and blend our talents with His, for the welfare of all Mankind. This is our purpose in this life. Attaining true and Divine happiness is then, perhaps, the purpose of eternal life.

"The longest day must have its close – the gloomiest night will wear on to a morning. An eternal, inexorable lapse of

moments is ever hurrying the day of the evil to an eternal night, and the night of the just to an eternal day."
– Harriet Beecher Stowe –

God is God from eternity to eternity.
What He does cannot be opposed, nor can it be reversed.

Ever since the world has been created, people have been able to see all that God has made – the earth, the sky, and the ever exciting things of nature. Through all of God's accomplishments that are visible to us, we can attest to His eternal power and divine nature. We have no excuse for not knowing God. He is all around us, in everything and in everyone we see.

"The essential part of our being can only survive if the transient part dissolves. Death is a condition of survival. That which has been gained must be eternalized by being transmuted, by passing through death they must return."
– Pir Vilayat Khan –

The thought of eternal life begins with faith. Only through our being tested, and proper response to the many trials and sufferings that we are given, can we attain our just reward. Death is merely the key that opens to us the gates of the Eternal Kingdom. We must forever grow spiritually, and have our eyes focused on the eternal, if we are to move towards, and arrive at our desired goal.

"Simon Peter replied, 'Lord, to whom would we go? You alone have the words that give eternal life.'"(Jn 6:68)

NEARING THE FINAL DAYS

Many have been soberly watching and analyzing world affairs, climate changes, plagues, and the intensity and the frequency of storms and disasters. According to what was prophesied, a broad pattern of events will affect our lives. Are we, or will we be, on the look out for these indications? Or, are we spiritually blinded? Are we to pay closer attention to these ever increasing calamities?

> "First, I want to remind you that in the last days there will be scoffers who will laugh at the truth and do every evil thing they desire. This will be their argument: 'Jesus promised to come back, did He? Then where is he? Why, as far back as anyone can remember, everything has remained exactly the same since the world was first created.'" (2 Pet 3:3,4)

We cannot deliberately choose to forget, that the heavens were made by the command of the word of God. He is the one that separated the earth from the water, and used the water for the mighty flood. It will also be at His command that the earth will be consumed by fire on the day of judgement, when the ungodly people will perish.

To the Lord time is of no consequence, as He lives forever in the present. But He has shown His patience for our sake in delaying what is to come. He is giving us more time to repent, time to turn from our worldly ways, and time to turn our lives over to Him. We know that when He comes, it will be unexpected, like a thief in the night. But when He does come everything will pass away with a terrible noise. Everything then will disappear in fire, and everything on earth will be exposed to His judgement. If these things are destined to happen, shouldn't we be living godly lives? Those that will have decided to, can look forward to the new heavens and the new earth that was promised us – a world where we will be right with God.

> "Today is the last day of your life – so far."
> – Author Unknown –

Our human society as we know it will be changed by Christ's return. What we consider now as our entertainment, our needs, our desires – these things will be chained, have an altered value, or might be gone forever. We are uncomfortable in thinking that our lifestyle as we know it will come to an end.

Some of the disciples, while at the Temple with Jesus, began talking about the Temple's beautiful stonework and the walls' memorial decorations. Jesus told them,

> "'The time is coming when all these things will be so completely demolished that not one stone will be left on top of another.' 'Teacher' they asked, 'when will all this take place? And will there be any sign ahead of time?'"
> (Lk 21:6,7)

Jesus then warned them not to be misled, that many would say that the time has come, or claim to be the Messiah. He told them that the end would not come when we hear of wars or insurrections, that we shouldn't panic, because these things must occur.

He told us that there will be in many lands, great earthquakes, famines and epidemics. That there will be miraculous signs in heaven, and terrifying things happening. Precluding these things there will be a time of great persecution, which will be an opportunity to tell others about Christ. He also warned that we would be betrayed by those closest to us, and would be hated because of our allegiance to Him, but not to despair, that He would take care of us. He said that we would know that Jerusalem's destruction will have arrived, when we see it surrounded by armies.

We are told to be on the look-out for strange events occurring in the skies concerning the sun, moon, and stars, and that the nations of the earth would be in turmoil over roaring seas and strange tides.

> "You should also know this Timothy, that in the last days there will be very difficult times. For people will love only themselves and their money. They will be boastful and proud, scoffing at God, disobedient to their parents, and ungrateful. They will consider nothing sacred. They will be unloving and unforgiving, they will slander others and have

no self-control; they will be cruel and have no interest in what is good. They will betray their friends, be reckless, be puffed up with pride, and love pleasure rather than God. They will act as if they are religious, but they will reject the power that could make them godly. You must stay away from people like that." (2 Ti 3:1-5)

"Keep a constant watch. And pray that, if possible, you may escape these horrors and stand before the Son of Man." (Lk 21:36)

GETTING READY

Being ready is to be prepared, supplied, or available with what is needed for action, use, or event; mentally or physically prepared for some experience or action; arranged or fitted for immediate use; quick in understanding or responding; likely to do something indicated; conveniently available; prepared for immediate use; willingly disposed; alert; dexterous; inclined; prompt; willing.

There are thousands who train and practice diligently, with the expectation of *qualifying* for the Olympics. Although their quest is to achieve the perfection needed, not all entrants will qualify or be accepted. Those that were the most serious about what was needed, applied the most attention, and spent the most time in the proper training, became better prepared, and resulted with exceedingly uncomparable qualifications.

"All Scripture is inspired by God and is useful to teach us what is true and to make us realize what is wrong in our lives. It straightens us out and teaches us to do what is right. It is God's way of preparing us in every way, fully equipped for every good thing God wants us to do." (2 Ti 3:16,17)

So it is, about getting ready for our eternal destiny – many are called, but few are chosen. Unlike the Olympics however, in our quest for eternal life, we are not, in this race, *competing* with one another, but we should be seriously *helping* each other through our trials, tribulations, and sufferings, in attaining our goal, so that all would become winners. We have to remember that we received all of these afflictions to test us, and to test our endurance.

Of importance, is not the journey – it is the destination.

Noah's faith and endurance was tested, but because he trusted God, he got His ark ready. Are we going to get our ark ready? Are we going to bring our loved ones and friends with us, two by two?

> "Happiness is not something ready made.
> It comes from our own actions."
> – Dalai Lama –

In order to get ready, our sights have to be on the reality of heaven, where Jesus sits at His Father's right hand, in the place of honor and power. When being in such company, we should be clothed with gentleness, humility, kindness, mercy, patience and tenderness. But our finest clothing should be love, which is what binds us all in perfect harmony. If we are adequately dressed, we will be ready for Him when He comes to knock at our door. We have to be *in* the world, but not *of* the world. God tells us that there will be special favor for those who get ready and are waiting for Him to come. Will He find us *well* with our souls? How much will we *cram*, getting ready for the final exam?

> "If you are pre-occupied with life and death
> then you aren't ready for heaven."
> – Author Unknown –

What is also included in *getting ready*, is to make sure that while we are here, for our temporary mortal journey, that we accomplish all what we were meant to accomplish. Not merely what *we* wanted to accomplish, but what *God* intended for *us* to accomplish, and accomplish *through* us. If we enjoy the worldly things, more than we are in getting ready for our next life, then we are not getting ready! Our enjoyment would be based on the wrong focus or perspective. We should constantly be *aware* of our soul, its condition, reputation, appearance, and especially its presence before God. In order to achieve this state of preparedness or readiness, we must rid ourselves of, and die of our old nature and habits, and be born again into a holier life through spiritual growth. We have to get ready, working toward becoming all that Jesus saved us for, and what He wants us to be. Time is running out, we must forget the past and look forward to what lies ahead. Once we finish the race, we will receive the prize for which God is calling us up to heaven through Christ. We can achieve this by standing true to what we believe, and by being courageous and strong.

> "I assure you, unless you are born again,
> you can never see the Kingdom of God."
> (Jn 3:3)

Our excitement in getting ready should start at youth. Good roots are formed in family life, by good example from the parents, and making sure that the children are well and properly educated, both academically and spiritually. When we attend church, all of us become as one family – there to honor our Father. The Father likes to have all of His children present for His exquisite meal that He prepares for us. Building spiritually together, unites the family, but a home divided, is doomed.

> "The door to heaven is narrow. Work hard to get in, because many will try to enter, but when the head of the house has locked the door, it will be too late. And note this: Some who are despised now will be greatly honored then; and some who are honored now will be despised then." (Lk 13:24,30)

What will be our presence – in the presence of God, about showing Him: adoration, devotion, praise and reverence? How will we feel about being around God's elect: the saints, the prophets, the angels, and the chosen few, for a life that will be everlasting?

> "You can't cross the sea
> merely by standing and staring at the water."
> – Rabindranath Tagore –

THE RAPTURE

The condition or the act of being carried away by overwhelming joy; the act of transporting, or of being transformed; state of being rapt; being out of oneself; spiritual or emotional ecstacy; bliss.

The word "rapture" comes from the Greek word *harpazo*, which would translate to English as "caught up", or "taken away".

There is an Aramaic expression *Maranatha*, that according as to how the word is divided, would mean either (maran'atha') "The Lord comes.", or (marana'tha) "Come! Lord!".

Rapture, as a popular Christian meaning, would imply, a name given to a future event when Christ would descend, accompanied by the spirits of His chosen saints, to bring with Him all of the believers.

This most important event which is yet to come, and would so drastically change the course of events or the nature of things, is not being given enough significance. All we know is that time is drawing closer to its occurrence.

> "People say that what we're all seeking is a meaning for life. I think that what we're really seeking is an experiencing of being alive, so that our life experiences on the purely physical plane will have resonance within our innermost being and reality, so that we can actually feel that rapture of being alive." – Joseph Campbell –

There is much discussion and disagreement about when this event will occur in relationship with the Tribulation. No one knows of its designated time. The views and opinions are threefold. The first is the belief that it will occur sometime before the Seven Years of Tribulation. The second would be midway through the Tribulation. The third proposed occurrence would be when Christ comes to establish the Kingdom of God, here on earth, to rule the world for a thousand years, a millennium.

> "For false messiahs and false prophets will rise up and perform great miraculous signs and wonders so as to deceive, if possible, even God's chosen ones. See, I have warned you."
> "So if someone tells you, 'Look, the Messiah is out in the desert,' don't bother to go and look. Or, 'Look, he is hiding here,' don't believe it! For as the lightning lights up the entire sky, so it will be when the Son of Man comes. Just as the gathering of vultures shows there is a carcass nearby, so these signs indicate that the end is near." (Mt 24:24-28)

> "I can tell you this directly from the Lord: We who are still living when the Lord returns will not rise to meet him ahead of those who are in their graves. For the Lord himself will come down form heaven with a commanding shout, with the call of the archangel, and with the trumpet call of God. First, all the Christians who have died will rise from their graves. Then, together with them, we who are still alive and remain on the earth will be caught up in the clouds to meet the Lord in the air and remain with him forever."
> (1 Th 4:15-18)

In the view that the Rapture would occur at *Pre-Tribulation*, some of those then, who had been left behind, and had accepted Christ, would be martyred during the Tribulation Period, because of their faith. Most of the American Evangelical Christians widely accept, and hold to the position of the Pre-Tribulation Rapture.

The *Pre-Wrath* view of the Rapture, would be when the Antichrist is revealed in the Temple.

The *Post-Tribulation* view, would place the Rapture at the end of the Tribulation period:

> "Immediately after those horrible days end, the sun will be darkened, the moon will not give light, the stars will fall from the sky, and the powers of heaven will be shaken."
>
> "And then at last, the sign of the coming of the Son of Man will appear in the heavens, and there will be deep mourning among all the nations of the earth. And they will see the Son of Man arrive on the clouds of heaven with power and great glory. And he will send forth his angels with the sound of a mighty trumpet blast, and they will gather together his chosen ones from the farthest ends of the earth and heaven." (Mt 24:29-31)
>
> "Take note: I will come as unexpectedly as a thief! Blessed are all who are watching for me, who keep their robes ready so they will not need to walk naked and ashamed." (Rev 16:15)

THE TRIBULATION

Tribulation is great affliction or distress; suffering; that which causes such distress; suffering, as from oppression or persecution; an occurrence of such suffering.

The duration of the Tribulation period is believed for most, to be Seven years, divided into two joined three-and-a half year periods. An occurrence of intense suffering for those who would be left behind, those who would be rebelling against the Antichrist's form of government – undergoing an extremely perilous time of immense sacrifice and suffering, unlike anything the world has ever seen.

There are different views among Christians that support the *Futurist* view of the Tribulation, and what will happen to them during this perilous time. It is said that the believers will be given a stronger faith to help them endure this time of testing.

Those that have the view of the *Pretribulationists*, believe that all living Christian believers, would be bodily taken up to Heaven during the Rapture, which would precede the Tribulation. Those that would become Christians following the Rapture would either survive or perish during the Tribulation years, after which Christ would return for the purpose of ruling over the world for a thousand years.

Those that have the view of the *Midtribulatinists*, believe that the Rapture will occur midway through the Tribulation, before its worst events. This would hold that the first half would be called the *beginning of sorrows*, and the following years, the *great tribulation* proper.

Those that have the view of the *Posttribulationists*, believe that Christians will be taken up to Heaven only at the end of the Tribulation.

The Rapture and the Second Coming of Christ are regarded as separate events for the Pretribulationists and the Midtribulationists, while the Posttribulationists regard them as being simultaneous. It would be the belief that there would be a third coming, according to the pretribulation and midtribulation beliefs.

There are some Theologians that rather believe of a time of social regeneration which will be led by the Antichrist.

Many of the events found in the Book of Revelation, that are said to come during the Tribulation, differ in opinions among Christians.

The *first* three and a half years would include: the Rapture; the Rising of the Antichrist; Jerusalem's Third Temple being rebuilt; the Rising of Babylon, The Rising of a false one-world religion; the Rising of the 144,000 Jewish evangelists; the Seven Seal Judgments; the Seven Trumpet Judgments.

During the *second* three and a half years, the events would include: the Bowl of Judgments; the Jews and Believers becoming martyrs; Babylon being destroyed; the Antichrist summoning the world's armies to Armageddon; the Battle of Armageddon; the returning of Jesus in Glory; the Antichrist and the False Prophet being thrown into Lake of Fire; Satan being bound for a thousand years; the Resurrection of the Tribulation martyrs.

At the *end* of the Seven Years of Tribulation, the following events would include: Christ establishing His thousand year Kingdom; Satan being released after a thousand years; the final Battle; the casting of Satan, Death, and Hell into the Lake of Fire; the Final Judgment of the Great White Throne; the New Heaven and Earth, the beginning of our eternity.

The following are the events of the *Seven Seals* as found in the Bible's Book of Revelation:

"As I watched, the Lamb broke the first of the seven seals on the scroll. Then one of the four living beings called out with a voice that sounded like thunder, 'Come!' I looked up and saw a white horse. Its rider carried a bow, and a crown was placed on his head. He rode out to win many battles and gain the victory." (Rev 6:1,2)

"When the Lamb broke the second seal, I heard the second living being say, "Come!' And another horse appeared, a red one. Its rider was given a mighty sword and the authority to remove peace from the earth. And there was war and slaughter everywhere." (Rev 6:3,4)

"When the Lamb broke the third seal, I heard the third living being say, "Come!' And I looked up and saw a black horse, and its rider was holding a pair of scales in his hand. And a voice from among the four living beings said, 'A loaf of wheat bread or three loaves of barley for a day's pay. And don't waste the olive oil and wine.'" (Rev 6:5,6)

"And when the lamb broke the fourth seal, I heard the fourth living being say, 'Come!' And I looked up and saw a horse whose color was pale green like a corpse. And Death was the name of its rider, who was followed around by the Grave. They were given authority over one-fourth of the earth, to kill with the sword and famine and disease and wild animals." (Rev 6:7,8)

"And when the Lamb broke the fifth seal, I saw under the altar the souls of all who had been martyred for the word of God and for being faithful in their witness. They called loudly to the Lord and said, 'O Sovereign Lord, holy and true, how long will it be before you judge the people who belong to this world for what they have done to us? When will you avenge our blood against these people? Then a white robe was given to each of them. And they were told to rest a little longer until the full number of their brothers and sisters – their fellow servants of Jesus – had been martyred." (Rev 6:9-11)

"I watched as the Lamb broke the sixth seal, and there was a great earthquake. The sun became as dark as black cloth, and the moon became as red as blood. Then the stars of the sky fell to the earth like green figs falling from trees shaken by mighty winds. And the sky was rolled up like a scroll and taken away. And all of the mountains and all of the islands disappeared. Then the kings of the earth, the rulers, the generals, the wealthy people, the people with great power, and every slave and every free person – all hid themselves in the caves and among the rocks of the mountains. And they cried to the mountains and the rocks, "Fall on us and hide us from the face of the one who sits on the throne and from the wrath of the Lamb. For the great day of their wrath has come, and who will be able to survive?" (Rev 6:12-17)

"When the Lamb broke the seventh seal, there was silence

throughout heaven for about half an hour. And I saw the seven angels who stand before God, and they were given seven trumpets.

Then another angel with a gold incense burner came and stood at the altar. And a great quantity of incense was given to him to mix with the prayers of God's people, to be offered on the gold altar before the throne. The smoke of the incense, mixed with the prayers of the saints, ascended up to God from the altar where the angel had poured them out. Then the angel filled the incense burner with fire from the altar and threw it down upon the earth; and thunder crashed, lightning flashed, and there was a terrible earthquake." (Rev 8:1-5)

The *Seven Trumpets* are the indication of the supernatural calamities that are said to be taking place: hail; fire; the burning of one-third of the earth; a burning mountain plummeting into the sea; one-third of the fish dying; a star, interported as a comet called Wormwood, disintegrating before striking the earth, poisoning the waters; the darkening of the stars, moon and sun by one-third; a plague of locusts imposing terrifying pain; one-third of the wicked on Earth killed by two hundred million horsemen; events of hailstorm, lightning and earthquakes.

Only God knows the mystery of the *Seven Thunders* which will be revealed when the seventh angel sounds:

"And he gave a great shout, like the roar of a lion.
And when he shouted, the seven thunders answered."
(Rev 10:3)

"When the seven thunders spoke, I was about to write.
But a voice from heaven called to me:
'Keep secret what the seven thunders said.
Do not write it down.'"
(Rev 10:4)

"For that will be a time of greater horror than anything the world has ever seen or will ever see again. In fact, unless that time of calamity is shortened, the entire human race will be destroyed. But it will be shortened for the sake of God's chosen ones." (Mt 24:21,22)

THE MILLENNIUM

Millennium is a term used to describe a length of time lasting a thousand years; a thousand anniversary.

The New Testament's Book of Revelation, reveals the one thousand year reign of Christ on earth, when holiness will be triumphant; a period of great joy; peace, and prosperity. A time of great government, and freedom from wickedness.

The understanding by Christian writers of the basic or primary idea of this future millennium, could be brought forward as: at the end of time, Christ would return to earth in all His splendor with His saints, gathering together the just; at which time He would destroy all hostile powers, and would found His glorious Kingdom here on earth, bringing the highest spiritual and material blessings. At the end of this thousand years, the saints would then enter heaven with Christ, while all of the wicked who will have also been resuscitated, would then be condemned to eternal damnation.

The duration of the event, is by no means as important an element, as what the period's essential occurrences will consist of:
– the return of Christ in all His Glory and Power;
– Christ establishing an earthly Kingdom with the just;
– the deceased saints being resuscitated and thus participating in the millennial reign;
– the powers of the hostile being destroyed;
– the universal resurrection and final judgement taking place at the end of the millennial Kingdom; the just will then enter heaven for eternity, while the unsaved will be consigned to hell, the eternal fire.

It was the hope of the Jewish people that the glorious Kingdom which had long been awaited, would be for a temporal Messiah and the Jewish apocalyptic. Guided by their political circumstances they expected that their people would be freed by an earthly character Messiah, that would free their people; freeing them from their oppressors, and restore Israel to its former splendor.

Scholars had a premise that if God had *created* all things in six *days*, and rested on the seventh *day*, that He would complete all things in *six* days, and rest on the seventh *day*. A *day* being noted as a thousand years, would then mean that God would complete man's existence on earth after six *days*, six thousand years, and rest on the seventh *day*, the thousand year millennium.

> "And you will live in Israel, the land I gave your ancestors long ago. You will be my people, and I will be your God. I will cleanse you of your filthy behavior. I will give you good crops, and I will abolish famine in the land. I will give you great harvests from your fruit trees and fields, and never again will the surrounding nations be able to scoff at your land for its famines. Then you will remember your past sins and hate yourselves for all the evil things you did. But remember, says the Sovereign LORD, I am not doing this because you deserve it. O my people of Israel, you should be utterly ashamed of all you have done!
>
> "This is what the Sovereign LORD says: When I cleanse you from your sins, I will bring people to live in your cities, and the ruins will be rebuilt. The fields that used to lie empty and desolate – a shock to all who pass by – will again be farmed. And when I bring you back, people will say, 'This godforsaken land is now like Eden's garden! The ruined cities now have strong walls, and they are filled with people!' Then the nations all around – all those still left – will know that I, the LORD, rebuilt the ruins and planted lush crops in the wilderness. For I the LORD, have promised this, and I will do it." (Eze 36:28-36)

SATAN'S FINAL DEFEAT

Satan chained for a Thousand Years. At the start of the Millennium, at the time Christ comes to rule the world for a thousand years, Satan will be thrown into the bottomless pit where he will stay during Christ's reign over the earth.

> "Then I saw an angel come down from heaven with the key to the bottomless pit and a heavy chain in his hand. He seized the dragon – that old serpent, the Devil, Satan – and bound him in chains for a thousand years. The angel threw him into the bottomless pit, which he then shut and locked so Satan could not deceive the nations anymore until the thousand years were finished. Afterward he would be released for a little while. (Rev 20:1-3)

The Defeat of Satan. After the thousand years, Satan will be released temporarily. He will, during that time, deceive many nations and bring them together in his demonic rage into a final battle.

> "When the thousand years end, Satan will be let out of prison. He will go out to deceive the nations from every corner of the earth, which we called Gog and Magog. He will gather them together for battle – a mighty host, as numberless as sand along the shore. And I saw them as they went up on the broad plain of the earth and surrounded God's people and the beloved city. But fire from heaven came down on the attacking armies and consumed them."
>
> "Then the Devil who betrayed them, was thrown into the lake of fire that burns with sulfur, joining the false prophet. There they will be tormented day and night forever and ever." (Rev 20:7-10)

> "The God of peace will soon crush Satan under your feet."
> (Ro 16:20)

THE DESTRUCTION OF THE EARTH

When we look at nature, and all of God's Creation, we feel and see the serenity of His nature. The beauty and balance of things that He alone has brought into being. People enjoy sitting on a shore gazing at the ocean's peacefulness, the mesmerizing sounds of the waves, or the ever changing colorful charm of the sunset. The captivating sight of a tiny bird visible from a window.

It seems virtually incomprehensible, that The Creator of these awesome wonders, the One who brought forth the sights of such splendor, would want to destroy such perfection.

> "However, no one knows the day or the hour when these things will happen, not even the angels in heaven or the Son himself. Only the Father knows." (Mt 24:36)

Death was not God's doing. He doesn't take any pleasure in it! He also doesn't take any pleasure in the extinction of the earth. He created us all to live an enjoyable and hopeful life. It was the devil and his envy that brought death into the world.

> "The earth has broken down and has utterly collapsed. Everything is lost, abandoned, and confused. The earth staggers like a drunkard. It trembles like a tent in a storm. It falls and will not rise again, for its sins are very great."
> (Isa 24:19)

Mankind brought to itself mortality, degeneration of culture, sinfulness, greed, and to a condition or place of great confusion and disorder. The world is quickly fading away, bringing along everything it craves. The other choice, doing the will of God, would have had man living forever. The destruction of the earth is not what God intended for us, even through our free will. He allowed us to make the choices that would bring us to our own destiny. We cannot say that we haven't been warned! God's word, and through His teachings during His presence with us here on earth, gave us all the indications of what would happen if we didn't adhere to His way of living. The choice was simply to be under the rule of our Creator – or under the rule of pride and vanity.

"I assure you, until heaven and earth disappear, even the smallest detail of God's law will remain until its purpose is achieved." (Mt 5:18)

The LORD told us the heavens will melt away as if disappearing like a rolled-up scroll, and that the stars would fall like withered leaves from a fruit tree – but His words will remain for ever.

"Look up to the skies above, and gaze down on the earth beneath. For the skies will disappear like smoke, and the earth will wear out like a piece of clothing. The people of the earth will die like flies, but my salvation lasts forever. My righteous rule will never end." (Isa 51:6)

"But the day of the Lord will come as unexpectedly as a thief. Then the heavens will pass away with a terrible noise, and everything in them will disappear in fire, and the earth and everything on it will be exposed to judgment."
"Since everything around us is going to melt away. What holy, godly lives you should be living! You should look forward to that day and hurry it along – the day when God will set the heavens on fire and the elements will melt away in the flames. But we are looking forward to the new heavens and new earth he has promised, a world where everyone is right with God." (2 Pe 3:10-13)

THE JUDGMENT

Judgment is the capacity to perceive, discern, or make reasonable decisions; the act of, or an instance of judging; the pronouncing of a formal decision or opinion; a conclusion reached after due consideration; a calamity sent by God, by way of punishment and justice; the result of being judged; discernment; discretion; justice; opinion; decision; the power of arriving at a wise decision; the act of determining what is judicially right according to law and justice; the decree, sentence, or mandate of God as the Judge of us all; God's or Christ's Final Judgment of Mankind; the Great Day of Judgment.

Every man or woman created were given a free will. A freedom to choose a particular way of living; a freedom to prepare for an everlasting destiny.

God sent all mortals certain trials, tribulations and sufferings. The way that we handled these difficulties will determine our faith, our belief, and trust in Him. This is the Final Examination! On the Day of Judgment, when the body and soul will be reunited, all the Books will be opened, including the *Book of Life*, in which will be written all of our earthly actions – good and bad.

He will then judge us with Divine Justice according to how we obeyed His laws, His Commandments, and His teachings. Whether we disciplined ourselves to the godly way of living, or if we chose a worldly way of life. Are we prepared? Will we *be* prepared? What will He say to us? What will we say to Him?

> "There is no judgment awaiting those who trust him. But those who do not trust him have already been judged for not believing in the only Son of God. Their Judgment is based on this fact: The light from heaven came into the world, but they loved the darkness more than the light, for their actions were evil. They hate the light because they want to sin in the darkness. They stay away from the light for fear their sins will be exposed and they will be punished. But those who do what is right come to the light gladly, so everyone can see that they are doing what God wants." (Jn 3:18-21)

We are now living in a time when few people listen to the right teachings. People either follow their own desires, or choose to listen to whoever will tell them what they want to hear. In following these strange myths, they will reject the truth. Not only should we keep a clear mind, but we should try to bring others as well, to the right path – the proper, loving thing to do. God has commanded us to love one another, there is no better way of showing love, than to help each other towards a glorious, *spiritual* destiny.

> God will let us take our proper values to eternity –
> not our earthly assets.

We should judge ourselves in the way we suppose that God is going to judge us. God wants us to recognize our shameful deeds, that we have sinned against Him, and done what is evil in His sight. God will be proven right in what He says, because His judgment is *fair* and *just*. The Son of Man will send his angels to separate the good crops from the weeds, removing everything that causes sin or do evil, and they will be thrown into the burning furnace. There will be much weeping. God warns us to understand that only the godly will shine like the sun in their Father's Kingdom. Some that night have thought to be first, will be last, and some that might have thought of being last, will be first. It will be *God's* decision!

> "The LORD Almighty says, 'The day of judgment is coming, burning like a furnace. The arrogant and the wicked will be burned up like straw on that day. They will be consumed like a tree – roots and all. But for you who fear my name, the Sun of Righteousness will rise with healing in his wings. And you will go free, leaping with joy like calves let out to pasture.'" (Mal 4:1,2)

ENJOYING THE GOOD LIFE

As we are now into the last chapter of this book, we are now also getting ready to write the last chapter in each of our own *Book of Life*. What will our life, our journey, have been comprised of? What will we have accomplished? Have we lived our lives conforming to the purpose that God had planned for us? What kind of person did we choose to be? What kind of decisions have we made? How much good have we done? How much have we helped others? How much love or forgiveness have we given? What would we go back and change, if we could? Whatever has been written, and once the cover has been closed, nothing inscribed inside will ever change. Life will have been what we had decided it to be!

The new life however, will be of a different nature – not only everlasting, and without any of this world's calamities, but it will be a time to rejoice. The primary reason for being joyful, is to experience God and His Kingdom. The joy that comes from enjoying a meal with Our Lord, the Saints, and the Prophets, at the Divine Table. The joy of experiencing our new body as oneness with our soul, and achieving a supreme fulfillment of our hope.

"And this is the way to have eternal life – to know you, the only true God, and Jesus Christ, the one you sent to earth."
(Jn 17:3)

As we look at the first fifteen hundred years of human history, lives routinely lasted for centuries. When we try to think of eternity, those few hundred years seem so extraordinarily small and insignificant.

We shouldn't let happiness be our only ultimate goal for eternal life. It will certainly be more than just "rollin' around heaven all day.' God will most definitely have new purposes in store for us, as we return to be with Him as His children. God had given Man dominion over the many creatures that were created. Adam, and his descendants in return, were made to care and cultivate the earth, and enhance and beautify the Lord's creative work. No longer will we have Satan to deceive us. We can now be helping Our Father with the talents that He has given us – each one of us joining the Saints and Angels for a particular Divine purpose. What excitement! Imagine being part of God's eternal work – being directed by our

Older Brother Jesus Christ! God promised us that if we had been faithful with smaller things, that He would put us in *charge* of many things. The many things, the many purposes, the many challenges are as endless as the universe. If we think of the joys of this world, or of our earthly accomplishments, they will have been in comparison, minuscule and superficial, as compared to the things awaiting us as part of God's family.

The first mention of God's name in the Old Testament was "Elohim." It was then used thirty-one times in the first Chapter of Genesis. It was used to define God as our Creator. This Hebrew name for God is in the plural form, proving that God is comprised of more than *one being*. The plural ending of this word signifies the plurality of beings. There is also biblical proof that "Elohim" should be understood to convey, not only the sense of a triune God, but of a God Family, *as a Divine Family of Beings*. We were made in the likeness and image of the Father and the Son, and He wants us to imitate Him – for a purpose.

> "And I will be your Father,
> and you will be my sons and daughters, says the Lord Almighty."
> (2 Co 6:18)

> " – what are mortals that you should think of us, mere humans that you should care for us? For you made us only a little lower than God, and you crowned us with glory and honor. You put us in charge of everything you made, giving us authority over all things – the sheep and the cattle."
> (Ps 8:4-7)

Having been made in God's *image*, we were made of the *God kind*. Christ being the *first* born of the Father, would mean that there will be *others* to be born of the Father. The Bible has taught us that we must be *born* again in order to share in the eternal life.

"And since we are his children, we will share his treasures

– for everything God gives to his Son, Christ, is ours, too. But if we are to share his glory, we must also share his suffering." (Ro 8:17)

We should be so thankful to God for the promised destiny, that He has planned for each and every one of us. We can only arrive at this ultimate fortune by overcoming our own human vanities and passions, and we have to become holy, because God told us we should *be* holy and righteous, because *He* is Holy and Righteous. True perfection will not occur in this life, but we must be making the appropriate progress, because we need to grow in the same kind of nature and character of God Himself. The relationship that Christ had with His Father, was one of love, service, and obedience; the type of relationship that produces peace and happiness, which abides in the spiritual law of God. Whatever we have to go through in order to achieve this, even through the sufferings of this earthly journey, is not to be compared to our promised reward.

"For God knew his people in advance, and he chose them to become like his Son, so that his Son would be the firstborn, with many brothers and sisters. And having chosen them, he called them to come to him. And he gave them right standing with himself, and he promised them his glory." (Ro 8:29,30)

The most wonderful, exciting, and awe-inspiring time of our lives is yet to come. The end of this mortal existence will be but the beginning of a most productive, stimulating, and increasingly fulfilling and purposeful experience.

"And after my body has decayed, yet in my body I will see God.
I will see him for myself.
Yes, I will see him with my own eyes.
I am overwhelmed at the thought!"
(Job 19:26,27)

Jesus said that we should imitate Him, and follow in His ways. He was obedient in following His Father's plan, through His mission and suffering while with us here on earth, in order to bring us Salvation. He showed us, and told us that He *was,* the way. As you follow in Jesus' path, may your life be blessed, and filled with excitement, joy, contentment, and may your eternal life be glorious, as you,

Enjoy The Good Life!

ENJOY THE GOOD LIFE

E ntering a new life, that Salvation acquired for us;
N ot compared in any way, to this earth's mortal exodus.
J ust, and honorable, will be our Celestial Ruler;
O bjectively showing us His abundant Love, for ever.
Y earning, waiting, and longing now, for a glimpse of Paradise;

T o a place, for which Our Dear Saviour, paid a Redeeming Price.
H appy, we all will be, sharing in the generous Bounty;
E ating, and sharing with Jesus, at His Table of Plenty.

G od, with His Angels and the Saints, in Majestic Adornment;
O bliging, unceasingly, for our pleasure and enjoyment.
O bserving Our Blessed Trinity, in Purest Reverence;
D iety, to be praised and adored, in their omnipresence.

L et's now imagine, the thought of Joy, Peace, and Tranquility;
I nsured to us in abundance, with Divine Serenity.
F ather, and LORD to us all, we will finally see Your Face;
E ternally residing, in Your Heavenly Dwelling Place.

PERMISSIONS

Scripture quotations were taken from the Holy Bible, New Living Translation, copyright © 1996. Used by permission of Tyndale House Publishers, Inc. Wheaton, Illinois 60189. All rights reserved. As found in BIBLESOFT PC STUDY BIBLE Version 4.2B copyright © 1988-2004. All rights reserved.

Letter *To My Grandchildren* used with applicable permission from Barbara Keffer.

Lyrics and music for the song *He Loves Me* Copyright © 2000 by Fr. Patrick A. Martin. Stafford Springs, CT 06076.

CPSIA information can be obtained
at www.ICGtesting.com
Printed in the USA
FFOW04n1300120116
20377FF